LITERARY CRITICISM AND CULTURAL THEORY

Edited by
William E. Cain
Professor of English
Wellesley College

A ROUTLEDGE SERIES

Literary Criticism and Cultural Theory
William E. Cain, *General Editor*

GENDERED PATHOLOGIES
The Female Body and Biomedical Discourse in the Nineteenth-Century English Novel
Sondra M. Archimedes

"TWENTIETH-CENTURY AMERICANISM"
Identity and Ideology in Depression-Era Leftist Fiction
Andrew C. Yerkes

WILDERNESS CITY
The Post World War II American Urban Novel from Algren to Wideman
Ted L. Clontz

THE IMPERIAL QUEST AND MODERN MEMORY FROM CONRAD TO GREENE
J. M. Rawa

THE ETHICS OF EXILE
Colonialism in the Fictions of Charles Brockden Brown and J. M. Coetzee
Timothy Francis Strode

THE ROMANTIC SUBLIME AND MIDDLE-CLASS SUBJECTIVITY IN THE VICTORIAN NOVEL
Stephen Hancock

VITAL CONTACT
Downclassing Journeys in American Literature from Herman Melville to Richard Wright
Patrick Chura

COSMOPOLITAN FICTIONS
Ethics, Politics, and Global Change in the Works of Kazuo Ishiguro, Michael Ondaatje, Jamaica Kincaid, and J. M. Coetzee
Katherine Stanton

OUTSIDER CITIZENS
The Remaking of Postwar Identity in Wright, Beauvoir, and Baldwin
Sarah Relyea

AN ETHICS OF BECOMING
Configurations of Feminine Subjectivity in Jane Austen, Charlotte Brontë, and George Eliot
Sonjeong Cho

NARRATIVE DESIRE AND HISTORICAL REPARATIONS
A.S. Byatt, Ian McEwan, Salman Rushdie
Tim S. Gauthier

NIHILISM AND THE SUBLIME POSTMODERN
The (Hi)Story of a Difficult Relationship from Romanticism to Postmodernism
Will Slocombe

DEPRESSION GLASS
Documentary Photography and the Medium of the Camera Eye in Charles Reznikoff, George Oppen, and William Carlos Williams
Monique Claire Vescia

FATAL NEWS
Reading and Information Overload in Early Eighteenth-Century Literature
Katherine E. Ellison

NEGOTIATING COPYRIGHT
Authorship and the Discourse of Literary Property Rights in Nineteenth-Century America
Martin T. Buinicki

"FOREIGN BODIES"
Trauma, Corporeality, and Textuality in Contemporary American Culture
Laura Di Prete

OVERHEARD VOICES
Address and Subjectivity in Postmodern American Poetry
Ann Keniston

OVERHEARD VOICES
Address and Subjectivity in
Postmodern American Poetry

Ann Keniston

NEW YORK AND LONDON

Published in 2006 by
Routledge
Taylor & Francis Group
711 Third Avenue
New York, NY 10017

Published in Great Britain by
Routledge
Taylor & Francis Group
2 Park Square
Milton Park, Abingdon
Oxfordshire OX14 4RN

First issued in paperback 2014

Routledge is an imprint of the Taylor and Francis Group, an informa business

© 2006 by Taylor & Francis Group, LLC
International Standard Book Number 13: 978-0-415-97627-5 (hbk)
International Standard Book Number 13: 978-1-138-83331-9 (pbk)
Library of Congress Card Number 2005031220

No part of this book may be reprinted, reproduced, transmitted, or utilized in any form by any electronic, mechanical, or other means, now known or hereafter invented, including photocopying, microfilming, and recording, or in any information storage or retrieval system, without written permission from the publishers.

Trademark Notice: Product or corporate names may be trademarks or registered trademarks, and are used only for identification and explanation without intent to infringe.

Library of Congress Cataloging-in-Publication Data

Keniston, Ann.
    Overheard voices : address and subjectivity in postmodern American poetry / by Ann Keniston.
       p. cm. -- (Literary criticism and cultural theory)
    Includes bibliographical references (p.) and index.
    ISBN 0-415-97627-8 (acid-free paper)
    1. American poetry--20th century--History and criticism. 2. Postmodernism (Literature)--United States. 3. Subjectivity in literature. 4. Plath, Sylvia. Ariel. 5. Merrill, James Ingram. Changing light at Sandover. 6. Gluck, Louise, 1943- Wild iris. 7. Bidart, Frank, 1939- Desire. I. Title. II. Series.

PS310.P63K46 2005
811'.509113--dc22   2005031220

Taylor & Francis Group
is the Academic Division of Informa plc.

Visit the Taylor & Francis Web site at
http://www.taylorandfrancis.com

and the Routledge Web site at
http://www.routledge-ny.com

For my parents

Contents

Acknowledgments — ix

Introduction
"The fluidity of damaged Form": Theorizing Postmodern Address — 1

Chapter One
Recovering You: Sylvia Plath's *Ariel* — 27

Chapter Two
Ghostly Projections: James Merrill's *The Changing Light at Sandover* — 51

Chapter Three
Buried with the Romantics: Louise Glück's *The Wild Iris* — 71

Chapter Four
Homo Faber: Frank Bidart's *Desire* — 95

Conclusion
"A dream of this room": Self-Effacement and Lyric Space — 121

Notes — 135

Works Cited — 157

Index — 165

Acknowledgments

This book would not exist without the encouragement and guidance of Bonnie Costello, my dissertation director at Boston University. Bonnie helped me develop the habits of mind of a scholar; she supported my early ideas, she modeled a rigorous and passionate mode of close reading, and she scrupulously noticed inconsistencies and weaknesses in my argument. My second reader, Leland Monk, offered many kinds of help in generous and exacting ways. John Paul Riquelme, David Wagenknecht, Rosanna Warren, and William Waters offered helpful suggestions for revision. Also at BU, William Carroll, Susan Mizruchi, Daria Donnelly, and Virginia Jackson supported my academic work at crucial moments.

I have been lucky to have colleagues and friends who provided me with intellectual and emotional support and practical help over the many years of writing and rewriting this book. Louise Harrison Lepera, Julia Lisella, and Sara Eddy gave me deadlines, read whatever I wrote, and gave me an excuse to get away from my desk. Jeanne Follansbee Quinn and Jane Thrailkill offered editorial insights and support. At the University of Nevada, Reno, Ann Ronald and Aaron Santesso gave me cogent and useable criticism of late drafts; Stacy Burton made sure I had the time to focus on revising the book; and Jen Hill, Jane Detweiler, Cheryll Glotfelty, and my other colleagues helped me stay sane.

I am also grateful to the care and patience of my research assistants, Sarah Hillenbrand and Mark Farnsworth; and to William Cain and Max Novick at Routledge, who turned this manuscript into a real book. I received financial support from the Boston University Humanities Foundation and Women's Guild and the University of Nevada, Reno Junior Faculty Research Grant Program.

My husband, Eric Novak, helped with countless rough spots in the text, listened patiently to my complaints and ideas, and willingly made many personal and professional sacrifices so that I could work. His love, humor, and faith not only helped me get the book done but more crucially let me derive pleasure from the process of writing it. My children, Jeremy and Paul, tolerated the absences my work on this book required and filled the hours when I was not working with humor, joy, and love. The book began in my conviction that when we call out to absent others, they do not respond, but Paul and Jeremy's quirky, tender answers to my questions proved something very different while reminding me of the pleasures of language.

My parents, Ellen and Kenneth Keniston, encouraged my love of reading and writing as a child and bought me poetry books when I asked for them. They let me explore my own passions, supported me when I needed help, and offered constancy and faith through this book's journey to completion. I owe my love of ideas to them, and I dedicate this book to them with gratitude and love.

A quite different version of the Introduction originally appeared in *Contemporary Literature;* a much shorter version of Chapter Four first appeared in *The Threepenny Review.* Grateful acknowledgment is made to these publications and especially to Thomas Gardner and Wendy Lesser for their editorial suggestions.

I also acknowledge permission to reprint the following texts:

Reprinted by permission of Farrar, Straus and Giroux, LLC: "This Room" from *Your Name Here* by John Ashbery. Copyright © 2000 by John Ashbery. UK/Commonwealth rights granted by Carcanet Press Limited.

Reprinted by permission of Farrar, Straus and Giroux, LLC: Excerpts from *Desire* by Frank Bidart. Copyright © 1997 by Frank Bidart. UK/Commonwealth rights granted by Carcanet Press Limited.

Reprinted by permission of Farrar, Straus and Giroux, LLC: Excerpts from *In the Western Night: Collected Poems 1965–1990* by Frank Bidart. Copyright © 1990 by Frank Bidart.

Reprinted by permission of Farrar, Straus and Giroux, LLC: "During Fever" from *Collected Poems* by Robert Lowell; copyright © 2003 by Harriet Lowell and Sheridan Lowell.

Reprinted by permission of HarperCollins Publishers: Excerpt from "The Untrustworthy Speaker" by Louise Glück from *Ararat*. Copyright © 1990 by Louise Glück. "The Deviation" (entire) in *Descending Figure* and excerpt from "Mock Orange" in

Acknowledgments

Triumph of Achilles from *The First Four Books of Poems* by Louise Glück. Copyright © 1968, 1971, 1972, 1973, 1974, 1975, 1976, 1977, 1978, 1979, 1980, 1985, 1995 by Louise Glück. "Matins 2" (entire) and excerpts from eleven poems from *The Wild Iris* by Louise Glück. Copyright © 1993 by Louise Glück. UK/Commonwealth rights granted by Carcanet Press Limited.

Reprinted by permission of HarperCollins Publishers: Excerpts from "Cut," "Ariel," "Lady Lazarus," "Daddy," and "Tulips" from *The Collected Poems of Sylvia Plath*, Edited by Ted Hughes. Copyright © 1960, 1965, 1971, 1981 by the Estate of Sylvia Plath. Editorial Material copyright © 1981 by Ted Hughes. Excerpt from *Letters Home by Sylvia Plath: Correspondence 1950–1963* by Aurelia Schober Plath. Copyright © 1975 by Aurelia Schober Plath. UK/Commonweath rights granted by Faber and Faber, Ltd.

Reprinted by permission of the publishers from *The Letters of Emily Dickinson*, Thomas H. Johnson, ed., Cambridge, Mass.: The Belknap Press of Harvard University Press, Copyright © 1958, 1986, The President and Fellows of Harvard College; 1914, 1924, 1932, 1942 by Martha Dickinson Bianchi; 1952 by Alfred Leete Hampson; 1960 by Mary L. Hampson.

From *The Changing Light at Sandover* by James Merrill, copyright © 1980, 1982 by James Merrill. From *Collected Poems* by James Merrill and J.D. McClatchy and Stephen Yenser, editors, copyright © 2001 by the Literary Estate of James Merrill at Washington University. Used by permission of Alfred A. Knopf, a division of Random House, Inc.

From *The Master Letters* by Lucie Brock-Broido, copyright © 1995 by Lucie Brock-Broido. Used by permission of Alfred A. Knopf, a division of Random House, Inc.

Excerpt from "To Psychoanalysis" by Kenneth Koch from *New Addresses,* copyright © 2000 by Kenneth Koch. Used by permission of The Kenneth Koch Literary Estate.

Introduction

"The fluidity of damaged Form": Theorizing Postmodern Address

The addressees of the most famous Romantic lyrics are generally both exalted and ethereal; they include invisible birds with piercingly beautiful songs, artworks that refuse to relinquish their secret messages, and a wind whose motion alludes both to the ravishing of all things mortal and to the unending realm of poetry itself. But the opening of Kenneth Koch's 2000 "To Psychoanalysis" (20–21), like many of the poems in the volume *New Addresses,* reads like parody:

> I took the Lexington Avenue subway
> To arrive at you in your glory days
> Of the Nineteen Fifties when we believed
> That you could solve any problem
> And I had nothing but disdain
> For "self-analysis" "group analysis" "Jungian analysis"
> "Adlerian analysis" the Karen Horney kind
> All—other than you, pure Freudian type—
> Despicable and never to be mine!

What Koch summons up is neither timeless nor transcendent: rather than calling on Psyche, as a Romantic predecessor might, he addresses Psychoanalysis, a concept allied with a particular historic moment, class, locale, and mindset. And while traditional apostrophe is associated with transport, soaring, and an often ambiguous sense of transcendence, Koch begins with mere transportation, and moreover with the subterranean, urban, dingy particularity of the Lexington Avenue subway line. Koch's insistence on his "disdain" for competing schools of analysis further reveals

1

the limitations of his act of address: his addressee can be defined only by contrasts with what it is not. The quotation marks around the names of these opposing schools of analysis situate the poem in the realm of technical jargon rather than the universalizing realm of traditional lyric. Apostrophe, the figure of address to inanimate, absent, or dead others, usually refers to what Jonathan Culler has identified as a "timeless present" that affirms only the "temporality of writing" (*Pursuit* 149); its vocative "O!" is identified by Culler with "undifferentiated voicing" and thus "the moment when poetic voice constitutes itself" (*Pursuit* 143). But Koch begins in a pedestrian, personal past tense: "I took the Lexington Avenue subway." By insisting on a recalled scene and in particular on the fact that the "glory days" of Psychoanalysis are long since past, the poem emphasizes separation and absence where most apostrophic poems affirm proximity. It is not surprising that when the speaker finally affirms his addressee, his allusion is in the form of an awkward appositive subordinated to the negative ejaculation that ends the poem's first sentence: "All—other than you, pure Freudian type—/ *Despicable* and *never* to be mine!"

"To Psychoanalysis" seems, then, to use apostrophe to undermine apostrophe's conventions. Its apostrophe is anything but seamless: it seems to mark the narrator's discomfort at relying on a figure that is anachronistic and pretentious. But although such awkwardness seems to conflict with the ease with which earlier poets reverted to apostrophe, Koch's poem nonetheless emphasizes features inherent in all apostrophe, which is, Culler claims, associated with "all that is most radical, embarrassing, pretentious and mystificatory in the lyric" (*Pursuit* 137). Koch's apparent embarrassment at his own apostrophe is, according to Culler's definition, a natural response to a figure allied with the excesses of lyric itself. Such a notion may help to explain not only why Koch has chosen to use apostrophe in "To Psychoanalysis," although the poem's narrative might as easily have unfolded in the indicative, but also why he insists on apostrophe throughout the volume in which the poem appears. As its title makes clear, *New Addresses* is a volume whose fifty poems are linked by their address of topics ranging from Sleep to Orgasms, from Kidding Around to his Father's Business to his Old (street) Addresses.

The possibility that apostrophe is neither dispensable nor peripheral to the poems of *New Addresses* is partly suggested by the transformations of the figure of Psychoanalysis through the course of "To Psychoanalysis." Apostrophe, as Culler makes clear, attempts to "will a state of affairs, to attempt to call it into being [. . .] to make of the objects of the universe potentially responsive forces" (*Pursuit* 139). Such an attempt is by definition doomed to fail, since the universe's objects are not alive, much less responsive. Yet Koch's

"*The fluidity of damaged Form*"

poem, for all its negations, is partly an enactment of the poet's ability to do just what Culler suggests is impossible: it animates psychoanalysis. At first, after the termination of the speaker's analysis, psychoanalysis lives only, and conventionally, within his consciousness:

> It was only one moment in a life, my leaving you.
> But once I walked out, I could never think of anything seriously
> For fifteen years without also thinking of you. [. . .]

But toward the poem's end, as the speaker shifts into the present tense, psychoanalysis becomes an autonomous, visible entity, albeit one that defies chronology: "Now what have we become?/ You look the same, but now you are a past You." By the last lines, psychoanalysis has become not only alive but nearly indistinguishable from the human, although Koch ends with a speculative future tense:

> [. . .] What shall we do? Go walking?
> We're liable to have a slightly frumpy look,
> But probably no one will notice—another something I didn't know then.

The moment is a crucial one, partly because it is ambivalent. The speaker succeeds in rendering psychoanalysis both autonomous and companionable, yet this act of animation is qualified: psychoanalysis persists only as a "past" or conditional companion, one that always draws attention to its artificiality. Such ambivalence is central to Koch's relation to apostrophe as well, as the opening's emphasis on classifications of discourse and the repeated references to poem writing and to the speaker's vocation suggest. The speaker's success in resurrecting the similarly frumpy, anachronistic figure of apostrophe itself is also ambivalent. To use apostrophe, Koch suggests, is to evoke the past, an act of recollection that inspires the impulse to mock as well as to renovate. What for the Romantics was associated with unequivocal longing, exaltation, and transcendence rather than—or, as Culler might suggest, as well as—unmitigated embarrassment is in Koch's version awkward and ironic but also, surprisingly, exuberant and comic, a way to evade sadness.[1]

Koch's poems are in numerous and significant ways distinct from those of Sylvia Plath, James Merrill, Louise Glück, and Frank Bidart, to each of whose work I devote a chapter below. Their address also differs from his: Koch's address is, among other things, lighter, funnier, closer to epithalamium than elegy. Yet Koch's volume powerfully, directly affirms two of the central claims I will advance in this book. As its varied, prolific address makes clear, apostrophe remains a viable and suggestive, if somewhat unnatural, figure for post-World War II American poets. And address—the term includes but is not limited to apostrophe—functions in particular, historically specific ways.[2] Postwar address does not merely reiterate earlier concerns or attitudes but, as Koch's concern with what might most simply be termed his belatedness makes clear, affirms a historically particular notion of what apostrophe can and cannot do.

As Koch's example suggests, apostrophe cogently articulates the poetic concerns and interests of postwar poets. Koch focuses so intensively on apostrophe throughout *New Addresses,* it seems, because this figure allows him to explore issues he finds pressing and poetically productive. The ambivalence I have identified in the address of "To Psychoanalysis"—the desire to go for a stroll with the apostrophized other along with the compulsion to acknowledge that it is long gone—informs nearly all the poems I will examine. Postwar apostrophe is concerned, that is, with the paradoxes of otherness, with the often irreconcilable conflict between the desire for others to be made present and the essential solitude of the lyric speaker. Address in this way allows postwar poems to enact and explore questions of desire. This desire is partly historical, a longing for a lyric mode that is, like Koch's pure psychoanalysis, hopelessly out of date. It is thus also generic: postwar poems often stand at the periphery of lyric, regarding it with a desire expressed through and corresponding to their desire for their addressee's embodiment.

Poems of address—including, but not limited to, apostrophic poems—recur in American poetry published since World War II. Apostrophe appears with particular intensity in the poems of the so-called confessionals and of the so-called language poets. While apostrophe by no means appears in the majority of postwar American poems, a glance at nearly any recent anthology or issue of an American literary journal suggests that American poets continue to rely—at times ironically or self-consciously—on address to absent others. Yet apostrophe has been generally seen as peripheral or insignificant to the preoccupations of contemporary poetry.[3] When critics discuss apostrophe, they generally emphasize the unabashed longing of Romantic lyric. This book redresses this silence. At the same time, by examining a group of poets not generally seen as similar, I wish to affirm a broader conception of literary kinship than has been traditionally allowed by readers of postwar American poetry, whose eagerness to distinguish the formally radical from the formally traditional, the experimental "postmodern" from the conservative "contemporary," the legacy of Emily Dickinson from that of Walt

Whitman or of Wallace Stevens from that of Ezra Pound tends to affirm variously defined antithetical or opposing "schools." It is doubtless true that the formalism of James Merrill can usefully be contrasted with the confessionalism of Sylvia Plath, Frank Bidart's long-lined, inclusive poems with Louise Glück's minimalist ones, Merrill's polished evasion of grief with Bidart's often abstract elaboration of the minutiae of emotional conflict, Plath's impulse toward extremism with Glück's toward self-erasure, Merrill's sprawling epic with Glück's carefully constructed lyric sequences. But my book, in including all four, suggests the important similarities revealed by their address.

Part of my aim is to connect, even reconcile, several critically opposed notions of contemporary poetry. Postmodernism, like any literary category, is difficult to define, but most theorists emphasize its use of language itself to undermine the authority of a prelinguistic or essential realm of experience or selfhood. Jeffrey Gray claims that language poetry, often seen as the most postmodern strand of postwar poetry, "reduce[es] or at least assimilat[es] the problem of subjectivity to the status of language [and so] attempts to purge poetry of origin, narrative voice, and affect" (714); Marjorie Perloff emphasizes postmodern poetry's challenge to fixed notions of genre.[4] In the case of language poetry, such a challenge is often enacted through disruptions of conventional patterns of syntax and meaning as well as of poetic form. Such disruptions are not obvious in the poems I examine, which tend to be formally and emotionally accessible and to contain relatively conventional markers of character, development, and closure. Nor do the poems of Plath, Merrill, Glück, and Bidart conform exactly to traditional notions of the confessional or postconfessional, which generally is seen to emphasize self-revelation, authenticity, and psychological pain.[5] Rather, these poems explore selfhood, love, loss, and memory—issues associated with confessional poetry—in ways that draw attention to the limitations of confessional assumptions about the stability of subjectivity. As their interrogation of the confessional draws on strategies associated with the postmodern, these poems also reveal the limitations of a postmodern poetics that attempts to do away altogether with subjectivity. The landscape of postwar poetry is, these poems thus imply, less bifurcated and more continuous than is often acknowledged. That these poems remain recognizable as lyric also challenges Perloff's alliance of postmodernism with the breakdown of generic categories. Instead, it is apostrophe, a figure explicitly identified with lyric, that these poets use to explore and interrogate poetic selfhood.

My analysis also emphasizes a question inarguably central to discussions of postwar—or what is often termed postmodern—American poetry, that of the position and stability of the lyric subject. This question is central to most earlier discussions of postmodern American poetry, although different studies often hold sharply divergent views. Some readers emphasize the continuity of the postmodern "I" with earlier, Romantic archetypes of selfhood, while others suggest—often but not always based on discussion of the works of different poets—that postmodern poetry has irrevocably dissolved fixed notions of selfhood.[6] Because my emphasis is not on the status of the lyric "I" but on the distinct yet adjacent position of the addressee or "you" of lyric, my study allows for an oblique vantage point on this old issue: a study of lyric address helps illuminate aspects of lyric that are difficult to see otherwise. In particular, by foregrounding the conflicts between desire and knowledge and the ways that postwar address questions the apostrophized other, I affirm subjectivity to be a central but contested preoccupation of this lyric. Because postwar lyric often defines self in terms of an always evasive other, it emphasizes the necessity of interrogating selfhood as a fixed or unified category. Its reliance on apostrophe, arguably the preeminent lyric figure, also allows this lyric to focus on the exact relation between lyric and selfhood. The lyric self, these poems ultimately suggest, exists by means of and in the service of the poem itself, yet this self also chafes against the generic structure to which it is captive.

Koch's emphasis on recollection and belatedness suggests the importance of a historically inflected reading of apostrophe, but the origin of its historically particular features is difficult to trace. The tendency of postmodern American poets to return to a figure associated both with the past and, as I will argue below, with elegy no doubt derives at least partly from tendencies in postwar American culture. Particularly compelling are explanations that emphasize the alienation deriving from postwar prosperity, complacency, and conformity; the increasing irrelevance of the written word in a post-industrial, post-literate culture and in particular the decline in the readership for poetry; and the enormity of the scale of human suffering and death following the Holocaust, other genocides, and the ravages of the AIDS pandemic. Yet the causal connection between such trends and literary works is nearly impossible to verify; such explanations also fail to account for the particular forms or genres of literary expression and for the ways that texts speak to and from their own generic histories. Perhaps for this reason, few earlier readers of postmodern poetry have attempted to locate its relation to particular cultural tendencies; rather, the dominant critical tendency has been to define postmodernism nearly entirely in terms of its adherence to or divergence from modernism.[7] But while postmodernism inarguably responds to what preceded it, postmodern poems do more than comment on their poetic

"*The fluidity of damaged Form*"

forebears. As a response to these two modes of explanation, my reading of postmodern apostrophe is neither wholly extraliterary nor wholly literary. My emphasis is on the ways that apostrophe allows postmodern poets to comment on lyric while articulating desires that, enabled by the capacities and limitations of the genre, transcend lyric.

If readings of lyric such as mine, which are both rhetorically and historically inflected, are relatively rare, this critical absence may reflect lyric's relation to temporality. Lyric is often defined in terms of its difference from narrative or epic poetry, from, that is, poems in which chronology or storytelling is central. In Sharon Cameron's terms, lyric is centrally preoccupied with "the anxieties of the temporal sequence" (24–5), with its own relation to the chronological, narrative, temporal world that surrounds it and that it nonetheless attempts to exclude. A similar conflict is also central to genre theory, which is concerned with transcending the apparent flux and variety of individual texts to devise a coherent, transhistorically valid notion of genre. The deconstructive readers who have more recently been interested in apostrophe and lyric figuration tend for different reasons to repudiate developmental, narrative, or historically based models of reading. In the case of apostrophe, this antihistorical tendency among readers has been particularly pronounced. Culler and most other theorists of apostrophe tend not to distinguish the apostrophe in poems from several centuries of English poetry.[8]

My explanation of why apostrophe remains a viable figure for postmodern American poetry relies on an analogy indirectly suggested by Koch's poem: part of the reason that apostrophe is so central to his volume, his fluid, half-articulated metaphor suggests, is that it resembles psychoanalysis. I argued above that Koch's notion of psychoanalysis as formerly idealized but now unobtainable cogently articulates the paradoxes confronting the post-Romantic apostrophic poet. More particularly, Koch's meditation on psychoanalysis includes a celebration of the mode of speech that psychoanalysis enables:

> I would free-associate. I would say whatever
> Came into my head [. . .
> . . . .]
> Ruined cities were as nothing to me
> In my fantastic advancing. I recovered epochs.

Although he insists that this form of speech "was not poetry it was something else," Koch here suggests that free association permits the recuperation of what might otherwise have been lost. Apostrophe does something similar:

its particular, vocative mode of speech enables the apostrophizer to make present or "recover" what is absent.

Apostrophe, I am suggesting, connects a way of speaking to an emotional content. By definition, apostrophe addresses, using the "you" of conversation, an entity known to be irrevocably absent; through the bravado of the second-person pronoun, it seeks to replace what is known with what is desired. As such, it requires a leap of faith, insisting that both speaker and reader radically suspend disbelief. Yet the fulfillment of apostrophe's wish—that the other hear the poem and respond—is antithetical to lyric, which is, according to most definitions, the utterance of a solitary voice. Lyric thus resists the incursions of dialogue and narrative; I am arguing, against the views of several critics, that apostrophe is distinct from, although it often craves, dialogue.[9] All apostrophe is built on a desire for the other's presence whose precariousness apostrophe itself recognizes, but apostrophe traditionally tends to conceal the impossibility of its desire. Postmodern address, as I will show, intensifies these often unacknowledged paradoxes, downplaying the optimism (or perhaps the delusion) of traditional apostrophe—the faith that the other *is* there and *can* hear—by foregrounding the absence of the addressee. This insistence on absence does not undermine the desire articulated by these poems; rather, the desire is intensified by being revealed to be illusory.

My notion that the structure of all apostrophe articulates a desire that cannot be fulfilled builds on and extends the observation by several readers that apostrophe shares features with Jacques Lacan's theory of how the child enters into language. According to Lacan, the infant begins to speak when his [sic] mother is not present: the removal of her breast or body impels the child to cry out to her, to "demand," in Lacan's terms, that she reappear. Yet as Barbara Johnson points out in a discussion of the relationship of this moment to apostrophe, "the mother addressed is somehow a *personification,* not a person" (198; emphasis added): the use of the word *mother* "inaugurates alienation" because it is distinct from the actual mother and cannot bring her back (198). Apostrophe, in Johnson's terms, can be imagined as "the fantastically intricate history of endless elaborations and displacements of the single cry, 'Mama!'" (199). More recently, Mary Loeffelholz has suggested a broadly similar analogy in the poems of Dickinson: she suggests that Dickinson's "very structure of address" echoes Lacan's notions of family triangulation and emphasizes Lacan's notion that "experiencing language as an inadequate substitute for an original 'presence' that itself is always already lost [. . . is] the condition of acquiring language at all" (59).[10]

What interest me are not so much the specifics of these analogies as the general connection between desire and apostrophe. The child's entry into language is not merely a "demand"—Lacan's term is grammatical—but the expression of a desire to restore the mother's presence, a wish that cannot be fulfilled because language is, in Loeffelholz's terms, "an *inadequate* substitute" for a presence that is "*always already* lost." Thus, utterance can only articulate a desire for closeness. Similarly, the use of "you" to address an absent entity articulates a desire to be heard, no matter what the content of the utterance. As the child's "Mama!" articulates her inability to regain her mother, apostrophe ultimately affirms the solitude of the lyric speaker.

The notion that the structure of apostrophe, rather than its particular mood or tone, articulates a necessarily unfulfilled desire for the other to appear also helps explain what is sometimes called the fictionality of lyric address.[11] Not only apostrophe but many of the tropes and figures of lyric create a similar fiction: prosopopeia (granting a name, face, or voice to the inanimate), catachresis (insofar as it often involves the naming, or misnaming, of objects with terms belonging to living beings), and even metaphor (insofar as through analogy it makes present something absent) all establish scenarios in which the speaker is not alone in an unresponsive setting but rather surrounded by others, albeit invented. A basic psychoanalytic reading might locate in the recurrence of this tendency something more resonant than mere pretending: lyric figuration, it could be argued, repeatedly articulates the desire for an end to the essential lyric condition of isolation. Address is concerned with actual others, as the range of possible lyric addressees—including the beloved, God, the reader, and others—implies. The "you" of apostrophe is not merely an externalized or split-off figure for the speaker or what Culler calls "an act of radical interiorization and solipsism" (*Pursuit* 146). Instead, address provides a way for the speaker of lyric to consider the extent to which others constitute the self.

By keeping my Lacanian reading of apostrophe general, I mean to avoid the kind of overly literal psychological models of apostrophe mocked by Culler (*Pursuit* 138), which careful readings of postmodern poems tend to belie. I am claiming neither that lyric addressees always represent the mother, nor that the various forms of apostrophe correspond in an exact or mathematical way to the stages of child development, nor that apostrophe always implies a narrative in which proximity is replaced by absence and solitude is overcome or denied.[12] Nor, though my reading emphasizes loss and absence, do I mean to imply that apostrophe is solely associated with elegy. Rather, as Koch's celebratory (if nostalgic) apostrophe makes clear and the chapters below suggest, postmodern poems treat the topic of loss in ways that engage a range of responses including antipathy (in Plath), humor (in Merrill), sarcasm (in Glück), and the transformation of absence itself into a source of consolation (in Bidart's elegies). These postmodern poets thus affirm that loss is productive poetic terrain, and in the process they affirm that apostrophe articulates more than the lyricality of lyric.[13] The very structure of apostrophe alludes to the paradoxes of desire.

More exactly, apostrophe suggests an analogy between two modes of desire. The desire to embody the other, to give the other a voice within the poem, tends to impel poems toward the periphery of lyric utterance. In this way, insofar as apostrophe attempts to unmake the lyric speaker's solitude, it invites the dissolution of its speaker as an autonomous and coherent entity and the entry of elements antithetical to lyric. Postmodern apostrophe thus emphasizes the risks that apostrophe poses to lyric integrity; by defying without eradicating lyric, apostrophic poems construct a position from which their speaker can desire lyric itself.

My notion that postmodern lyric is alienated from a lyricality toward which it yearns partly recalls Herbert Tucker's identification of a "yearning after the condition of lyric" (230) or a "nostalgia for lyric" (238) in the dramatic monologues of Robert Browning. Tucker's retrospective argument relies on his observation of actual changes in the lyric; he concludes that dramatic monologue ultimately undermines its lyric moments both by marking them as the utterances of particular characters and by "enfolding [them] into a narrative history" (227). But postmodern poetry, perhaps because it cannot see what it is evolving toward, foregrounds and lingers on the *situation* of unmediated desire. The most striking example of this tendency in my study is James Merrill's narrative-epic-dramatic *Changing Light at Sandover*, which seems to undermine or transcend lyric completely. But while the dead, summoned up by ouija board, respond directly to the narrator's appeals, the poem also acknowledges a distinctively lyric solitude, which is rendered more poignant by the speaker's remove from the lyric mode. Plath's assertion in "Ariel" that her speaker as solitary entity no longer exists and Glück's insertion of narrative elements into her lyric sequences also transgress lyric in different ways; these poems too construct from these transgressions scenarios of longing.

I mean by laying out this equivalence between the desire within the poem (for the other to appear) and the desire enacted by the poem (for lyric) to link notions roughly analogous to what Tucker calls the intersubjective, or the relation among the poem's characters, and the intertextual, or the relation of the text to earlier texts.[14] Tucker emphasizes the overlap of and connections between these two modes of reading in dramatic monologue. My point is roughly analogous: apostrophe too connects the desire within the text and the desire of the text. Its represented scene of address—speech to an invisible, listening other—approximates the scene of lyric speech, which requires a reader absent from the scenes both of composition and utterance. As Koch's representation of psychoanalysis as longed-for, old-fashioned, and slightly ridiculous articulates his feelings about apostrophe itself, the longing conventionally associated with the apostrophized other expresses the postmodern poet's feelings about lyric.

Tucker's essay alludes to and builds on John Stuart Mill's 1833 assertion that "eloquence is *heard,* poetry is *overheard*" (qtd. Tucker 226, Mill's emphasis). Mill's image suggests the reader of poetry—his subsequent statements make it clear that he is referring to lyric poetry in particular—to be an eavesdropper, someone not addressed. In Northrop Frye's amplification of Mill, "the poet, so to speak, turns his back on his listeners" (250). Yet both theorists also suggest that this concealed presence is necessary to lyric; it helps define the lyric genre. Lyric thus seems to be a nearly theatrical speech act, performed for an audience that resembles the audience for drama, except that lyric, according to Frye, requires "the concealment of the poet's audience from the poet" (249).

As my book's title suggests, a similar notion of lyric overhearing underlies my claim that apostrophic desire resembles or articulates the desire for lyric. More exactly, the situation of apostrophe—in which a solitary speaker addresses an absent other—resembles that of writing—in which a solitary author sits at her desk, imagining her absent, potential readers. The exact nature of the analogy between the relation of speaker to poet and of addressee to reader is imprecise, as several other critics have made clear.[15] Apostrophe addresses directly an other meant to hear, whereas the reader of lyric is generally not spoken to and so remains removed from the utterance. And while apostrophe is fictional address, lyric, at the most pragmatic, literal level, requires actual readers. Yet the lyric "you" nonetheless at least partly resembles the reader, as many of the poems I examine below imply; in William Waters's cogent terms, "it avails nothing to discuss poetry's pronouns without involving the question of the reader's experience" (*Poetry's* 14).

Such analogies extend, though they seem to contradict, Frye's notions about lyric and audience. Although Frye claims that lyric "does not address a reader directly" (4) but "avoids [even] the mimesis of direct address" (25), he does acknowledge the centrality of address to lyric utterance, even when the speaker seems to be alone: "the lyric poet normally pretends to be talking to himself or to someone else: a spirit of nature, a Muse [. . .], a personal friend, a lover, a god, a personified abstraction or a natural object" (249). This emphasis on the simultaneous invisibility and presence of the reader, from whom the poet turns away while also speaking loudly and distinctly enough that his speech will be overheard, recalls the ways I have been characterizing the lyric speaker's relationship to the absent addressee. Moreover, the distinction Frye makes between apostrophic hearing and lyric overhearing is undermined by the fact that apostrophe is meant to be overheard by the poem's actual audience.[16] Frye does suggest that the relationship between poet and reader is at times characterized by a kind of partial dialogue: even as the poet turns away from his listeners, he acknowledges, he "may speak for them, and [. . .] they may repeat some of his words after him" (250). Thus Frye's notion of lyric raises questions about the other's identity and autonomy that are also central to apostrophe.

Although it does not allude to Frye, Tucker's rereading of Mill raises analogous questions about agency. Tucker's concern is not with the listener who overhears the poem but rather with the position of the Victorian poet himself as overhearer:

> To the most ambitious and original young poets of the day [. . .] the sort of lyricism Mill admired must have seemed "overheard" in a sense quite other than Mill intended: heard overmuch, overdone, and thus in need of being done over in fresh forms. (227)

Tucker's notion of lyric overhearing adds a historical or narrative element to the apparently simultaneous scene of Frye's overhearing: the Victorian poet hears poems that have already been spoken. This historicizing element is central to Tucker's assertions about dramatic monologue: "What gets 'overheard' in [. . .] Victorian monologues is history dramatically replayed," a history that comes to "include" lyric (228).

Postmodern lyric is caught between Frye's and Tucker's notions of overhearing. Its speaker experiences an exclusion similar to that of Frye's; prohibited from intimacy with his reader, she is also impelled, like Tucker's poet, to hear reiterations of the same old sounds. Often refusing simple or straightforward reader address, many postmodern poems employ an unidentified or ambivalent "you" that implies both the reader and the addressee of apostrophe, and in the process emphasizes absence. Postmodern address keeps looking back at lyric, hearing it not so much as an inescapable and therefore oppressive rhythm but as a marker of the desire for proximity. As a result, postmodern poems affirm neither Frye's disinterestness nor Tucker's defiant weariness. Rather, these poems affirm the pathos of overhearing: straining to hear the responses of their apostrophized others, their speakers also overhear the apostrophes that preceded theirs, which they comprehend and toward which they yearn but which they can no longer easily inhabit. This pathos itself contains contradictions—the term refers both to the unmediated identification of spectator with what a work of art conveys and to the maudlin or ironic excesses of that identification—and as such connects the intersubjective with the intertextual.[17] Overhearing is pathetic in that it seems to unmake the self's solitude even as it affirms that solitude. Positing the possibility of identification and union, it insists on exclusion.

Two apostrophic poems drawn from the outer reaches of my study's chronology—the first was published in 1959, the second in 1995—by poets whom I do not discuss below directly thematize overhearing and in the process elaborate its pathos. The juxtaposition of these different poems also allows me more fully to connect intersubjective to intertextual representations of this pathos. The first poem, Robert Lowell's "During Fever," foregrounds the connection between its own apostrophe and its various intersubjective scenes of overhearing; in the second, Lucie Brock-Broido's "Her Habit," the impulse to make the apostrophized other present echoes the intertextual wish to revive the voice of a dead poet and to recall a lyric mode outside which this prose poem remains.

"During Fever" (*Collected* 181–2) is generally read as a meditation on the inescapably erotic relationship between parents and opposite-sex children. Yet the poem emphasizes—through a repeated apostrophe acknowledged by very few readers of the poem—both renunciation and physical exclusion. Several scenes of overhearing within the poem suggest the speaker's preoccupation with questions similar to those that preoccupied Frye at nearly the same time.[18] To rely on the anachronistic figure of apostrophe, Lowell suggests, requires of the postmodern poet a turning away that is if anything more extreme than Frye's, since it undermines the central lyric fiction that the speaker of the poem is its represented "I."

Like Koch's lighter "To Psychoanalysis," "During Fever" emphasizes psychoanalysis and in particular the relationship between psychoanalysis and invocation. But while Koch suggests psychoanalytic and apostrophic desires to be analogous, Lowell's juxtaposition of oedipal with apostrophic desire distinguishes them.[19] It is certainly true that the speaker recalls his relationship with his mother in terms that emphasize exclusionary intimacy:

> Often with unadulterated joy,
> Mother, we bent by the fire
> rehashing Father's character—
> [. . . . .]

> Mother, your master-bedroom
> looked away from the ocean.
> [. . . .]
> Gold, yellow and green,
> the nuptial bed
> was as big as a bathroom.

The enormous bed that the mother seems permanently to inhabit emphasizes the son's physical smallness but also the vastness of his desires; that the same or a similar bed is the scene of marital sex in another poem in the volume ("Man and Wife" [*Collected* 189]) intensifies the sense of transgression in his bedside visitations. Yet while these stanzas apostrophize the mother, these early invocations fail to summon her: the speaker's attempt to replicate through apostrophe the past bodily closeness between mother and son does not bring the mother back.

That the addressee would remain silent throughout an apostrophic poem is conventional, but like psychoanalysis in Koch's poem, which rises up and takes a walk with the speaker, Lowell's fourth and final stanza, in defying this convention, revises the anachronistic figure of apostrophe itself:

> Born ten years and yet an aeon
> too early for the twenties,
> Mother, you smile
> as if you saw your Father
> inches away yet hidden, as when he groused behind a screen
> over a National Geographic Magazine,
> whenever young men came to court you
> back in those settled years of World War One.

Here the mother not only appears, but she is smiling, apparently at her son's mode of recollection in this stanza. The fulfillment of the speaker's apostrophic desire to see his mother, though, requires several renunciations. The speaker does not appear in this final stanza as a character. Instead, he distances the parent-child bond from himself by describing his young mother and her father before his own birth. Moreover the peripheral, concealed figure of the father here affirms not the mother's romantic relations with her paramours but rather the force of paternal prohibition.

The assertion of this paternal prohibition—the frustration of the son's rivalry with his father, the son's conversion of his own desire for the mother into something that resembles identification with his father—is consistent with Freudian notions of the oedipal relation of son to father. Yet the poem affirms not so much the son's desire for the mother as his renunciation of that desire. Similar notions of refusal and prohibition are central to Barbara Johnson's notion of apostrophe, as I suggested above: the cry of "Mother, Mother!" at the opening of "During Fever" strongly evokes Johnson's notion that the cry of "Mama!" underlying all apostrophe marks not proximity but the speaker's knowledge that proximity cannot be attained. (Peter Sacks affirms something similar when he claims that elegy always renounces oedipal desires [*English* 7–8].) That this narrative of loss involves a critique rather than a simple embrace of psychoanalysis is suggested by the allusion in the poem's last lines to Freud:

> Terrible that old life of decency
> without unseemly intimacy
> or quarrels, when the unemancipated woman
> still had her Freudian papá and maids!

This final sentence of the poem is marked by multiple negations: the mother is unemancipated; the glory days of Freudianism are, as in Koch's poem, long since over; and their heyday itself was "terrible" because it required a denial of the "unseemly" truths of "intimacy" and "quarrels." These nearly excessive strategies of distancing imply that the speaker's repudiation of the Freudian involves a struggle. Lowell's version of Freud is far more conflicted than Koch's somewhat impersonal eulogy, which contains few intimate disclosures about its speaker and whose addressee is a personified abstraction rather than, as in Lowell's poem, an actual person. Lowell insists that the lyric desire for the other's animation can be fulfilled only through the renunciation of actual filial desire. Far more directly than Koch, then, Lowell links apostrophe with turning away.

The poem's several scenes of overhearing intensify this sense of renunciation and also of pathos. The father in the poem's final stanza eavesdrops on the conversation between his daughter and her suitors, a scene that imperfectly repeats an earlier scene of paternal overhearing. In the second stanza the speaker's father, unbeknownst to the speaker and his mother, overhears their gossip about him yet fails to make his presence known to them:

> Often with unadulterated joy,
> Mother, we bent by the fire
> rehashing Father's character—
> when he thought we were asleep

> he'd tiptoe down the stairs
> and chain the door.

The appearance of these two scenes in a poem preoccupied with the efficacy of apostrophe evokes Mill's association of poetry with overheard speech. Yet the relation of overhearing in "During Fever" to the speaker's more straightforward desire that his apostrophe be heard is difficult to parse without incriminating Lowell's obscurantism and insisting, as does one of Lowell's readers, that lyric, in opposition to Mill, ought to be "heard, not overheard" (Kramer 82).[20] Such an inversion of Mill partly reflects common assumptions about the supposed accessibility of confessional poetry, but it also highlights the fact that Mill's notion of poetry, like Barbara Johnson's of apostrophe, emphasizes the failure of direct communication. "During Fever" represents overhearing inconsistently, incompletely laying out an equivalence between the poem's represented overhearers, its apostrophized other, and its audience. In this way, it enacts something similar to the multiple exclusions that for Johnson, Mill, and Frye are essential to lyric. Lyric is in this way tropological: when it describes overheard speech, it is partly describing its own status as overheard speech. To adapt Tucker's notion of overhearing, to apostrophize is to recollect a past mode of lyric; apostrophe sets both the speaker and the poet into a position of overhearing that affirms the instability of apostrophic utterance itself. "During Fever" presents several models of recalling the past; its apostrophe is caught between recollection and defiance. Lowell as apostrophizer is, to use different terms, both listener and poet, and these doubled roles, the poem makes clear, involve conflict.

The poem's two scenes of overhearing juxtapose two different kinds of fathers, the first powerless and timid, the second more powerful as well as more sympathetic to the speaker, who lingers behind the screen with him.[21] More significantly, though, both scenes define speech as a triangular act, requiring the presence not only of speaker and hearer but also overhearer. Both scenes also obstruct simple mechanisms of communication in ways that recall the doubleness of pathos, which undermines as it insists on the possibility of sympathetic identification. The effect of these third, silent figures is different in the two scenes, yet in both they complicate erotic intimacy. The mother's father at the end of the poem, in suppressing unseemly erotic talk, in fact affirms his own "Freudian" relationship with his daughter; the fact that early on the speaker, if not the gossiping son, is aware of the father's trip downstairs seems retrospectively to imbue his recollection of the fireside scene with an added thrill. Both scenes of overhearing also reveal the limited perspective of their participants. The earlier scene emphasizes the distance between the son, unaware of his father's presence, and the narrator, who is essentially omniscient; the final scene more directly expresses a kind of pitying contempt for the innocence and repression of by-gone days. The presence of an overhearer, that is, reveals the limitations of direct speech; the suitors' self-conscious attempts at wooing the mother are not even represented.

The poem's apostrophe affirms a similar preoccupation with prohibition: to ensure the mother's response, the speaker must absent himself from the recollected scene, and when he does so he is allowed to see her body, or at least her synecdochic smile. Just as the scenes of overhearing emphasize the stagedness or artificiality of dialogue, the machinery surrounding the invocations of the mother—one in each stanza, each requiring a different, elaborate scene—reveals the artificiality of invocation itself. What makes it worse is that apostrophic speech requires overhearers: just as the poem's scenes of speech require a listening father, Lowell needs us to be his listeners.

"During Fever" in these ways qualifies the apparent triumph of the final stanza's successful summoning up of the mother. The poem enacts Lowell's uncertainty about relying on apostrophe, a figure that is both pathos-filled and pathetic and that suggests the enormity of yearning even when that yearning seems to have been fulfilled. Summoning up the Freudian papá while insisting on his anachronism, insisting on the discrepancy between credulous character and recollecting poet, and repeatedly invoking a mother who, when she finally appears, has no interest in the speaker, Lowell reveals his ambivalence toward apostrophe. Apostrophe is, the poem makes clear, archaic and naïve, but it remains, it seems, capable of expressing the poem's disproportionate feeling.

The analogy "During Fever" implies between overhearer and apostrophizing poet qualifies Frye's notion that the poet disdains his readers by turning deliberately away from them. Lowell implies that the poet, like the overhearer, is powerless, not fully able to master his poems or turn away from the troubling scenes that he is compelled to transcribe. In this way, Lowell affirms what Tucker calls intersubjective overhearing—the scenes of overhearing that occur within the parameters of the fictional world established by the poem—while diminishing the power and integrity of the speaker, whom Tucker sees as central to this mode of overhearing.

A similar qualification of the conventional power of the poet is evident in Lucie Brock-Broido's "Her Habit," but in a different realm. The poem expands Tucker's notion of intertextual overhearing, revealing the dependence of poetic speech on the overhearing of various kinds of voices, including those contained in earlier texts. Like Lowell's poem, Brock-Broido's links overhearing to pathos, to both the emotionality and the excess of invocation, by relying on apostrophe to an other who is not only absent, as in "During Fever," but also undefined. "Her Habit" considers issues similar to "During Fever," including erotic desire, death, and a desire to reanimate the other. But while Lowell stresses the connection between apostrophic and erotic desire, Brock-Broido links apostrophic desire to the desire for lyric itself.

Central to Brock-Broido's challenge to conventional notions of address is an insistence on what she calls a "form" that is not lyric. "Her Habit," like many of the poems in *The Master Letters,* the volume in which it appears, is a prose letter, a genre that undermines the lyric distinction between hearing addressee and overhearing reader: unlike lyrics, letters speak directly to their readers, although, as Waters suggests, they do so at a physical and chronological remove.[22] Yet Brock-Broido qualifies this distinction in the volume's Preamble, calling its poems, in the phrase of Dickinson's editor Thomas Johnson, letters whose "Recipient" is "Unknown" (vii). As she wrote the volume's poems, she claims, her addressee "took on the fractured countenance of a composite portrait, police-artist sketch" until he was at once "editor, mentor, my aloof proportion, the father, the critic, beloved, the wizard—he was beside himself" (viii).

Brock-Broido in this way emphasizes the relation between genre (the poem-letter) and the intersubjective realm (the relation of "me" to "him"). The gesture evokes Tucker's challenge to the illusion of self-containment generally fostered by lyric. "Her Habit" does something similar in its first few paragraphs: it affirms an archetypal stance of longing but then undermines the illusion of solidity on which that longing relies.

Master—

Because I was in the habit of you & because I have an ardor for the lie, *I cannot speak until I know.*

I have watched for you up & down the long clay path, demi-daily. Sometimes I think I hear you in the solemn bark of birds, or the cantering of dogs as they bring home their quarry—gently—in their mouths, no pierced skin, no feathers askew, only the unbruised slant of a neck broken by fear, limp now & perfect in the fluidity of damaged Form.

The addressee at first seems to be an absent lover for whom the speaker longs: "I have watched for you [. . .] Sometimes I think I hear you." But not only is the speaker unsure of whether she actually hears the Master's voice ("*Sometimes* I *think* I hear you"), the representation of this voice is indirect and shifting, apparent both "in the solemn bark of birds" and also—their doglike "bark" provides a connection—in the hunting dogs who bring home other, dead birds. Thus, the speaker's attempt to represent the Master's voice creates both birds and dogs, two distinct, even opposed entities which ultimately distance him from the speaker.

This distancing also involves the speaker's transformation of the poem's initial scene of hearing. The speaker's first analogy emphasizes the equivalence of sounds: the Master's voice, it seems, is audible in the birds' barking songs and in the sounds of the dogs cantering. Yet the resemblance to the human voice diminishes as the sentence proceeds: the sound of the dogs running resembles human speech less than the birdsong does. Then the speaker abandons the analogy of sound altogether, focusing instead on the visual image of the silent dead birds. These shifts seem to distract the speaker—by lingering on the perfectness of the dead birds' bodies, she seems to forget her desire to hear the other's voice—but they also imply a connection between hearing and obliteration. Insofar as the dogs' cantering represents the sound of the master, their quarry must partly represent the speaker. Within the poem's represented scene, then, Brock-Broido emphasizes the evanescence of scenes of hearing and the tendency of such scenes to unmake the categories of listener and speaker.

This representation of partial or indirect hearing occurs, of course, in the midst of the speaker's attempt to unmake the addressee's absence: she speaks directly to the Master, asking that he read about (or hear) her representation of herself in a position of overhearing him.[23] In this way, the poem suggests that the speaker's inability to summon up her addressee depends both on her identification of herself with him as hearer and on her transformation of him into something unfixed and inhuman. Like Lowell in "During Fever," Brock-Broido is concerned with the relationship between apostrophe and scenes of hearing and overhearing. But while Lowell's poem emphasizes the multiple, if mutually exclusive, desires involved in apostrophe, "Her Habit" unmakes its speaker's desire for proximity. The pronoun "you" does not recur in the last third of "Her Habit," although apostrophe is in *The Master Letters,* as in Koch's *New Addresses,* the dominant and unifying figure.

The poem's emphasis on the instability of address and hearing is more dramatically affirmed by its representation of the overhearing of earlier lyric. As its title suggests, *The Master Letters* is modeled and draws on Dickinson's three passionate letters to an addressee unidentified except as "Master."

Scholars of Dickinson have long been baffled by the identity of the letters' addressee: the actual "Recipient" of the letters, to echo Brock-Broido's Preamble, remains "Unknown" because the only known copies of Dickinson's letters are drafts, found among her papers after her death. Thus, like all the belated, incidental readers of Dickinson's letters, Brock-Broido overhears them: she is not their addressee. This accident of reception becomes the guiding principle of Brock-Broido's volume. In the process, Brock-Broido revises Dickinson's words, often in ways that further dislocate Dickinson's addressee from her reader. In "Her Habit," for example, Brock-Broido eradicates the distance in a condolence letter of Dickinson's between the dead friend and the letter's addressee. Dickinson's letter reads, "I winced at her loss, because I was in the habit of her [. . .] but to all except anguish, the mind soon adjusts" (187). Brock-Broido initially heightens the sense of the other's proximity by addressing the dead friend (Dickinson's "her"): "Because I was in the habit of *you*." But the penultimate paragraph of Brock-Broido's poem, "To all except great dread, the heart adjusts," converts Dickinson's anguish to an aversion to future contact and thus diminishes the sense of immediacy of Dickinson's letter. Such revisions of Dickinson attempt to summon her up, revealing the extent to which Brock-Broido's overhearing of Dickinson—in Tucker's sense of excessive hearing—engenders her poems. Here, as in "During Fever," pathos inheres in Brock-Broido's failures at invocation, as well as in her enactment of the partial, isolating quality of overhearing itself. That Brock-Broido does not always acknowledge her borrowings from Dickinson and other authors within the poems—although she does so in the endnotes—further blurs Brock-Broido's speaker with the authors on whom she relies and thus also blurs hearing with speech.

Tucker's notion of intertextual overhearing supports his more general claim that Victorian dramatic monologue longed for the lyric mode its practitioners so incessantly, excessively overheard. Brock-Broido's poem represents a similar generic longing, although in her case, the analogy between overhearing and desire is more complex than in Tucker's example of Browning. Dickinson does not provide an example of generic fixity against which Brock-Broido rebels: the addressees of Dickinson's poems are themselves undefined and shifting, and Dickinson's writings are generically fluid in that her letters at times prosodically resemble poems, while poems are embedded in her letters. In "Her Habit," longing is repeatedly linked to questions of form. The poem insists that the process of granting form involves damage or loss: the dead birds possess a "fluidity of damaged Form"; the speaker's recent cessation of meat-eating is "a deference to form," which is itself a "form of

Prayer." These references draw attention to Brock-Broido's formal choices in "Her Habit": distinguishing recipient from reader, the poem alludes to or, in the terms of the first line, reveals its "habit of" lyric even as it refuses to confine itself to lyric's lineated form. The fluidity of the poem's shifts of tone and image derives, to extend Brock-Broido's description of the dead birds, from its damaged form: like the birds, this poem cannot sing as lyric once did, although it refers to this lyric past.

Thus, Brock-Broido's poem suggests the realm of lyric to be circumscribed and therefore unobtainable. In the Preamble, Brock-Broido calls the letter "the impure, irresistible form of prose which lies on top of poetry" (vii). The image is ambivalent, yet it suggests poetry to be a mostly concealed element of Brock-Broido's letter poems, a trace of which is apparent in the speaker's allusion in "Her Habit" to her "innumerable habits":

> In truth, I have innumerable habits; I was a-Bed today. My world is as ordered as if—as if I had stacked the stars in the nightsky's orchard, senseless as crates of fish stacked glimmering, one-eyed & blank, one atop the other of them, cold as Rome apples or a new moon.

Her habit of "order[ing]" her world by turning it into a series of symmetrical boxes laid "one atop the other" evokes the prose poem's right-justified paragraphs. Their physical position on top of one another also evokes Brock-Broido's analogous earlier image: the prose-letter poem "lies on top of"—evoking, desiring, remaking—"poetry."

As I have been suggesting, Brock-Broido's image of the bird corpses recalls the various apostrophized singing birds of lyric. Unlike those of the Romantics or even the artificial or ordinary birds of modernists like W. B. Yeats and Robert Frost, Brock-Broido's birds cannot sing. The image, though, does more than evoke what Brock-Broido's poem can no longer attain: it also affirms, if indirectly, the position of the reader. Although their necks have been broken "by fear"—by their own agency—the dead birds are not only damaged but "perfect": they are defined by the way they appear to a witness. The image evokes Mill's implication that the overhearing reader is necessary to lyric. Despite—or perhaps because of—its preoccupation with unmaking the conventional relations between poet, speaker, addressee, and reader, Brock-Broido affirms that the spectacle of her poem requires a witness. In this way, Brock-Broido like Lowell insists on the existence of an other, even if that other cannot be placed or identified. The gesture of addressing this other or allowing the implied other who reads the poem to overhear is often sad; it requires the speaker to acknowledge the limitations of speech. But it also affirms the persistence of faith in an other, even if the other, in the terms of Dickinson cited by Brock-Broido in the Preamble, remains a negative presence: "We pray to [God], & He answers 'No.' Then we pray to him to rescind the 'No,' & He don't answer at all" (viii; Dickinson, *Letters* 290).

The poems of Plath, Merrill, Glück, and Bidart represent the pathos Lowell and Brock-Broido thematize in terms of overhearing: the intersubjective dynamics dramatized by the situation of apostrophe become, in different ways, opportunities to examine the intertextual problem of relying on a figure linked with a lyric tradition that seems obsolete. The pathos inheres for these four poets as it does for Lowell and Brock-Broido in problems of affect, and in what follows I will focus on the intensity, awkwardness, and embarrassment of being in the position of yearning for something unobtainable. The poems I will examine do not refer to scenes of overhearing as explicitly as do the examples with which I have begun. Yet just as the postmodern address of Koch, Lowell, and Brock-Broido elaborates a presence yearned for but known to be illusory, Plath, Merrill, Glück, and Bidart confirm, despite and through their apostrophe, their speakers' solitude. In a different way, each poet resists the essential isolation of lyric; taken together, the following chapters suggest a range of ways postmodern poets critique and extend lyric as well as a range of theoretical approaches useful in interpreting postmodern address. One outcome of my decision to include four poets who inhabit what might be called the center of American postwar poetry rather than those who represent opposing "camps" or "schools" is this heterogeneity: these poems suggest a range of voice, tone, and theme while revealing a common preoccupation with linguistic complexity and emotional risk-taking, a combination that may partly explain the sensitivity of these poems to questions of otherness.[24] At the same time, these poets help affirm qualities that keep the lyric engaging as a genre; they share both a preoccupation with redefining lyric subjectivity and, perhaps more importantly, with delineating, challenging, and extending the parameters of lyric itself. The chapters below are also linked by my method of reading, which I have partly exemplified through my discussion of "During Fever" and "Her Habit": throughout, I closely read selected poems alongside but also against rhetorical and psychoanalytic theory.

Chapter One, "Recovering You: Sylvia Plath's *Ariel*" reevaluates a volume whose recurrent violence, often directed at the speaker herself, is not so much a reflection of Plath's biography as an outcome of her rhetorical choices, especially her insistent apostrophe. The central themes of Plath's late work—the blurring of longing with rage, speaker with addressee, transcendence with destruction, and the speaker's simultaneous insistence on her power and her compulsion to relinquish it—have often been associated with her confessionalism. Yet they are also issues central to apostrophe. By focusing on the ways that Plath manipulates and alters conventional notions of apostrophe, I argue that her poetry is both more complex and more allusive than is often thought. Plath's poems violate the empathy essential to much apostrophe: often addressing an enemy, they are both pathos-filled (they enact extremes of suffering and yearning) and contemptuous of this pathos. The reader is thus both starkly excluded from and complicit in the poems' utterances. Although Plath's extended exploration of the relation between violence and apostrophe, in the end, resists biographical readings, it does not dissociate lyric figure from suffering self. Rather, Plath's late poems emphatically affirm the relevance to lyric figuration of psychological imperatives.

While my discussion of Plath focuses on her use of fairly conventional apostrophe, I turn in Chapter Two, "Ghostly Projections: James Merrill's *Changing Light at Sandover*," to a poem that is neither lyric nor apostrophic: *Sandover* is more than 600 pages, chronicles several years of its narrator's life, and includes long passages of dialogue, often represented in dramatic format. These features suggest a very different relation to loss than do those of *Ariel*: Merrill's animation of the dead affirms an aesthetic of evasion, play, and substitution that challenges Freudian notions of absence and conventional models of elegy. Yet the address in Merrill's epic emphasizes a longing for response that is central to apostrophe. The poem's attempt to fulfill and thus eradicate longing is ultimately imperfect: Merrill's apparent avoidance both of the need to mourn and of the strictures of apostrophe is qualified by a residual yearning for the lyric mode he seems to have abandoned. My reading of the poem's ending identifies the solipsism and loneliness that ultimately derive from Merrill's insistence on inventing, then embodying his addressee. By emphasizing the similarity between the apostrophizer seeking a lost beloved and the poet attempting to locate a reader, Merrill allows something approximating apostrophe to articulate the uncertainties involved in his own undertaking as a poet. Including his listeners within the poem, Merrill nonetheless emphasizes the kinds of exclusion and separation crucial to apostrophe. The poem's pathos inheres most poignantly in its representation of—and yearning for—lyric itself.

Implicit in the address of Plath and Merrill are doubts about the integrity and autonomy of the invoked other. Chapter Three, "Buried with the Romantics: Louise Glück's *The Wild Iris*," argues that Glück structures her sequence of apostrophic lyrics around such doubts. *The Wild Iris* is intensely apostrophic. Its various speakers insistently implore, cajole, and command their others. Yet these speakers are also ferocious in their critique of apostrophe: they represent it as both obsolete and pathetic in the sense of being ridiculous, as the poems' often strained reliance on personification or pathetic fallacy makes clear. Yet Glück does not relinquish apostrophe, which ultimately marks not self-involvement as much as an ambivalent, embarrassed yearning for an actual responsive other and thus for a lyric mode that Glück represents as unobtainable. This awkward posture of yearning leads in Glück's poems not merely to an affirmation of lyric longing but to an extension of apostrophe to both narrative and dramatic purposes.

Although very few critics have seriously examined the poems of Frank Bidart, I claim in Chapter Four, "Homo Faber: Frank Bidart's *Desire*," that Bidart's poems clearly articulate not only the link between apostrophe and loss but the dilemmas central to much contemporary poetry. Insisting that elegiac apostrophe articulates a desire enabled by absence, Bidart's poems invert Merrill's resistance both to elegy and to lyric, embracing the illusion that Plath and Glück resist. The possibility of overhearing the dead may be a fiction, as Bidart's speakers acknowledge, yet that fiction nonetheless offers consolation. The poems thus enact pathos—an intense emotionality based on identification—far more openly than the others I examine. Bidart's volume is unabashedly elegiac, yet, like Merrill, Bidart also revises conventional notions of elegy. Bidart's speakers do not cease desiring the dead; it is their desire itself, their inability to forget or transform their recent losses that ultimately consoles them. In this way, Bidart affirms a lyric that insists on repetition, juxtaposition, and contradiction rather than on narratives of healing or relinquishment.

Bidart's poems affirm the solitary mode of lyric while refusing to valorize conventional notions of lyric selfhood: his speakers are defined but also eradicated by their desire for absent others. In my conclusion, " 'A dream of this room': Self-Effacement and Lyric Space," I locate my discussion of address within more general questions about lyric subjectivity. I begin with an examination of a recurrent tendency in the poems of Plath, Merrill, Glück, and Bidart: the speaker often refers directly to self-effacement. But this self-effacement is not linked to violence, annihilation, or despair. Nor does it lead to a systematic dismantling of the notion of self. Rather, self-effacement leads in these poems to a kind of stillness, which enables the possibility of proximity: to unmake the coherence of the self is, it seems, a necessary step in inventing the illusion of intimacy, an illusion through which the poem, however tenuously, comes into being. By emphasizing a self defined by its willingness to be unmade, these poems affirm selfhood to be constituted by desire. And by focusing on the paradoxes of this desire, they suggest that selfhood itself exists within and in the service of lyric. I turn in the second half of the chapter to a reading of a poem by John Ashbery that considers the repercussions of this self-effacement. Imagining the reader in a position as tenuous as that of the addressee of many of the apostrophic poems I have examined, Ashbery's "This Room" makes explicit the extent to which postmodern poems use apostrophe to define their relationship with their actual, if unrepresentable, readers. By depicting a speaker whose identity is fragmented in ways that resemble those of the addressee, Ashbery permits the possibility of an identification, albeit highly contingent, between reader and speaker. At the same time, his representation of a vivid but imaginary space or "room" recalls a notion central to the book as a whole: lyric itself is powerful because it is artificial. It creates an intact, beautiful realm alongside the actual and familiar.

Chapter One
Recovering You: Sylvia Plath's *Ariel*

For readers weary of biographical analyses of Sylvia Plath's late poems, Louise Glück's intelligent, idiosyncratic reading of *Ariel* comes as a relief. Glück, herself a poet influenced by Plath, instead focuses on the function of address in these poems, an issue discussed by very few critics.[1] Glück's basic claim is that the negativity with which Plath's speakers address others within the poems exposes a similarly negative conception of the poems' actual readers, whom Glück argues Plath ultimately "exclu[des]" from the poems. In the process of elaborating this argument, Glück implies several general questions both about lyric address and about Plath's poems. What is it about Plath's late poems that so forcefully implicates and disturbs their readers? What is the relation between this vehemence and Plath's reliance on address or more exactly on apostrophe? What does the condition of exclusion condemned by Glück reveal about Plath's conception of lyric? And what does it reveal about the relation of apostrophe to reader address more generally?

    In this chapter I will answer these questions by examining three of Plath's late, apostrophic poems. One of my central claims is that these poems make stark an exclusion and also a pathos inherent in all lyric. They offer, that is, a particularly vivid example of dynamics concealed but present in other poems. At the same time, focusing on Plath's address changes her poems. This is my second main point: although few readers have noticed the predominance of apostrophe in Plath's final volume, *Ariel,* attention to this apostrophe renders these poems less solitary than they often seem, and also more crafted and more allusive.[2] The poems' apostrophe also reveals their emotional terrain to be subtler and more diverse. Plath's apostrophe reveals desire as well as rage, the wish to possess as well as to repudiate, and a speaker who is solitary but also constituted by her interactions with others. This range suggests something more crucial. The formal and rhetorical choices that impel Plath's poems define—indeed they are a source of—their emotions. Plath's late poems are not merely or wholly chronicles of her life experiences, interpersonal struggles, memories, or mental instability; of her attempts to articulate a personal system of mythology; of her attempts to overcome the restrictions of her gender or her era; or of her political convictions.[3] Rather, although they allude to such situations, the psychological conflicts in these poems also derive from her rhetorical decisions. Plath's poems in this way help reveal why poets apostrophize at all. My aim in drawing attention to Plath's concern with renewing and altering lyric is both to examine ways that Plath "recover[s]," in the terms of her poem "Daddy," a series of particular addressees or "you[s]" and also to recover "you" or apostrophe itself as a crucial element of Plath's poems.

Glück's objections to Plath, and in particular to "Lady Lazarus" (*Collected* 244–7), derive from what she perceives as the equivalence of the poem's addressed audience—its "you"—and its actual readers. Glück claims that because Lady Lazarus, the poem's speaker, distinguishes herself from an audience she reviles, the poem itself "renounce[s] human aid, human analogy" ("Invitation" 119), presenting a "taunt" (120) rather than a genuine invitation or point of entry to the poem's readers: its "success depends on the unbridgeable distance between artist and audience" (120–1). For this reason, Glück claims, the poem "exiles the reader" (122); "the whole force of this poem is bent on exclusion" (121). Glück asserts more generally that "to overhear [a poem] is to experience exclusion," to be made "superfluous, [. . .] marginal" (115). Glück's preference is for something more intimate and open, for poems that "need to be heard, in that they postulate [. . .] a listener" (115).

Glück's terms strikingly recall John Stuart Mill's claim that "eloquence is *heard*, poetry is *overheard*" (qtd. Tucker 226). We are, according to Mill and others, inevitably excluded by, turned away from in, and forced to overhear poetry, rather than being addressed or invited in. The situation of overhearing or exclusion against which Glück chafes in Plath is thus the same situation many critics have associated with all poetic utterance.

Glück in this way advances an aesthetic that seems to repudiate the sense of alienation that for Mill and others inheres in lyric. Paradoxically, although she condemns Plath's poems based on this aesthetic, her reading of "Lady Lazarus" unmakes this sense of exclusion. Instead, Glück engages in an unacknowledged act of identification. "Lady Lazarus" is the poem in *Ariel* whose "you" is most directly identified as an actual audience; the poem recounts the reincarnated speaker's "big strip tease" before a greedy, jostling, "peanut-crunching crowd," a group of "Gentlemen, ladies" whom she also addresses.[4] The poem is highly apostrophic, but its address is both inconsistent and shifting; the "you" changes, as does the presence of address.[5] These inconsistencies disrupt Glück's equation of the audience within "Lady Lazarus" with the poem's actual readers. While the crowd clamoring for a glimpse of an illicit performance within the poem evokes the poem's voyeuristic readers, Plath stops short of reader address: the gentlemen and ladies are particular spectators at a scene to which the reader, like the reader of any lyric poem, is granted only indirect access. But by setting herself and other readers into the poem and finding a way for the poem to speak—even if contemptuously—to them, Glück implies that the reader is not only drawn into but compelled to mimic the dynamics of the poem. Her reading thus paradoxically inserts identification into the poem's apparent assertion of exclusion; the situation of overhearing lyric is not for Glück as lonely as it seems.

I have elaborated the implications of Glück's reading of Plath at such length because they reveal several key elements of Plath's apostrophe, although Glück does not refer directly to this apostrophe. Questions of connection, identification, exclusion, and desire are central to Plath's poetics: readers struggle with the poems partly because the poems themselves enact similar struggles, often between their speakers and their apostrophized addressees. Plath's poems both confront and exclude us; our response as a result cannot be dispassionate. The intensity of Glück's distaste for Plath in this way enacts the pathos of overhearing Plath's poems. We are pulled in although we know, as Glück insists she knows, that we will also be humiliated.

"Daddy" (*Collected* 222–24) is undoubtedly Plath's best-known, most anthologized, and most discussed poem, partly because of the ferocity with which it violates conventions of both filial obedience and consistency of tone and partly because its many oppositions are at times vexingly difficult to resolve. The poem's essential conflicts, as many earlier readers have asserted, have to do with control, subservience, imprisonment, revenge, and escape. These are the same problems expressed—generally in far tamer form—by apostrophe. Examining the emphatic apostrophe of "Daddy"—the pronouns "you" and "your" recur 31 times in the poem's 90 lines, often at the line end—draws attention to the conflicts about power implied by all apostrophe, although apostrophe often conceals these conflicts beneath a rhetoric of desire.

As is often the case, perhaps especially with Plath, several persistent critical debates about the poem expose its underlying dynamics. One area of disagreement focuses on the identity of both its protagonists. Readers have often disagreed about the poem's speaker. Some see her as essentially autobiographical and others as wholly fictitious; some find her essentially a victim, while others celebrate her resistance not only to victimhood but to fixed notions of identity.[6] Debate about Daddy's identity more directly emphasizes questions about power. Some critics, in arguments recalling Culler's claim that apostrophe is always concerned with "radical interiorization and solipsism" (146), see in Daddy a double or alterego for the speaker, someone who cannot be extricated from her, while others see him as an autonomous character whose opposition to the speaker remains extreme.[7] It is unsurprising that readers would also differ about the poem's movement. Most readers locate a fundamental undecidability in the poem's final assertion that the speaker is "through."[8] Some, though, insist that the speaker triumphs in the end, "exorcising" Daddy, to recall a recurrent critical term, by impelling him back into immobility.[9] Others argue that the speaker is herself annihilated by her attempt to free herself from Daddy or converted into a "copy" of him no less indistinguishable from him than her husband is.

"Daddy" itself prevents such disputes from being resolved; in fact, uncertainty about who is in control is central to the poem. The poem's apostrophe heightens this uncertainty. Apostrophe by definition involves a speaker who makes himself known through his representation of the addressee, along with an addressee who exists only within the speaker's utterance. The situation of apostrophe thus challenges the autonomy of both "I" and "you"; it establishes a situation of dependency in which the threat of annihilation is always visible.

The apostrophe of "Daddy" thus cogently articulates the confusions about mastery that have, it seems, impelled the speaker to utter the poem at all. Apostrophe also intensifies these confusions by setting forth the fiction that Daddy is present despite the speaker's repeated attempts to vanquish him. In this way, the poem's apostrophe both elaborates and resists its argument. And the poem's thematics explore but also undermine the implications of its apostrophe. Such dynamics end up intensifying the poem's central struggle.

The poem's apostrophe, like all apostrophe, is in this way ambivalent. It alludes to yearning and desire even as it insists on distance. If the poem's apostrophe were removed—if "Daddy, I have had to kill you," for example, became "I have had to kill him"—some of the ambivalence, the sense of coercion of the original would remain. But missing would be much of the uncertainty and therefore the tenderness. The speaker's father is, of course, long since dead, yet her use of the second person—particularly combined with the ambiguous time frame implied by the present perfect—denies his death. Although some of the speaker's actual words to him are filled with antipathy, the *structure* of the apostrophe expresses the wish for dialogue and reveals that the speaker remains in Daddy's power despite her claim to have killed him. The fact that she must kill him though he is already dead—or have his newest incarnation killed—intensifies the paradox essential to the poem's address. Since the speaker restages his death three times—"I have had to kill you"; "You died before I had time—"; and "There's a stake in your fat black heart"—Daddy must seem to the speaker somehow alive. These repetitions recall Barbara Johnson's claim that apostrophe is preoccupied with unmaking absence (it is the child's cry to the absent parent) even as it ultimately affirms the permanence of death. The poems Johnson discusses, addressing aborted children, raise the question of the mother's culpability for their death. Plath's alliance of yearning with murderousness is more extreme, yet it is consistent with Johnson's notion that apostrophe's apparent attempt to animate absent others often reveals an opposing impulse to deanimate.

A related conflict is central to Jahan Ramazani's reading of the poem as elegy. Although many readers see "Daddy" as more or less exclusively enraged, Ramazani argues that the poem alludes to and revises the lyric convention of elegy by melancholically refusing to relinquish the dead.[10] The speaker's bereavement for Ramazani is both vengeful and grief-stricken: Plath is "participating in [. . .] a genre that allows her, like other poets, both to mask and to reveal grief, to dramatize and to disclose it" ("Daddy" 1143). Plath's apostrophe articulates for Ramazani the speaker's "melancholic ambivalence[, . . .] her desire to revive yet revile the dead man, to reach yet relinquish him" ("Daddy" 1153). Ramazani's emphasis is mostly on the negative features of this apostrophe. Rather than impelling Daddy to return to life, as does much apostrophe, for Ramazani Plath's apostrophe "hammer[s] her dead father into oblivion" (1153). Ramazani suggests that the speaker's longing for Daddy and her desire to unmake her separation from him may have led her in the past to do whatever she could to join him: "At twenty I tried to die/ And get back, back, back to you"; "I made a model of you,/ [. . .]/ And I said I do, I do." Yet the poem for Ramazani chronicles the speaker's change in attitude: she realizes that her future happiness requires not proximity to but freedom from him. The speaker's realization that Daddy is not "a bag full of God" but "a swastika," "a brute," and "a devil" impels her to cast him away from herself.

The poem's final scene, though, can be read not only as the culmination of a narrative of revenge but as a more ambivalent, even tender account. Significantly, the speaker does not perform the poem's final act of murder; instead, her inability to kill him recalls her earlier wish to "get back to" him:

Daddy, you can lie back now.

There's a stake in your fat back heart
And the villagers never liked you.
They are dancing and stamping on you.
They always *knew* it was you.

Here the villagers gleefully, angrily stomp on the father-as-vampire, both recognizing and annihilating him. The speaker, though, is merely a witness, not a participant, recusing herself at the last moment from driving in the stake which she notes, impersonally, is "There [. . .] in your fat black heart."

The poem's language also suggests an alternative to Ramazani's implication that the poem chronicles a narrative in which tenderness is transformed into vengefulness. By describing Daddy using imagery and syntactic patterns distinct from those through which she describes herself, the speaker affirms an unchanging realm characterized by the persistence of her dependency on Daddy. In the process, she draws attention to her own linguistic power.

The poem's almost dogged insistence on its "I" has been several times noted.[11] Many of the poem's sentences begin with assertions about the speaker's relation to Daddy:

> I have had to kill you.
> I used to pray to recover you.
> I never could talk to you.
> I thought every German was you.

This recurrent syntactic pattern emphasizes the speaker's immobility. Her attempts to assert herself always affirm her dependence on Daddy; he is the object of each of her sentences.[12]

In contrast, Daddy is more changeable. The poem's "you" flits from one body and identity to another; he is described nearly wholly through analogy, by means of a string of metaphors, similes, and metonymies.[13] His transformation from inanimate black shoe to bag full of god to Nazi to devil to vampire reveals the speaker's shifting vision of him. At one level, these transformations affirm Daddy to be the poem's most powerful figure, since he keeps changing in form and through these transformations threatening to master the victimized speaker, who would not be speaking at all without the impetus of her antagonism toward him. As the poem's use of "you" establishes a situation in which response is invited, the speaker's repeated attempts to locate herself in relation to Daddy reveal her desire to gain proximity to him.

Daddy ultimately exists, though, only because the speaker has animated him. Much has been made of the speaker's reversion to babytalk and the poem's enactment of the breakdown of language as a means of poetry and communication. But the narrator is also verbally dexterous—she can imagine Daddy in many forms—and thus not entirely in Daddy's thrall. Instead, her ability to manipulate rhetorical figures, including apostrophe, frees her from the subjection of self to other implied by the apostrophe itself. Identity in the poem, the opposition between poet and protagonist in this way suggests, derives at least partly from the capacity to use poetic language.

That issues of artistic representation are central to the poem is emphasized by the speaker's description of Daddy. It has been several times noted that, amid the rapidly shifting figures and characters that Daddy becomes in the course of the poem, only one evokes the actual man, professorial, mild-mannered, nonthreatening, unmythologized: "You stand at the blackboard, daddy/ In the picture I have of you." Although this moment is striking in its lack of judgmentalism as well as its brevity—the speaker moves immediately back to castigation and mythologization—it also implies that the actual, living Daddy is unrepresentable. Instead, Daddy is revealed through a picture, a mediating image, humanly made and partial. The other images in the poem, this moment implies, are similarly constructed, incomplete, and artificial.

The image of the picture recalls at least one of the critical arguments to which I alluded above, between those who feel that the poem's speaker is defined by Daddy and those who feel that the father is invented and animated by the daughter. At one level Daddy clearly constitutes the speaker, who would not be speaking at all without the impetus of her longing and antagonism toward him. But at the level of artistic making or language, the father exists only because the speaker has summoned up his spirit and granted him power. The poem's reliance on trope—the repeated drawing of analogies between Daddy and other entities—reminds the reader that the poem is constructed and the "you" in the end is merely textual. Plath's extreme, almost ecstatic chain of analogies describing and ultimately containing Daddy linguistically enacts the kind of violence the poem describes: it confines Daddy and robs him of power. To put the issue in terms of another critical debate about the poem, the speaker's reliance on apostrophe and trope distinguishes the author from the persona in the poem. Disempowered within the poem, struggling toward a victory that is highly qualified at best, the poet is ultimately not limited, as is the speaker, by her stuttering or nursery rhyme–like rhythms and rhymes. Rather, she is able to draw on all the tricks that lyric offers. The poem's many references to silence ("The tongue stuck in my jaw") and its stammering attempts at defining selfhood ("Ich, ich, ich, ich") enact a struggle toward a speech that paradoxically establishes the daughter-poet as devious master of the father's brute strength. The poem's *rhetorical* figures—including apostrophe—thus express and also help define the *psychological* ambivalence of the poem.

I have thus far been focusing on the poem's psychological or intersubjective dynamics, on how apostrophe helps define the speaker's relation to Daddy. The poem also invites another, intertextual mode of reading that expresses a similar ambivalence. "Daddy" is, like many of *Ariel*'s poems, a prelude to dialogue. As lyric, though, it is not dialogue but rather the speech of a single voice, an invocation which, as Culler has implied, works ultimately as a kind of lonely echo, affirming not only the speaker's imaginative power but her solitude. The mixture of antipathy and longing, nostalgia and parody in "Daddy" derives from this doubleness; the speaker seems convinced that what is gone is inaccessible, yet she keeps trying to regain it. What Ramazani calls a melancholic refusal to let go of the dead helps explain Plath's relation to apostrophe itself. Just as "Daddy" keeps resurrecting and killing Daddy, the poem both clings to apostrophe and does it violence. "Daddy" in this way ambivalently elegizes Plath's forebears, and in particular the highly apostrophic Romantics, by bluntly invoking what Romantic apostrophe more delicately presented as it expresses contempt for Romantic yearning.

I am not alone in emphasizing the connection of Plath's poems to earlier literary models, although most readers have focused on her connection to modernist, female, Victorian, or contemporary authors.[14] John Keats's "Ode to a Nightingale" (205–7) bears striking similarities to "Daddy." Both poems emphasize the connection between transcendence and death. At the end of Keats's ode, the speaker is alone, having chosen solitude not because he wants to remain amid "the weariness, the fever, and the fret" of the mortal but because he understands that transcendence is linked with death, with the threat of becoming a "sod." "Daddy" ends with a similar gesture, more violently presented: the speaker also escapes the claims of the apostrophized Daddy, a figure who, like the nightingale, cannot or will not die. But her method of escape is far more extreme. The villagers kill him or his vampirelike, husbandlike manifestation. Keats's speaker turns reluctantly away from the prospect of "easeful death" to his "sole self." "Daddy" ends similarly, with a speaker who, like Keats's narrator, has overcome her own earlier suicidal wish to get "back, back, back" to Daddy. Her solitude, though, renders her both more triumphant and more desperate than Keats's speaker. The various meanings of the poem's final word, *through*, suggest an equivalence between transcendence—the ability to pass "through" the temporal realm of suffering—and annihilation, being "through" or finished. Keats's ode is in some ways a consideration of the danger of excessive or unqualified apostrophe; Plath's revision of Romantic apostrophe contains a more extreme ambivalence about apostrophe itself. In both poems, the wish to join the apostrophized other marks an impulse toward self-erasure, but the endings not only of "Daddy" but of other poems in *Ariel* tend toward violent—rather than, as in Keats, resigned—assertions of the speaker's solitude.

I have proposed, then, two adjacent ways of reading the apostrophe of "Daddy," the first connecting the emotional ambivalence of the poem with its rhetorical structure and the second considering the poem's melancholic relation to the lyric tradition. Both these models suggest that Plath is preoccupied with questions of power, dependency, and communication. My discussion of "Daddy"—foregrounding emotional ambivalence and the struggle for the power to speak—bears little resemblance to most characterizations of confessional poetry, which tend to emphasize an isolated, injured self.[15] But these issues seem quite consistent with Michel Foucault's notion that confession is concerned with power and domination. Foucault argues that confession bestows power not on the confessing supplicant—the focus of virtually all discussion of "confessional poetry"—but rather on the interlocutor who possesses the power to absolve:

> The confession is a ritual of discourse in which the speaking subject is also the subject of the statement; it is also a ritual that unfolds within a power relationship, for one does not confess without the presence (or virtual presence) of a partner who is not simply the interlocutor but the authority who requires the confession, prescribes and appreciates it, and intervenes in order to judge, punish, forgive, console, and reconcile; a ritual in which the truth is corroborated by the obstacles and resistances it has had to surmount in order to be formulated; and finally, a ritual in which the expression alone, independently of its external consequences, produces intrinsic modifications in the person who articulates it: it exonerates, redeems, and purifies him; it unburdens him of his wrongs, liberates him, and promises him salvation [. . . .] By virtue of the power structure immanent in it, the confessional discourse cannot come from above [. . .] but rather [comes] from below, as an obligatory act of speech which, under some imperious compulsion, breaks the bonds of discretion or forgetfulness [. . . . .T]he agency of domination does not reside in the one who speaks (for it is he who is constrained), but in the one who listens and says nothing; not in the one who knows and answers, but in the one who questions and is not supposed to know. (61–2)

Although Foucault is speaking neither of confessional poems nor of apostrophe, his model evokes the tensions enacted by Plath's apostrophe: Daddy is, like Foucault's listener, "not simply the interlocutor but the authority." The poem wrestles with and works to appropriate "the agency of domination" seemingly possessed by Daddy.

Foucault's characterization of confession also helps link my reading of dynamics within the poem—the relation between the speaker and Daddy—to the position of the reader and Plath's particular readers. When a poet adapts the posture of someone making a confession, even if the poem represents a fictional protagonist before a fictional audience, she invites her readers to become "not simply the interlocutor but the authority" and demands that they "judge, punish, forgive, console, and reconcile," apparently contradictory roles all of which affirm the reader's power, the fact that "the agency of domination [. . .] reside[s . . .] in the one who listens and says nothing." In responding negatively, in identifying themselves as actual readers with the poem's represented audience, critics including Glück may be misreading, but they are also revealing the revulsion and fear that Foucault suggests are common responses to confession. The poet, in allowing the listener to overhear, grants power to that listener; the poet's apparent turning away from the reader disguises his dependency on this reader, who is after all the only listener the poem will have. In a sense, then, Glück is not misreading but rather fulfilling a role "Lady Lazarus" has granted her, seizing power that Plath herself has offered.

Yet such power can be terrifying. Apostrophe flirts with self-destruction, both in "Ode to a Nightingale" and, more extremely, in the poems of *Ariel:* to become one with the longed-for other involves a diminishing or loss of self. Self-obliteration is in some ways a necessary risk of apostrophe. In Keats's ode, as Cynthia Chase has argued, the central question is "how can I live without *thee?*" (223), in which "*thee*" is not so much the particular addressed nightingale as the stance of addressing an other as if it were alive. The poem for Chase chronicles the speaker's coming to terms with the "futility" (216) and also the fictionality of his invocation. If this is the case in Keats, it is not surprising, given what I have just suggested about "Daddy," that Plath would approach such questions with more violence and less restraint. To recall but reverse the terms of my discussion of "Daddy," a focus on the rhetorical—the tendency of apostrophe to undermine the "sole self" of lyric—offers a way of making sense of the violence of Plath's late poems and particularly their recurrent imagery of suicide. This imagery is often read through Plath's actual suicide, as a kind of poetic foreshadowing. But if apostrophe is always concerned with and drawn toward self-obliteration, then the recurrence of suicide in Plath's late poems may affirm the power of her rhetorical choices as much as her actual compulsion toward death. Suicide, that is, may be the most extreme ending point of an apostrophic poem or more exactly of a poem that fulfills apostrophe's desire for union.

Plath's "Ariel" (*Collected* 239–40)—as the title poem of Plath's last volume, it is particularly significant—is preoccupied with the problems of a particularly lyric union. By insisting on the "one[ness] of the speaker and the poem's other—the horse Ariel on which she rides—the poem radically extends and even violates the lyric convention of an autonomous, singular speaker. It is this violation, this insistence that "I" can be subsumed in "we," that leads to the destruction of the poem's conclusion. By its end, the plural pronoun has vanished, leaving the speaker alone. Yet this ending neither restores her to chastened solitude nor permits her triumphantly to affirm selfhood. Instead, the speaker is at the end of "Ariel" defined by a series of analogies to inanimate others. The "suicidal" nature of her final flight is thus not so much the effect of a preexisting mental instability in Plath herself as the outcome of the speaker's early insistence that autonomous selfhood is obsolete.

In "Ariel," apostrophe has been rendered obsolete. "God's lioness," the poem's first acknowledgment of a living presence in the poem, a phrase that might function as an appositive, is immediately followed by "how *one we* grow," a phrase that excises the autonomy of the lioness.[16] When the first-person singular pronoun appears in the first half of the poem, it is generally in the position of object or subordinate clause (as in "Something else/ Hauls me through air" or "the neck I cannot catch"). This post-apostrophic situation—in fact, Plath in revising excised the apostrophe from an early draft (van Dyne 121)—reveals the most radical way Plath altered the apostrophe of her Romantic precedecessors.

In passing, Marjorie Perloff has called "Ariel" "a modern variant" of "Ode to a Nightingale" ("Angst" 117). Perloff locates her analogy between the two poems in the similarity between the sensuous representation of the wish for death at the end of "Ariel" and Keats's "Now more than ever seems it rich to die" ("Angst" 117). A more complete list of the similarities between the two poems might also include the numerous parallels in imagery and structure. Both poems suppress the visual ("Stasis in darkness," begins Plath; Keats's speaker sits in "embalmed darkness") and both emphasize imagery of flight (Keats's "for I will fly to thee" becomes Plath's present-tense "I/ Am the arrow,// The dew that flies"). In both, the speaker is flattened, nearly annihilated. Keats's speaker is near oblivion from the outset (he feels "as though [I . . .] Lethe-wards had sunk") while in Plath's poem the pronoun "I" occurs only twice in the first half of the poem. The emphasis in both is on merging with the other: Keats's speaker's emotions are defined by and exaggerate the nightingale's (he is "too happy in thy happiness") while Plath's speaker has nearly merged with the other at the poem's outset: "God's lioness,/ How one we grow." The speaker's identification with the other leads both poems toward an embrace of death: the "full-throated *ease*" of the nightingale evokes for Keats's narrator "*easeful* death"; Plath's speaker marvels—the referents are herself and her horse—at "how *one* we grow," but by the poem's end she is "at *one* with" a force associated not only with death but also with suicide (all emphasis added). Both end with ambiguous imagery heralding temporal change, Keats's with the famous "Fled is that music! Do I wake or sleep?" and Plath's with "I/ Am the arrow// [. . .] that flies/ [. . .]/ Into [. . .]// [. . .] the cauldron of morning."

Given these parallels, the differences in the narratives of the two poems are particularly significant. The moment Perloff cites as evidence of Keats's kinship to Plath, "Now more than ever seems it rich to die," occurs not at Keats's poem's end, where it might mark its culmination, but midway through. Just after articulating his yearning for death, Keats's speaker imagines the problems that would result from achieving that wish:

> Now more than ever seems it rich to die,
>   To cease upon the midnight with no pain,
>   While thou art pouring forth thy soul abroad
>   In such an ecstasy!
>   Still wouldst thou sing, and I have ears in vain—
>   To thy high requiem become a sod.

On the verge of entering the realm of the nightingale, of achieving his apparent wish to become one with it, the speaker realizes the danger: in dying, he would become inanimate, a "sod" unable to hear the song or sing himself. This revelation helps him, by the poem's next stanza, to pull back more definitively. The realization that the timeless, magical realm represented by the bird is "forlorn" draws the speaker "back from thee to my sole self!" By the end of the poem, having bid the nightingale "Adieu!" with a mix of triumph and regret, the speaker is alone.

Keats's poem first imagines union with the nightingale in the future ("for I will fly to thee") and through an apostrophe that emphasizes the speaker's separation from as well as yearning toward the nightingale. He then shifts to the present tense of attainment or desire ("Already with thee! tender is the night"). But Plath's poem begins at a state of Keatsian "already with." In Plath's poem, the initial sense of merging—"God's lioness,/ How one we grow"—intensifies as the poem progresses rather than being drawn back from. As the poem proceeds, the speaker sheds her old self, first "unpeel[ing]," then becoming a series of objects (wheat, seas, arrow, dew). This transformation, like Keats's into an inanimate "sod," projects her into a place linked with death. While Keats turns away from death, though, Plath continues headlong forward.

Perloff affirms something similar in her discussion of "Ariel," arguing that the inanimate—or more exactly the animal realm of the horse—replaces the poem's speaker: the speaker is erased as a self through her identification with the horse she is riding ("Angst" 116–7).[17] This notion is consistent with the power dynamics I have been associating with Plath's apostrophe; Perloff emphasizes the dependence of the poem's speaker on the invoked other.[18] But while Perloff is one of the few critics to discuss *Ariel*'s figurative patterns, especially its use of animation or prosopopeia, she does not consider the ways that the speaker's identifications and mode of self-representation change during "Ariel."[19] The poem describes a temporal and physical journey. Beginning in darkness, it ends with the rising of the red sun; it passes through a varied landscape. In the process the speaker's animation of and oneness with her horse become a oneness with the drive into morning's red eye. The speaker begins by blurring the boundaries between herself and the horse. "Pivot of heels and knees!" refers to the speaker's body but also to that of the horse to which her body seems to have nearly fused; the image emphasizes the bodily connection, even confusion, of horse with rider. The surroundings too are animated through the speaker's analogy—the term "sister" refers to living beings—between field and horse neck:

[. . .] The furrow

Splits and passes, sister to
The brown arc
Of the neck I cannot catch[.]

This impulse toward animation takes a very different form by poem's end. Here, the speaker's concern is no longer with the horse's body, which drops out of the poem as does the pronoun "we." Instead she describes her transformation into what she sees around her: "And now I/ Foam to wheat, a glitter of seas." She then defines herself ("I/ Am") through analogies with a series of inanimate objects removed from the landscape she is passing through: she becomes first arrow, then dew whose motion, it seems, transforms her into a personified, boiling sun or at least "the drive/ Into the red// Eye, the cauldron of morning." Unlike Keats's powerless sod, which cannot hear the nightingale singing much less respond to it, Plath's speaker's transformation into an object involves an acquisition of power: the poem's final images invest her with a force and autonomy she lacked earlier.

The poem thus represents the speaker's transformation in ambivalent terms. The poem moves grammatically toward an assertion of self. In the first half—about the horse ride—the syntax is fragmentary, the first-person pronoun nearly absent, and the verbs missing or embedded in subordinate clauses. But then the syntax changes: "I" is the subject of all three of the last sentences: "I unpeel"; "I/ Foam"; "I/ Am." As Susan van Dyne has noted, the placement of "I" at line endings—Plath relineated the poem as she revised it—emphasizes the ascendancy of the speaker's self (123). As the "I" emerges at the poem's end, however, Plath deanimates it, defining the speaker in terms of her equivalence to a series of things. Early in the poem, Ariel is defined as "God's lioness" and the furrow is her neck's "sister," but the speaker has by the end "unpeel[ed]" herself not only from what is dead in her but from her femininity. As many readers have noted, the tone of triumph at the end of the poem comes at least partly from its sense of phallic, indeed military, trajectory.

The terms in which I have laid out the poem's movement—in which an undefined ego blurred with a female other yields to a more straightforward, independent, phallic assertion of "I" as subject—evoke in some ways a fairly orthodox Freudian notion of ego development rather than a model derived from or relying on apostrophe. The entry of the child into the oedipal or symbolic stage, in which he becomes capable of independent thought, of seeing himself as an autonomous being who is part of a wider community and subject to its laws, is heralded by the presence of the father, a third term interrupting the mutuality of the mother-child pair. The protagonist of "Ariel" is by the end of the poem moving arrow-like toward the sun, an entity not present at the poem's beginning; the horse has become not the object of the speaker's attention but merely a way she gains proximity to this new desired object. Yet such an account fails to consider the connection between the speaker's trajectory and her self-objectification. The speaker's journey away from mutuality yields, that is, not to the autonomy celebrated by the Freudian paradigm of development nor even to the more ambivalent Lacanian notion that autonomous selfhood is itself a delusion relying on a series of delusions about the other. Rather, Plath's vision is far more absolute: the speaker's taking on of power links her with the inanimate and ultimately deanimated. Whereas the Lacanian Symbolic involves the repression of the son's desire for patricide and an internalization of paternal prohibition, the speaker's journey summons up, indirectly, a desire for suicide.

These features of the poem link it to the claims I have been making about apostrophe, although the poem itself lacks apostrophe. "Ariel" affirms the need for the kinds of limitations—the necessary distance of other from self—essential to apostrophe. It does so through negative example, by revealing that without these limitations, lyric selfhood, and lyric itself, become impossible. In some ways, "Ariel" evokes not the early Freud of the seduction theory nor the later Freud of the Oedipus complex but his very late, more fragmentary *Beyond the Pleasure Principle,* which posits, in addition to a pleasure principle or life instinct, a reality principle or death instinct antithetical to gratification and eros (63–4). (I will consider the relevance of this work to lyric models of mourning further in relation to James Merrill.) But "Ariel" also complicates Freud's opposition of eros to death.[20] The paradox enacted by the poem's simultaneous movement away from merging with Ariel and into self-inflicted death recalls Barbara Johnson's decision to exemplify her general claims about apostrophe through a study of poems which chronicle a different kind of deliberate killing—the decision to abort a fetus. Johnson's essay begins by considering a question central not only to "Ariel" but to the study of lyric more generally: what is the relation of lyric figure and trope to "real-life" considerations of mortality, suicide, and the like? In Johnson's terms, is there "any *inherent* connection between figurative language and questions of life and death, of who will wield and who will receive violence in a given human society" (184)? Apostrophic poems, Johnson claims, insist on animation even as they "act [. . .] out a *loss* of animation" (186), often in the speaker. All apostrophe is thus preoccupied with the limitations of its attempts at animation; poems addressed by mothers to aborted children intensify the conflict by emphasizing a death for which the speaker is responsible. Yet as long as the mother keeps talking to the aborted child, she "keep[s it] alive" (192) and so undermines her identity as murderer. Johnson thus connects the uncertainty of apostrophe about the other's status to an uncertainty about "the precise degree of human animation that existed in the entity killed" (189). While Johnson's argument is in many ways inapplicable to "Ariel"—most obviously because, as I have been arguing, Plath's poem is not apostrophic—"Ariel" emphasizes the connection between what Johnson calls "figurative language and questions of life and death." The poem's last sentence both affirms and annihilates the speaker as animated subject. Having implied apostrophe to be unnecessary, the speaker is nonetheless preoccupied with the intersection of death and address, but the death it considers is the speaker's rather than the addressee's. Plath's poem thus extends as it inverts Johnson's analogy. Rather than identifying apostrophe as a response to a deliberately chosen death, Plath suggests suicide itself to derive from the impossibility of apostrophe. In "Ariel" as in Johnson's model, the self cannot persist once its desire for the other has been rendered unnecessary.

Johnson's connection of apostrophe, animation, and death relies on Paul de Man's more general notion that prosopopeia affirms both "the fiction of the voice-from-beyond-the-grave" and the certainty of the speaker's death (*Rhetoric* 77). A similar paradox is central to Johnson's formulation: the poems she examines both affirm and deny death. De Man's implication is that autobiography—which for him includes poetry (*Rhetoric* 68)—functions like posthumous utterance. This analogy evokes the shifting and ambiguous time frame of "Ariel" and the more general tendency of Plath's late poems to chronicle their speaker's death as if recalling it. Yet such apparently posthumous narration inevitably reveals its "fiction[al]" nature: the possibility that the speaker of "Ariel" is dead is undermined by the poem's vibrancy of voice; its speaker's suicide is, like the speaker's paralysis in "Daddy," rhetorical. The fact that the speaker is engaged in a suicidal *flight* at least partly contradicts the stasis of death. Her flight continues past the last line of the poem, and Plath the author can keep writing poems. Similarly, though the speaker emphasizes the analogies between herself, Ariel, and the landscape through which she passes, the poem at the most basic level distinguishes the speaker from the world; it is, in the end, a kind of personal meditation inspired by a landscape of the kind favored by Plath's Romantic predecessors.[21]

The word "suicidal" in the poem's last sentence is often read as crucial to the poem's movement, although it has been interpreted differently by different readers.[22] In fact, Plath added the word late in the revision process (van Dyne 121). Moreover, the syntax of the last sentence of the final version is ambiguous: the dew's suicidal trajectory is never connected directly to the speaker herself:

> And I
> Am the arrow,
>
> The dew *that* flies
> Suicidal, *at one with* the drive
> Into the red
>
> Eye, the cauldron of morning. (emphasis added)

By interjecting arrow, dew, drive, and eye between herself and the cauldron, the speaker separates herself from the adjective "suicidal," whose antecedent is unclear: it may be associated with the dew, its flight, or the drive. That an arrow's flight is less quickly met with obliteration than dew's heightens the confusion.

In "Ariel," then, as in "Daddy," Plath's preoccupation with problems of separateness and merging reveals her speaker's psychological state. The poem also shows Plath's attempt to work out—through a kind of negative example—her relation to the traditional notion that the speaker of lyric must be both solitary and whole. As I have been arguing, Plath is here concerned less with modifying the Romantic prototype than with bursting through its limitations.

Her attempt to render apostrophe obsolete, though, ends up affirming something not so different from what more conventionally apostrophic poets have found: it is impossible to forsake the lyric subject. While the poem attempts to transcend separation and thus desire, absence persists, a failure of merging that recalls Lacan's emphasis on the lost, yearned-for figure of the mother: "mourning" inheres in the final image of "morning." Longing is particularly apparent in the apostrophe excised from an early draft of the poem's last sentence: "O bright// beast, I/ Am the arrow" (qtd. van Dyne 121). The apostrophe explicitly links the speaker's acknowledgment of her bond with Ariel to her transformation into the arrow. By deleting the apostrophe, Plath severs this connection, affirming in its place the speaker's connection only to her own self-multiplications; she is both grammatical subject and object in the last sentence, both herself ("I") and others. Adapting a familiar poetic pun, the last sentence of "Ariel" connects the witnessed, seeing "red// Eye" of the sun to the "I" or solitary self.[23] A similar equivalence is central to apostrophe, which constitutes the speaker in terms of vision (or hearing): to exist as a subject or "I," the apostrophizer must see the other and imagine being seen by him. Here, though, the eye with which the speaker becomes one is not that of an actual other human but the personified eye of the inanimate sun. The eye/I equivalence affirms the speaker's isolation in ways that compactly recall the problems of apostrophe and more generally of the lyric subject. The apostrophizer must imagine an other (she must detect an "eye" in the process of perceiving her) in order to exist as a subject or "I." Plath's pun does not reveal vision or equivalence. Rather, it exposes the inadequacy of her speaker's attempt to equate self with other. The gesture is rendered particularly poignant in juxtaposition with an autobiographical essay cited by Perloff. Plath's early realization "I am I," she recalls, marked the end of "my beautiful fusion with the things of this world"; this realization was the "awful birthday of otherness" ("Ocean" 269). "Ariel" seems to posit an alternative to this otherness by imagining the fusion of "I" and "you," the transformation of "I" into "eye," yet the fantasy fails; the poem affirms the self to be constituted by a desire for a perceiving other who cannot, in the end, perceive. In this way, paradoxically, the poem recalls the lyric that it seems to repudiate, affirming through the impossibility of its own final vision something like the solitude or even the desolation that may, after all, be essential to lyric.

My extension of Perloff's observations suggests that a rhetorical analysis of Plath's late poems raises concerns about selfhood, isolation, autonomy, grief, and attachment that are commonly seen as psychoanalytic. Indeed, Plath's apostrophe is not wholly or even primarily about itself. The *Ariel* poems instead connect the violence of rhetorical figuration to actual bodily violence, insisting that its speakers turn to apostrophe to articulate impulses that originate outside language. Apostrophe's etymological association with turning away suggests that apostrophe and rhetorical figure more generally permit a turning away from or avoidance of what is distasteful or painful. In Christina Britzolakis's slightly different terms, apostrophe is "an obsessive gesture, a magical charm which wards off the narcissistic fear that one will *not* see oneself reflected in objects" (106–7).

As Kenneth Koch and Lucie Brock-Broido, who rely on apostrophe in multiple poems within a single volume, reveal the range of ways the pronoun "you" can function, different poems in *Ariel* use "you" in different ways. "Daddy" emphasizes the pathos involved in the separation of speaker from addressee, while "Ariel" reveals the untenableness of their union or "oneness." In "Cut" (*Collected* 235–6), the "you" is not truly separate from the "I"; the poem instead uses address to split off part of the speaker's body—her thumb—from herself. The poem's structure is also different: instead of recounting a story of union or separation, "Cut" sets forth a series of analogies for the cut thumb and its nearly severed tip. This string of personifications, as Perloff suggests in what remains one of few critical discussions of the poem, corresponds to the disappearance of the "I" from the poem.[24] "Cut" in this way explores the artifice of its address, its compulsion to convert self into other.

The verbal proliferation of "Cut" in some ways inverts the emphasis on death in both "Daddy" and "Ariel." In "Daddy," Daddy's deadness underlies the speaker's transformations of him; the last sentence of "Ariel" converts the speaker from a subject (she begins "And I/ Am") to a series of objects. The animation and apostrophe of the inanimate thumb in "Cut," though, reveal not an underlying failure of life but rather something more psychological—that the speaker wants to separate her self-inflicted injury from herself.

Perloff's emphasis on animation and deanimation in "Cut" and the other poems of *Ariel* raises the question of why Plath so often obliterates her speakers, bestowing their aliveness onto objects.[25] A poststructuralist reader like de Man might respond that Plath's recurrent thematics of violence, mutilation, and death derives from her apostrophe and prosopopeia themselves:

her poems enact the violence inhering in these figures. Prosopopeia, many critics agree, works by setting up analogies or metaphors between unlike entities. In the process, though, it recalls the differences it attempts to elide between the living and the dead, the animate and the inanimate. The etymology of "prosopopeia," de Man points out, refers to the "confer[ring of] a mask or face" on what is "absent, deceased, or voiceless" (*Rhetoric* 75–6). But, he goes on, prosopopeia also removes that face; it is preoccupied "with the giving and taking away of faces, with face and deface, *figure,* figuration and disfiguration" (76). Making someone else speak confirms the speaker's own speechlessness (122); the animation of something outside the self marks not the poet's impending death but for de Man the fact that he is already dead. Death itself is for de Man "a displaced name for a linguistic predicament" (81).

Such notions help explain the restlessness of a poem like "Cut." By jumping rapidly between different modes of prosopopeia and metaphor, the speaker affirms the inadequacy of her own analogies. (In the same way, the negations running through "Daddy" articulate in part the speaker's frustration with her ability to devise and sustain effective tropes.) Yet while the poem is, as de Man would predict, preoccupied with death, it ultimately denies rather than confirms the possibility of the speaker's mortality. Moreover, the poem's figuration is rooted, as are de Man's attempts to explain it, in the physical world.[26] Here, then, as in a poem like "Daddy," Plath is concerned with the interaction between the extratextual and the figurative. "Cut" reveals that Plath is not concerned exclusively with the ramifications of her tropes and figures; instead the poem, like "Daddy," examines the ways these figures express and also complicate psychological states.

It is certainly true that "Cut" is filled, according Jon Rosenblatt's assessment of Plath's poems, with imagery of "physical dissolution and dismemberment [and in particular] of knives, operations, amputations, blood, lost limbs, and cutting" (30). Confronted by the bleeding and nearly-severed tip of her thumb, the speaker first describes it in psychologically dissociated terms:

> What a thrill—
> My thumb instead of an onion.
> The top quite gone
> Except for a sort of a hinge
>
> Of skin[.]

She then moves to apostrophe, addressing the thumb as a soldier involved in a series of conflicts described chronologically; it is first a "Little pilgrim/ [. . .] scalp[ed]" by an Indian, then a "Kamikaze man," then a "Ku Klux Klan/ Babushka," and finally, in the last stanza, a "Trepanned veteran." The transformation of the thumb into "you" impels what began as an apparently self-inflicted, if accidental, injury into a realm emphatically external to the self.[27] The first lines, despite the absence of the pronoun "I," present the speaker as both victim and perpetrator: she has cut her own thumb. Plath then splits these two roles, imagining the thumb as the victim of military violence.

The poem keeps reminding us, though, of the underlying situation it attempts to deny, as midway through, when the speaker describes a series of redcoats:

> Out of a gap
> A million soldiers run,
> Redcoats, every one.

Here the term "Redcoats" evokes the redness of the speaker's actual blood-covered thumb; the pun forces her back to the body, and also to her initial confusion about agency: "Whose side are they on?" Similarly, at the end of the poem, the hitherto masculine addressee is first refeminized ("Dirty girl") and then identified directly ("Thumb stump"). Such moments suggest that she is speaking so prolifically, so erratically, to displace or conceal from herself not only the gruesomeness of the injury but, more centrally, the fact that she has injured herself.

The notion that Plath's prosopopeia undermines itself, that its act of projection fails, evokes the endgame of "Ariel," in which the rhetoric of suicide derives at least partly from Plath's attempt to overcome apostrophe's estrangement and loneliness. In "Cut," self-harm—what might be seen as a milder version or precursor of suicide—is the poem's impetus. Yet, in contrast to "Ariel," here the rhetoric of suicide remains submerged. Neither the prosopopeia nor its final unraveling lead to death or even to a rhetoric of death. Rather, the poem's rhetorical structure obscures and ultimately prevents suicidal impulses. The poem in this way celebrates the processes of projection and displacement that poststructuralist readings attempt to demystify.

Thus far, I have said little about the gendering of Plath's speakers—the allusions to the familiar characters of subservient daughter and avenging wronged woman in "Daddy," the archetypal feminine merging of "Ariel"— although much sensitive criticism on Plath deals with such issues.[28] In

"Cut," though, Plath's insistence that rhetorical figure derives from the bodily raises a series of urgent questions about the connections between gender and rhetorical figuration. "Cut" begins with a bodily wound, a kind of metaphorical severing of the integrity of a phallic appendage. Dealing explicitly with privation, denial, and negation, the poem seems to invite a reading that emphasizes the Freudian notion that to be female is to perceive oneself as castrated or incomplete. Yet Plath's treatment of this event challenges Freudian paradigms. The speaker's chronicle of her injury does not affirm her exclusion from the male realms of voice and power; rather, her description of her wound reveals her verbal prolixity, a phallic impulse to disperse. It also allows her to abandon the cramped, feminine space of the kitchen in which the poem begins. Coopting a series of masculine personae, she enters the expansive, public, male realm of battlefields, weaponry, and warfare. Imagery of mutilation, removal, and disfigurement—the terms are central to de Man's notion of prosopopeia——permits the speaker to acquire or at least expose her power. "Cut," like "Daddy," records its speaker's imaginative power: the injury does not paralyze her because she converts it into a poem.

It is plausible to read "Cut" both as a critique of the militarism on which patriarchy relies and, not necessarily in contradiction to this reading, as an affirmation of the subversive effect of challenging received notions of gender. What is most central to my reading of the poem, though, is that Plath's unstable representation of gender mirrors the poem's rhetorical structure. The extreme, almost parodic quality of the poem's apostrophe and prosopopeia reveals both the speaker's compulsion to deny injury and the limits of that denial. That a similar dynamic occurs in relation to the speaker's representation of femininity—it is denied but reappears in the poem's final image of the thumb as "Dirty girl"—suggests that the mechanism of denial for Plath inheres in a particularly female body. The poem's mockery of gender stereotypes paradoxically affirms Plath's dependence on them. Something similar is true of her reliance on apostrophe and prosopopeia: these figures, "Cut" reveals, mark hilarity, parody, and what is denied. Apostrophe originates not only in the relatively unhindered realm of desire but also in revulsion and fear. Plath's late poems repeatedly inscribe a similar revulsion toward the terms on which they rely—death, pure femininity, self-revelation, transcendence. Beginning in the implausible, the antiquated, and the impulse to deny, apostrophe too grants the speaker access, paradoxically, to what really matters.

"I am writing the best poems of my life; they will make my name," Plath wrote to her mother in the midst of composing the poems of *Ariel* (*Letters* 468). This sentence has been often cited as evidence of Plath's preoccupation with and prescience about her future fame. But the wording, in the context of my discussion of the ways "Daddy," "Ariel," and "Cut" define self in terms of other, suggests something more complex. Plath imagines herself, her comment implies, currently to be nameless, anonymous; it is the poems that will remove her from this invisibility. A similar implication links my readings of Plath's three poems: their linguistic dexterity, I have argued, ultimately exalts their maker as a manipulator of language distinct from the confined speaker within the poem. Plath's earlier poem "Tulips" affirms the connection between facelessness, self-obliteration, and the poetic compulsion to personify. Caught "Between the eye of the sun and the eyes of the tulips," she claims, "I have no face, I have wanted to efface myself" (*Collected* 161). The passage from Plath's letter contains none of the overt prosopopeia of "Tulips," yet prosopopeia is implied: the poems, in granting identity, possess the power of something alive.

Her poems, the letter also suggests, can release her from mortality. Part of the resonance of Plath's comment comes from its certainty about the future. The line offers an absolute statement about the connection between art, death, and identity; it reads as a kind of epitaph. The fact that Plath committed suicide four months after writing this letter only increases its power. Plath seems, in hindsight, to be linking death with writing, implying that now that these poems have been written, she can die. The letter thus seems to extend de Man's association of prosopopeia and apostrophe with foreknowledge of death by insisting on a causal relation: death is enabled by poem-writing; poems facilitate not only identity but death. The dynamic implied by Plath's letter thus evokes the argument I have been making about Plath's apostrophe. Unlike much apostrophe, which is occasioned by and attempts to unmake death, Plath's late poems insist that apostrophe can also lead to death. Plath's letter grants to her poems the power of naming and thereby conferring identity. Her poems grant a similar power to their "you." Apostrophe and prosopopeia, they suggest, constitute her poetic speakers.

Our understanding of this dynamic in Plath's letter depends on our position as overhearers and so recalls Glück's reading of "Lady Lazarus." To read letters addressed to someone else is to violate them, as Brock-Broido's letter-poems make clear. Part of the intensity that Plath's letter now possesses derives from the juxtaposition of its assertive, absolute tone with its author's apparent inability to imagine anyone other than her mother reading it. It is embarrassing for us to read this sentence partly because Plath's musings are so immodest, partly because, to recall Glück's terms, they exclude us even as they let us overhear. The embarrassment Culler connects with the experience of reading apostrophe is similar. We are embarrassed by apostrophe because it seems both excessive and private, because we are both overhearing and meant to overhear.

Plath's letter, though, also offers a way out of the apparent conundrum raised in different ways by Culler and Glück. On the one hand, the exclusion of apostrophe is irrevocable. The intensity with which Plath's poems speak to someone particular, even if inhuman or inanimate, sets us outside their intimacy. Yet in this act of address, the lyric speaker is ultimately alone, powerless, caught in an attitude of beseeching. Our position as excluded readers is similar: we resemble not only the appealed-to addressee, as Glück maintains, but also the speaker attempting to deny her isolation through incessant talk. In the case of Plath, this possibility is disturbing: we want not to be like her. Or, like Glück, we want to insist that our own identity, our subjecthood, derives from a source antithetical to the objecthood into which Plath's poems seem to place us. But by setting us, as does any apostrophizer, outside the lyric frame, Plath's poems offer a kind of mirror, in which we can see our resemblance to her.

seem more natural.) Moreover, while apostrophe is solitary speech, its desire for presence marked by the use of the imperative or subjunctive, the ouija board offers true dialogue, or the fiction of it. Merrill chronicles not only the protagonists' attempts to communicate with the dead (something like apostrophe) but their increasingly elaborate responses in the simple past of reportage. The strategy seems to impel the reader to take it all straight, to believe that all this really happened. But, as JM himself frequently acknowledges and as the skepticism and bafflement to which the poem's actual readers often admit reveal, it is difficult to do so.[4] The hesitation of these readers, though, tends to be mixed with, if not unmade by, pleasure. The board, many acknowledge, is witty as a poetic device precisely because it is so indeterminate.

To associate apostrophe or invocation with what is inarticulate, artificial, and uncertain is to allude to loss. This is what Julia Kristeva suggests in a discussion of melancholia:

> the depressed person has the impression of having been deprived of an unnameable, supreme good, of something unrepresentable, that perhaps only [. . .] an *invocation* might point out, but no word could signify. (13)

For Kristeva, invocation is associated with the failure of representation itself: it does not, as does Ramazani's melancholic apostrophe, pretend that the absent other is present, nor does it put forth, as does Culler's elegiac apostrophe, the temporary illusion that absence can be unmade.[5] Instead, for Kristeva invocation converts an actual or perceived loss—"the impression of having been deprived of an unnameable, supreme good"—into something that is impossible to signify.

Kristeva is speaking about depression rather than lyric. But her characterization of invocation as preoccupied with its own fictionality helps clarify the position of loss in *Sandover*. JM's desire for the dead to be made present is inextricable from his consciousness of the estrangement that the act of writing both requires and creates. The pathos of the poem derives from this relationship; compelled to represent his desire for presence in language, JM is also compelled to enumerate the ways language fails both to evoke others and to describe the desire itself. But Merrill's poem also offers a corrective to Kristeva's model's absolutism. *Sandover* acknowledges the limitations of its own rhetoric, yet it also affirms that even imperfectly signifying speech, originating in and reiterating absence, can provide pleasures and consolations of its own.

Standing outside apostrophe, then, allows Merrill to expose its artificiality; standing outside but alluding to lyric, Merrill also reveals something about what is essential to lyric. The poem reveals an affinity, even a nostalgia for lyric. David Kalstone has compellingly argued that *Sandover* incorporates short lyrics within an essentially narrative structure.[6] Like Brock-Broido's prose poem "Her Habit," though, Merrill's narrative-epic does not merely contain traces of lyric; rather, it presents a large-scale exploration of essentially lyric desires. Paradoxically, its estrangement from lyric shields the poem and its speaker from losses that might otherwise be overwhelming. The poem is filled with the raw materials of elegy; it repeatedly attempts to gain access to and grow intimate with the dead.[7] Yet the poem does not mostly grieve, nor does it need to.[8] If Plath's mode is to invent some vehicle that will impel her speaker into the red eye, Merrill's is to evade, substitute, contradict his own assertions so they reveal their implausibility. Having already lost, the poem's narrator is in a sense free. Loss, bereavement, and isolation persist, yet their inexpressibility lets Merrill distract himself with words.

I am making, then, two central claims: Merrill's poem illuminates the mechanisms of all apostrophe by drawing attention to their artifice. And Merrill's exaggerated and artificial not-apostrophe ends up offering an alternative to narrative models of loss and consolation often associated with elegy. For Merrill, loss neither resists nor cedes to consolation. Instead, loss and retrieval alternate, or in another of Merrill's recurrent visual models, the loss remains inside or beneath the avoidance of loss.

I will explore and elaborate these claims in this chapter by focusing on several passages from the sections of *Sandover* generally considered most "lyric."[9] I will first consider Merrill's relation both to address and to narrative by examining his most direct treatment of the problem of his poem's credibility in the poem's first volume, "The Book of Ephraim." Although he alludes directly to the Freudian narrative of the oedipal struggle, JM's insistence on evasion, denial, equivocation, and turning away throughout the poem evokes a psychoanalytic model not addressed by previous critics—the non-narrative alternation of Freud's fort/da game, a game motivated, like apostrophe, by the impulse to displace bodily absence and one that offers an alternative to Freudian models of mourning.[10] Merrill's characteristic reliance on puns throughout the poem reveals a related impulse. As the fort/da game both denies and recapitulates absence, the poem's puns permit an indirect approach to losses not fully acknowledged, illuminating "matter[s] hitherto/ Overpainted" (83) without forcing the speaker to linger on them. While the passages I discuss in the first part of the chapter focus on scenes of interpersonal contact, in the last section I consider several representations of isolation, exclusion, and bereavement. Such scenes undermine, always indirectly, the possibility of reunion and companionship. When, in *Sandover*'s "Coda,"

JM introduces a bereft, solitary figure, he recalls a lyric realm of unmitigated loss that he has apparently forsaken.

It is unsurprising that JM at one point in "The Book of Ephraim" considers a psychoanalytic explanation for the presence of Ephraim, "a Greek Jew/ Born AD 8 at XANTHOS" (8; in the poem's typography, capitalization indicates the actual words transcribed from the ouija board) and the sole character in the trilogy's first volume to respond through the board. Apostrophe tends to be found in close proximity to psychoanalysis in the postmodern American consciousness, as the poems of Koch, Lowell, and Plath in different ways reveal. Psychoanalysis's ability neatly to explain the conflicts essential to address—including the compulsion to cling to what is absent—renders psychoanalysis appealing, if also suspect.

JM's description of his visit to his "ex-shrink," Tom, occurs nearly midway through the twenty-six consecutively lettered sections of "The Book of Ephraim," in section I (29–32); according to the poem's punning logic, this section deals with and returns to JM himself. In a scene much cited by critics eager to confirm their own doubts about Ephraim's identity, JM acknowledges the coincidences between Ephraim's areas of expertise and weakness and his and DJ's; he asks whether Ephraim's "lights and darks were a projection/ Of what already burned, at some obscure/ Level or another, in our skulls."[11] Tom agrees with JM's analysis, offering a straightforward oedipal explanation of Ephraim and the ouija board. Ephraim is, he confirms, a psychological, rather than an actual ghostly, projection, and JM and DJ have been engaging in a "folie à deux" which, however "harmless," nonetheless represents an avoidance of deeper issues. It is JM who completes the analysis, dutifully accepting the truth of what Tom has encouraged him to articulate and converting his homosexuality into a kind of childish disobedience which foregrounds his failure to have children, the expected outcome of heterosexual marriage:

> I stared, then saw the light:
> "Somewhere a Father Figure shakes his rod
>
> At sons who have not sired a child?
> Through our own spirit we can both proclaim
> And shuffle off the blame
> For how we live—that good enough?" [. . .]

JM here confirms an acceptance of the basic tenets of Freudian psychoanalysis that he has already embraced.[12] And indeed, the events that precede

JM's visit to Tom seem to support Tom's analysis. JM explains at the section's opening that he and DJ have been involved in a cosmic mix-up. Ephraim has been punished for JM's errors, reporting that his higher-ups are "FURIOUS [. . .] Ephraim they've brought/ Before a kind of court." Once he has reported the anger of his superiors, Ephraim says no more: he has apparently been forbidden to speak to his earthly friends. Ephraim, it seems, is like JM a disobedient son, and his angry, prohibiting superiors resemble JM's own internalized "Father Figure shak[ing] his rod." The recurrence of forbidding and angry fathers and sons who defy them at their peril here recalls the Oedipus complex, a model associated with Freudian thought at its most orthodox and perhaps, to contemporary readers, outdated. It is also a model Peter Sacks has associated with the process of elegiac mourning, partly because, as Tom makes clear, it involves a therapeutic narrative in which infantile pleasures (the "folie à deux," the "marvelous nightly pudding" of Ephraim's visits) must be replaced with more mature and realistic concerns.

JM does not unequivocally embrace Tom's analysis, partly because he seems to recognize Tom himself as a self-important father figure. Instead, JM gently mocks him: Tom does not merely reveal but "exud[es] insight"; the image of the father figure shaking his phallic rod is more ridiculous than potent. More crucially, Tom's explanation of Ephraim's provenance fails utterly to vanquish Ephraim. That very evening, Ephraim returns. This event fulfills JM's wish— "Our beloved friend/ Was back with us!" he effuses—while undermining Tom's attempt to unmake Ephraim's seductiveness. In fact, Ephraim's first words concern Freud: he has, it happens, located Freud in the afterworld and reports that "FREUD [. . .] DESPAIRS/ OF HIS DISCIPLES & SAYS BITTE NIE/ ZU AUFGEBEN THE KEY/ TO YR OWN NATURES." The image also suggests Freud is not altogether pleased with Tom's application of his ideas. His suggestion that JM and DJ persevere and be true to themselves implies that Tom's words have removed them from their "OWN NATURES." JM seems relieved to turn away, in the section's last lines, from rational analytic discourse toward an embrace of the pleasure offered by Ephraim's regular visits, even if—or because—they defy "Plain dull proof":

> The point—one twinkling point by now of thousands—
> Was never to forego, in favor of
> Plain dull proof, the marvelous nightly pudding.

Tom's view is here reduced to one possible interpretation among "thousands"; JM in contrast prefers to focus on the coexistence of multiple points, along with pleasures that can be "nightly" or repeatedly indulged in.

JM's evasion of the narrative, analytical model represented by Tom typifies his mode of response throughout the poem. JM tends throughout "The Book of Ephraim" to sidestep rather than directly to confront difficult issues; he avoids confrontation by undermining absolute claims of all kinds. The poem's narrative facilitates such evasiveness: Ephraim in section I has vanished, but he then reappears. In the first section of "The Book of Ephraim," JM defines the poem's theme in terms of "an old, exalted [theme]:/ The incarnation and withdrawal of / A god" (3). In fact, the poem involves multiple incarnations and withdrawals; throughout "The Book of Ephraim," Ephraim keeps disappearing and returning as JM and DJ keep resolving but finding themselves unable to put away the ouija board for good. In this way, the plot of "The Book of Ephraim" is more circular than linear; it is concerned with repetition as much as with forward motion.

This interplay of incarnation and withdrawal, proximity and solitude recalls a Freudian model of loss and absence seldom associated with literary texts and very different from Tom's narrative of oedipal renunciation and the model of elegy with which it is sometimes associated. In *Beyond the Pleasure Principle,* Freud describes the actions of his eighteen-month-old grandson after being left alone by his mother: the boy devised a game that involved repeatedly casting a spool away while saying "fort" or "gone" and then reeling it back while saying "da" or "there" (9). As Freud notes, the game both refuses and repeats the loss of the boy's mother; it converts what might otherwise be sadness at her departure into a form of play in which grief has no part. As such, the game is profoundly ambiguous as a strategy for dealing with absence. It unmakes the child's powerlessness: while he can do nothing to bring back his mother, he is the absolute master within the game, banishing and recalling the spool at will. His actions also undermine the narrative closure of the mother's leavetaking. What was a one-time event permits an infinite number of reiterations of both absence and retrieval.[13] But while the game in these ways permits the child to assert his mastery of absence, it also perpetuates the loss, repeating the trauma of separation and failing to restore the lost mother. As such, although the game has been read as a preoedipal "rehearsal" for mature, oedipal mourning (Sacks, *English* 9), such readings ignore the fact that the game is fundamentally irreducible: it is both a strategy for mastering loss and a perpetuation of that loss.[14]

I do not mean by linking Freud's model to Merrill's poem to imply that Freud's model explains Merrill's poem nor that Merrill was conscious of it when he wrote the poem. Rather, the fort/da game illuminates the predominant mood of the poem and thus its strategies for representing loss and in particular bodily absence. JM's evasive, shifting mode of speech allows the poem to contain contradictions. The pleasures afforded by Ephraim's company (something like Freud's "da") alternate with sadness at his departures (something like the "fort"). The alternation also keeps JM from needing to describe the more fundamental absence that underlies this interplay, the fact that Ephraim is, in the end, not real. Like the addressee of apostrophe, he is a verbal construct disguising a loneliness that JM's fiction of responsiveness and reciprocity—like Freud's grandson's game—conceals.

The poem also helps clarify the more general relation of invocation to loss. The game offers a substitute for apostrophe; it prevents the child from having to call out to his absent mother. JM's revision of apostrophe does something similar. By allowing his invocations to be answered, JM renders apostrophe unnecessary. Yet this strategy also recalls the psychological projections implicit in apostrophe. To call out to a mother who has already left pretends that the mother can hear and respond. Apostrophe too is a hopeful gesture, which defies both the fact of absence (the fact that, being out of earshot, the mother cannot be made to hear) and the laws of chronology or narrative (the fact that, having departed, she cannot be made not to have departed).

Language, as Barbara Johnson has argued in relation to apostrophe, originates in a bodily (more exactly a maternal) absence it cannot unmake or express; it must fail, in Kristeva's terms, to "signify." In a sense, then, apostrophe is speech that has been severed from speech's conventional signifying or communicative function. Rather than truly speaking to anyone else, it alludes to what has been removed and thus to its own processes of displacement and projection. In this way it always hints at what has been taken, as the signifiers "fort" and "da" allude to the maternal body without speaking of them directly and thus mark the child's alienation from bodily presence.[15] Apostrophe is not utilitarian speech, although it transforms desire into reality; in Culler's terms, it "attempt[s] to call [something] into being" (*Pursuit* 139). It is, as Kristeva indicates, alienated and incommensurable. But for this reason, apostrophe and language more generally are freed from the compulsion to represent.

Such is the model of language implied by JM's frequent meditations on his own utterance. And language itself—or more exactly the poem—is, unsurprisingly, what matters most: whatever happens to JM gives him what he calls "'material.'" Not only Ephraim's withdrawals (roughly analogous to the mother's departure) but also his returns further the poem. Always bodiless, making his presence known only by the planchette's movement from letter to letter, Ephraim is a wholly linguistic being and thus represents for JM, as section I explains, a kind of protolanguage:

> We, all we knew, dreamed, felt and had forgotten,
> Flesh made word, became through [Ephraim] a set of
> Quasi-grammatical constructions which
> Could utter some things clearly, forcibly,
> Others not.[. . .]

As a "set of/ Quasi-grammatical constructions"—a kind of syntax or primitive vocabulary—Ephraim lets JM articulate knowledge and dreams that might otherwise remain unsayable. JM acknowledges the obstructions involved in this model. What Ephraim offers is only "quasi-grammatical"; it sometimes fails to engender clear or forceful speech. JM's syntax itself is here difficult to parse, partly because it lacks a subject or agent: it is not clear who is doing the uttering and who is being uttered. This slipperiness, though, is what makes language worthy of veneration, as JM goes on to explain:

> [. . .] Hadn't—from books, from living—
> The profusion dawned on us, of "languages"
> Any one of which, to who could read it,
> Lit up the system it conceived?—bird-flight,
> Hallucinogen, chorale and horoscope:
> Each its own world, hypnotic, many-sided
> Facet of the universal gem.

The image evokes JM's response to Tom, in which a single point is juxtaposed with "thousands" of other, possibly conflicting ones. There JM clings to his own preferred interpretation (the choice of the marvelous pudding over the duller explanation offered by Tom). But here there is no need to choose, master, or parse a single language. Rather, what Ephraim reveals is the abundance of languages. Even the language of "The Book of Ephraim" is, as the previous passage makes clear, second-hand, borrowed from or imperfectly filtered through Ephraim. And, although JM acknowledges the beauty of these languages—each language or facet is "its own world, hypnotic, many-sided"— the gem that these facets together constitute remains inaccessible. JM celebrates language and its power to create or "conceive" understanding, but he insists that he refers not to actual languages but rather to more removed, perhaps more metaphoric "languages."

This sense of alienation is revealed in the passage's central image. Language is, JM suggests, like light. Yet the light is metaphorical, not real; the gem and its facets are vehicles invented by the poet struggling to embody the ineffable. The act of rendering the languages solid, present, and real, JM here acknowledges, requires an act of projection, imagination, and hope.

Merrill's poems are sometimes condemned for their verbal facility—he is seen as a dazzling but somewhat cold formalist—but the analogy to the fort/da game suggests that the formal patterns in "The Book of Ephraim" reveal JM's impulse to turn away from without abandoning absence, desire, and loneliness. Merrill's reliance on puns here—as in many of his other poems—enables him with particular concision to enact the evasiveness I have been tracing thematically in Section I and throughout "The Book of Ephraim." Frequently, JM turns away from some topic only to allow it to recur, indirectly and below the surface, by means of a pun. JM's puns, especially in section X (83–86), which directly explores dynamics of X-raying, covering, and burying, allude to what he directly calls "meanings" seemingly at odds with the realm of surfaces to which puns generally allude. In fact, puns for Merrill, in ways that contradict several earlier readings of his work, function metaphorically, allowing repressed or concealed losses partially to emerge.[16]

The fort/da game converts a one-time event (the mother's departure) into something multiple (it includes both departure and return) and repeated. Puns occupy a somewhat analogous relation to time. A pun by definition involves simultaneity: it alludes, through a single word, to multiple and often contrasting meanings. In perceiving or "getting" the pun, we shift back and forth between these meanings and thus are reminded, in Walter Redfern's terms, "both of our mastery and our lack of control over language" (123). Puns thus retard forward progress; one meaning yields to another, then back. As Redfern notes, they impel us to "read in slower motion and backtrack" (25).

Section X's puns operate in similar ways. They also suggest another spatial model, one antithetical to the realm of pure verbal play with which puns are often associated. In fact, Merrill's puns tend to allude to depths, to what has been concealed or covered over. The correspondence Merrill is interested in is not between two mutually exclusive meanings but rather between the literal meanings of certain words and their deeper, concealed significance.

The nature of this correspondence is revealed at the opening of Section X, which describes two versions of Giorgione's painting *The Tempest*. The painting, X-rays reveal, originally depicted the story of Saint George and the dragon. But the now-visible painting revises this narrative into a more static image: the dragon central to the original painting has been "relegated/ To a motif above a distant portal." The speaker's knowledge of the painted-over scene, though, alters the finished painting's significance, "hint[ing]/ At meanings we had missed by simply looking." To look beneath or inside changes the surface; knowing what is concealed offers a new range of "meanings."

This scene of overpainting and X-raying is more significant, JM makes clear, because it has to do with maternity. In the original, now painted-over version, Saint Theodore reclines "at ease [. . .] after rescuing/ His mother from a dragon—'her beauty such,/ The youth desired to kiss her,' as the quaint/ Byzantine legend puts it." The excised proto-oedipal and apparently harmonious depiction of mother-son union is also revised in the poem; the painting reminds JM of "a matter hitherto/ Overpainted—the absence of my mother from these pages."[17] The mother's absence permits, fort/da-like, her return, but in another form: St. George's mother becomes JM's own, although JM's allusion to her renders her present *through* her absence and in textual rather than physical form.

As physical absence here permits linguistic resurrection, in the verse paragraphs that follow, JM punningly explores the possibilities of restoring what has been concealed. His mother is present, JM explains, only via her letters. But while she is available in this textual, displaced form, JM's description focuses, unlike the fort/da game, on her actual body:

> [She] has been, letters tell, conspicuously
> Alive and kicking in a neighbor's pool
> All autumn, while singsong voices, *taped, unreel,*
> *Dictating* underwater calisthenics. (emphasis added)

The mother's patient and repetitive motions are the last direct glimpse we get of her in section X and in "The Book of Ephraim." The next verse paragraph seems to discuss something altogether different, although this new topic too has to do with physical loss and textual reclamation, since JM retells the plot of his lost novel, converting it in the process to verse. Puns, though, recall the mother:

> The novel would have ended with surveyors
> Sighting and *measuring* upstream from the falls.
> A *dam* projected. (emphasis added)

The unreeling measuring tape evokes the mother's unreeling audio tapes; the measurements recall the musical measures; and the dictatorialness that the novel's pueblo elders, the next lines explain, are powerless to resist recalls the dictated calisthenics. Most crucially, the dam both evokes and transforms her.

JM relies on similar puns throughout the section and in the process affirms the slipperiness of language as he alludes to what is apparently lost or forsaken.[18] Merrill's wordplay is thus both playful and scientific. The puns show the poet's power: it is he who can convert and transform the mother. Puns are, like child's spool, possessed by the poet, who manipulates them at will. Yet the impetus, the starting point, is the mother's absence.

JM's allusions to his mother gradually recede in section X; his puns represent the most verbally disguised of his attempts to hold her. His attention turns, late in the section, to the absence of Ephraim himself. Ephraim now seems permanently to have withdrawn; the voice that has sustained JM and DJ has become silent. The metaphoric logic is here less clear: have the references to the mother enabled JM to disguise and defer his real concern with Ephraim's absence? Or does the drama of Ephraim's disappearance externalize a deeper (and also more Freudian) grief at the mother's absence? The poem does not let us decide, and in the process it destabilizes the distinctions between surface and depth that have unified the section. But this is in fact the point. Ephraim's absence, JM directly insists, is in fact not a loss but a transformation, one that, like the section's puns, allows apparently abandoned subjects to recur:

> Back underground he sinks, a stream, the latest
> Recurrent figure out of mythology
> To lend his young beauty to a living grave
> In order that Earth bloom another season.

By being transformed, the absent Ephraim is allowed to persist. His origin in myth renders him "recurrent"; he is only the "latest" of a series of figures that will, perhaps, continue to be transformed. At the same time, his death allows a different mode of continuance, this one bodily: his corpse nourishes the earth and enables its springtime renewal.

Given this imagery of persistence, it is unsurprising that JM directly acknowledges that he cannot imagine the way, without Ephraim in it, the story will end. He considers the possibility that he will "come lighter-hearted to that Spring-tide/ Knowing it must be fathomed without a guide" but then lapses into a groping, self-contradicting mode whose negations and unstable pronouns ("no one, nothing along these lines [. . .]/ It can't simply be written off") suggest that without Ephraim, he will fail to be autonomous, a subject who can "think for myself."

The section also ends without true closure. Instead, it punningly conflates ellipsis, the visual marker of the failure to end, with elision, an omission or removal. JM's verse itself, he explains in cosmic terms, creates through its alternation of "Gassy expansion and succinct collapse" a series of black holes that provide "Vanishing points for the superfluous/ Matter elided (just in time perhaps)/ By the conclusion of a passage thus. . . ." The ellipsis that ends the passage is itself a series of black holes, which signify not conclusion or finality but the removal or elision of "superfluous/ Matter" or the material realm itself. The pun here succinctly equates the solid matter of the poem's punctuation with the excised or elided text that ellipses conventionally mark. In this case, what is elided or omitted is the ending itself; the need to end permits its own deferral.

Underlying Merrill's proclivities toward dialogue, storytelling, and play, then, are impulses that evoke the interplay of absence and presence central to apostrophe. Several moments in *Sandover* more directly explore an isolation seemingly at odds with the poem's emphasis on conversation. In section V of "The Book of Ephraim," for example, JM describes, cameraless and alone in Venice, watching tourists posing for one another's photos.

> Who are these thousands entering the dark
> Ark of the moment, two by two?
> Hurriedly, as by hazard paired, some pausing
> On the bridge for a last picture. Touching, strange,
> If either is the word, this need of theirs
> To be forever smiling, holding still
> For the other, the companion focusing
> Through tiny frames of anxiousness. There. Come. (75)

What is here touching is not merely the tourists' need to preserve what they see but their mutuality. The adjective "touching" is ambiguous. It suggests at first reading that the couples are physically touching. Instead, though, their intimacy involves separation: they enact their bond by standing separately and allowing the camera to intervene between them. JM is here the unnoticed observer of scenes that affirm the essential solitariness of love. The sense of solitude is intensified by the invitation "There. Come." Spoken not by the photographers but by JM himself, these words are ineffectual; they confirm his solitude. The couples pausing on the bridge, like apostrophized others, cannot hear him and do not come.

Significantly, JM is here a spectator: he is invisible, and his detachment lets him comment on the scene. JM's preference for this position recurs throughout "The Book of Ephraim": he tends to shun the role of author, preferring the more passive position of reader or interpreter, as section I's description of reading various languages makes clear. This tendency recalls JM's more general insistence that he is not in fact the poem's real or only author.[19] It also here poignantly marks an exclusion, a powerlessness in relation to others that recalls the loneliness and desire that impel apostrophe itself.

The trilogy's final scene more poignantly and fully lays out this connection between spectatorship and exclusion. At first glance, "The Ballroom at Sandover," in *Sandover*'s "Coda: The Higher Keys" (556–60) seems simple. JM describes himself squinting at the mirror which gives him access to the other world; he sees a group of people enter a ballroom, greet one another, gossip, and sit down. JM recognizes most of them as illustrious dead writers. They are assembling for a performance, and what they are about to hear, JM realizes, is his own about-to-be-completed poem. But this is not a group of strangers; rather, they are the poem's dramatis personae, who have appeared in the course of its unfolding. JM adjusts the light and surveys the crowd. He has become not solitary poet but performer, and the poem's ghostly addressees have become, explicitly, its audience.

In this way, "The Ballroom" seems to vanquish doubts that JM has been intermittently articulating about the reality of Ephraim and the other ouija board characters. The poem's addressees are physically present and visible, and the issues that seem insurmountable to lyric and central to apostrophe—problems of temporality, mortality, solitude—seem to have been unmade. The scene thus seems explicitly to confirm W. R. Johnson's assertion that the lyric "you" is a metaphor for readers of the poem, a notion that lyric can never directly confirm, since neither addressee nor reader can be embodied within the lyric frame. Because *Sandover* is not lyric, though, it can make this connection explicit.

In this context it seems at first merely distracting when an uninvited guest appears. Once the dead spectators have all been seated, one chair remains empty. Then the actual doorbell of JM and DJ's apartment rings. It is Vasíli, a friend whose newly dead wife, Mimí, has been glimpsed among the ouija board's assembly. Vasíli is distraught at Mimí's death—he "can't eat, can't sleep,/ Can't weep"—and JM and DJ offer to put away the board, since as DJ says, "just as this life takes precedence/ Over the next one, so does live despair/ Over a poem or parlor game." Vasíli demurs: he agrees to fill the last chair and listen to the reading of the poem. He thus seems to represent an actual physical embodiment of audience. But despite his willingness to be a mere audience member, his presence threatens to dismantle the poem's final scene of celebration and, more crucially, the scene's apparent equivalence of addressee with audience and thus the fiction of presence on

Ghostly Projections

which the poem has largely relied. As the fort/da game enacts the child's unexpressed grief at his mother's absence, Vasíli represents a return of JM's repressed fear that his preoccupation with the ghostly world has kept him from participating in the actual one, that "written for the dead/ This poem [will] leave a living reader cold."

That Merrill is compelled to bring Vasíli into his poem's final pages suggests his consciousness of the denial on which the trilogy's repudiation of absence has relied. Vasíli stands for the mortal realm of loss, unmitigated by the ouija board's illusion of presence: although Mimí persists on the poem's stage-set, Vasíli's grief cannot be so easily unmade. Vasíli recalls the realm of elegy JM has worked to avoid throughout the poem, in which apostrophe remains unanswered and the dead stay dead.

It is not surprising, given Vasíli's association with the solitude of lyric, that JM describes Vasíli's relation to loss in terms that echo Keats, the archetypal poet of apostrophe.[20] Although Keats's role in the poem as a whole is negligible, earlier in the trilogy, in section Y of "The Book of Ephraim," JM echoes Keats directly:

> And here was I, or what was left of me.
> Feared and rejoiced in, chafed against, held cheap,
> A strangeness that was us, and was not, had
> All the same allowed for its description,
> And so brought at least me these spells of odd,
> Self-effacing balance. Better to stop
> While we still can. Already I take up
> Less emotional space than a snowdrop.
> My father in his last illness complained
> Of the effect of medication on
> His real self—today Bluebeard, tomorrow
> Babbitt. Young chameleon, I used to
> Ask how on earth one got sufficiently
> Imbued with otherness. And now I see. (89)

The reference here is to Keats's "chameleon poet" who, Keats claims, has "no identity [. . .] no self" (279, letter to Richard Woodhouse 27 Oct 1818). Keats is evoked in the context of JM's reflections on the loss of his father's "real self" and JM's own apparent desire to become "Imbued with otherness." Such self-effacement, this passage suggests, is not a threat to the self; it leads, after all to "balance." What JM "see[s]" in the end, it seems, is that being a chameleon is not the point. Instead, the passage's repeated shift into and out of the plural pronoun suggests that becoming "sufficiently/ Imbued with otherness" allows "self" to become, paradoxically, more fully itself.

It is perhaps appropriate, since Keats is here associated with a lack of ego, that he is seldom referred to again in the trilogy; he does not appear in the poem's final audience, although a fragment from "Ode to a Nightingale" is cited in the trilogy's third volume (331). The last lines of the "Coda," and of *Sandover*, nonetheless strongly recall Keats's Nightingale ode:

> DJ brighteyed (but look how wrinkled) lends
> His copy of the score to our poor friend [Vasíli]'s
> Somber regard—captive like Gulliver
> Or like the mortal in an elfin court
> Pining for wife and cottage on this shore
> Beyond whose depthless dazzle he can't see.
> For *their* ears I begin: "Admittedly . . ."

Vasíli's solitude recalls that of Keats's speaker, who finds himself among similarly deathless personified presences, "the Moon cluster'd round by all her starry fays"; Vasíli too is the lone mortal in a realm of immortals. Vasíli's isolation is caused partly by his grief: he is "pining for wife and cottage" just as in Keats's seventh stanza a similarly solitary mourner in a strange place similarly longs: "Ruth [. . .], sick for home/ [. . .] stood in tears amid the alien corn." Ruth's appearance in Keats's poem impels the narrator to realize that the "faery fields" he is staring at are "forlorn," a revelation that "toll[s] me back [. . .] to my sole self," to an abandonment of apostrophe and an acknowledgment of his mortality (206–7). Vasíli's forlornness is caused by a somewhat more complex sense that he is caught between realms: he is both "captive" in the elfin court and caught "on this shore," the mortal shore, from which he cannot see Mimi. Keats's narrator's reununciation of the nightingale, according to Cynthia Chase, is also a renunciation of the poem's illusion that the other can hear and respond (216). *Sandover*, perhaps most acutely in this final scene, similarly acknowledges the limitations, even the impossibility, of the inhabited, responsive realm it has conjured into being.

These limitations are more definitively recalled by an allusion to another poem by Keats, "When I Have Fears," in which apostrophe is also abandoned. Vasíli's position "pining [. . .] on this shore" recalls Keats's sonnet's last lines: "on the shore/ Of the wide world, I stand alone, and think/ Till love and fame to nothingness do sink" (133). And as Keats's sonnet concerns its narrator's "fears" about his mortality, Vasíli's presence makes JM acknowledge his "worst fear," of abandoning his actual, "living" readers. It is not enough, the allusion here suggests, to hope for a "Fame" based solely on appealing to illustrious dead authors. Vasíli disrupts the poem's coziness with the dead: he is not merely alive, but utterly removed from their wit and grace.

Vasíli's solitary, unconsoled presence also draws attention to the gaps in JM's embodiment of his audience. JM does not describe the audience's response to his performance of his poem; the poem ends with the first word of the reading and of "The Book of Ephraim." Furthermore, the reference to the text as a "score" reminds us that the poem's audience is evanescent: each of its members will in the course of the performance become an actor or singer. More radically and also more subtly, the italicized pronoun in the poem's last line renders the identity of JM's audience profoundly ambiguous: "For *their* ears I begin." Italics are generally used for clarification—in this case they would be expected to distinguish one group of spectators from another. But the referent is ambiguous: it may be DJ and Vasíli, sitting together, or the gathered immortals, whose last words have been "NOW POET, READ!" The italicization also affirms that the poem's actual readers are not *them* but *us,* ourselves, to whom JM ought to be referring in the second person. "*Their*" thus distinguishes the audience embodied within the poem from the poem's actual readers: *Sandover* refuses to reserve us a chair, to include us in its seemingly capacious roomful of spectators. In Frye's terms, the poem, like lyric, turns away from its actual readers.

In this way, "The Ballroom" reveals the importance of desire. The audience at the end of *Sandover* ultimately represents not the poem's actual readers but the poet's desire for those readers. That Merrill should also desire lyric is not, after all, so startling. Lyric, as the figure of Vasíli suggests, cannot help desiring what it has given up or acknowledged to be lost. Merrill's poem in this way is poised on a shore of its own. Having shifted in its last scene from written text to performance piece, it cannot help looking, or trying to look, back to the realm of lyric that it has forsaken, from which Vasíli is a kind of emissary.

In emphasizing the conjunction of JM's invocation with desire, I am recalling Kristeva's more radical dismantling of the efficacy of invocation as a means of bringing about change. In the end, though, *Sandover* does not, as Kristeva insists invocation must, undermine the possibilities of signification. Instead, it celebrates translation—the substitutions, the artificiality effected by language, or what Kristeva might call the signifier. Merrill is concerned throughout *Sandover* with metamorphosis, doubleness and mirroring, and the collapse of multiple characters into singularity. This tranformation of one thing into another evokes the substitutions effected by language, the ways that, as Merrill's poem "Lost in Translation," originally published in the same volume as "The Book of Ephraim," lays out, loss can be remade by being "translat[ed]": "But nothing's lost. Or else: all is translation/ And every bit of us is lost in it/ (Or found[)]" (*Divine* 284). Here, it seems, translation, which does not so much convert loss into its verbal equivalent as eradicate everything outside language, permits the modulation of being lost into being found or at least their juxtaposition, as the repeated "or" implies. Because loss exists "in" translation, it becomes, it seems, less acute. In the same way, the "self-effacing tree" located by the speaker "in that loss" is both consoling and unreal: it is a textual rather than a real tree, a tree in a poem for whose lost translation the speaker has been searching throughout his own poem.

Translation, Merrill here implies, sets forth a realm distinct from the actual or nonverbal experience of loss or trees. It is in this way like apostrophe. Merrill has explained in an interview that the habit in poems of speaking to the dead improves the poems:

> Poems get written *to* the person no longer reachable. Yet, once dead, overnight the shrewish wife becomes "a saint," frustrations vanish at cockcrow, and from the once fallible human mouth come words of blessed reassurance [. . .] Given the power—without being Orpheus either—would I bring any of these figures back to earth? (*Collected* 88)

Merrill seems to be affirming the poem's power: its linguistic constructions can create a reality distinct from the actual realm of longing. But the passage also suggests that language itself is circumscribed and inadequate. Just because he has written the dead back into life within his poem, Merrill does not mean to imply that he actually wants them back on the real earth. Language replaces or translates what is gone not into some version of that lost entity but into its own grammar. It cannot effect real changes in the world. Even so, Merrill suggests, language shields us from emotions that, unarticulated, might overwhelm us. Offering a substitute for loss, it also offers a way loss can be made comprehensible to someone else.

In a memoir of Elizabeth Bishop, Merrill includes a vignette which helps clarify his notion of both the limitations and the power of language:

> Late one evening, over old-fashioneds by the stove, a too recent sorrow had come to the surface; Elizabeth, uninsistent and articulate, was in tears. The young painter [a Brazilian, also a houseguest], returning, called out, entered—and stopped short on the threshold. His hostess almost blithely made him at home. Switching to Portuguese, "Don't be

upset, José Alberto," I understood her to say, "I'm only crying in English." (*Collected* 233)

The moment is strikingly similar to one in "Lost in Translation" where the young protagonist delineates his governess's divided emotions by language. Bilingual, biracial, she confides to him her "French hopes, her German fears" (*Divine* 4). In both cases, switching languages permits the emotions themselves to change. And by implication language (or the particular languages employed by the multilingual) defines emotion. We feel through language. It is not merely that our emotions seek to be expressed or even that once they are expressed, they change. Rather, our emotions exist only through and in and because of language, although language also saves us from excesses of feeling; switching to Portuguese, Bishop can cease to cry.

In both these passages, Merrill positions himself as a listener. His anecdote about Bishop hinges on what he "understood her to say," on his comprehension despite what he makes clear is his imperfect Portuguese. What is significant, he implies, is exactly this imperfectness, the things that cannot be wholly understood. As listeners, we always comprehend language imperfectly; we are constantly reminded of language's failure to communicate. Merrill, or at least JM, persists in putting himself in the position of reader, in framing and reframing questions of audience and readership because language's limitations are central to *Sandover*. Speech, the poem makes clear, is always indirect, elliptical, punning; it is not transparent. The difficulty of Merrill's poem is an outcome of what it struggles to articulate; and if longing is at its origin, that longing must keep, fort/da-like, repeating itself. "It's madness to think of an audience," Merrill has said in an interview. "It's also madness not to think of one" (*Collected* 141).

Chapter Three
Buried with the Romantics: Louise Glück's *The Wild Iris*

The poetry of invocation, some might argue, keeps coming up against the same problems. Apostrophe, the calling out to what is by definition absent, inanimate, or dead, is by the same definition doomed from the outset: it is a partial or ersatz dialogue, whose cries and appeals (from "Hear!" to "Speak!") are never acknowledged. Beginning in various impulses—a desire for companionship or a powerful feeling of joy or desolation or a compulsion to express love or a wish for revenge—poems of address tend, in the end, to express a relatively narrow range of feelings. They tend, that is, to get stuck in complaints about unrequited desire. In this way they affirm a version of self-pity that ultimately eradicates the other, the putative object of desire, and transforms the impulse toward identification, empathy, and pathos into a merely pathetic series of complaints closer to whining than true lament. Because the apostrophized other can never be summoned up or impelled to respond, such an argument might conclude, this other is ultimately revealed to be a nothing more than a projection of the speaking subject, a partial, flawed mirror in which the speaker, like the child in the Lacanian Imaginary, believes himself to be perfected.

Not all poets see apostrophe this way, as both inescapable and paralyzing, a figure that affirms, as Louise Glück says in another context, "the knowledge of [. . . one's own] passion's impossibility" ("American" 10). I have been arguing that Plath and Merrill articulate an ambivalent relationship to apostrophe, recognizing its problems but refusing to abandon it. Plath's late poems exaggerate the destructiveness usually concealed by apostrophe by demolishing the summoned-up other, although the eradication is always incomplete. James Merrill's *The Changing Light at Sandover* avoids the rage of Plath's lyrics but undermines apostrophe more radically by allowing the addressee to materialize and speak in defiance of the strictures of lyric. But the isolation and loneliness in *Sandover* recall apostrophe itself. It is difficult, then, to determine whose critique of apostrophe is more pointed. Plath expresses violent and negative feelings without abandoning apostrophe; her challenge to apostrophe is tonal rather than formal. Merrill, in forsaking lyric, is formally more extreme, yet his tone is equivocal, imbued with more wistfulness than wrath.

The doubts about apostrophe I have been describing focus on the mechanisms of identification in lyric, the often creaky, artificial, or anachronistic means by which the lyric speaker invokes and attempts to embody others within the lyric frame. While a poet like Merrill reveals apostrophe's anachronism by turning away from apostrophe, Louise Glück's Pulitzer Prize–winning *The Wild Iris,* the volume that definitively established her as a major poet, adopts a different strategy. Nearly all the poems in this sequence of linked lyrics address a silent "you," variously beseeching, instructing, chastising, and complaining; many address an unknowable, unresponsive God.[1] Moreover, they are preoccupied with the nature and problems of identification, the extent to which a truly distinct other can or should mirror the self. As a result, the work of her precursors seems partial and evasive in contrast with Glück's sustained, direct, multipart critique of apostrophe. If apostrophe is, as I have been arguing, implicit in Merrill's trilogy, a partly buried or concealed motif (to use the terms of section X) apparent only in a ghostly or displaced form (insofar as JM seldom apostrophizes in the poem), it is in Glück's sequence the formal manifestation of the volume's central theme. Yet Glück uses apostrophe to critique apostrophe. The volume condemns apostrophe in terms similar to those with which I began this chapter—directly, in a sustained and often sarcastic manner. Apostrophe is, these poems assert, outdated— it is associated with the Romantics—and often ridiculous, yet it persists despite the volume's systematic examination of its flaws. Glück's critique of apostrophe thus emphasizes, more directly than the poems I have thus far examined, the self-absorption of lyric. In the process, *The Wild Iris* directly considers the possibility that the other is in fact not there. Glück's exploration of the addressee's absence pushes her poems in a different direction from Merrill's. By juxtaposing poems spoken by different characters, her sequence approaches dialogue—an impulse that recalls *The Changing Light at Sandover*—but refuses to abandon lyric.

Glück's ambivalent relationship to apostrophe is clarified, as in *Sandover* but more explicitly, by an engagement with a concept drawn from psychoanalysis, although as in Merrill's poems the equivalence is not absolute.

While Merrill's focus is on the problems of the Oedipus complex (to which he explicitly refers in section I) and the alternative virtues of an evasiveness reminiscent of the fort/da game (to which he does not refer), Glück's volume can be read as a response to the notion of narcissism, which she elaborates in an essay published several years after *The Wild Iris*. While Merrill's evasiveness enacts the limitations of oedipal models, Glück is more direct: her poems consider, even as they sometimes enact, the narcissistic tendency to convert others into mirrors of the self. Apostrophe, these poems suggest, involves a longing that is solipsistic and self-pitying, that unmakes the autonomy of the other.

The intensity of Glück's engagement with problems related to narcissism is not surprising given her vehement response to Plath's "Lady Lazarus," which I discussed above. Her claim there that "to overhear is to experience exclusion" ("Invitation" 115) paradoxically relied, as I have argued, on identification, on a blurring of invitation and exclusion, participant and reader that evokes her complex depiction of narcissism in *The Wild Iris*. Moreover, Glück's earlier poems reveal a similar ambivalence toward address and identification. From the austere assertions of *The House on Marshland* (1975) to the mordant mutual criticisms of a pair whose marriage is unravelling in *Meadowlands* (1996) to the recollections of unions past and desired in *The Seven Ages* (2001), Glück's poems have always meditated on the temptations and perils of desire, imagining sexual and spiritual merging to be a threat as well as a culmination, as some of her best-known lines, from the poem "Mock Orange," make clear:

> [. . .] I hate sex,
> the man's mouth
> sealing my mouth, the man's
> paralyzing body—
>
> and the cry that always escapes,
> the low, humiliating
> premise of union— (*Triumph* 3)

Here the cry can't help escaping; the speaker's lack of control over it is part of what makes sex itself hateful.

Glück's poems often rely on a similar tension. "The Deviation," the fourth part of the five-part poem "Dedication to Hunger," is one of Glück's most cogent statements about her poetics. Here, Glück links the poet's need to resist her own sexuality to the rigors required by poem-making:

> It begins quietly
> in certain female children:
> the fear of death, taking as its form
> dedication to hunger,
> because a woman's body
> *is* a grave; it will accept
> anything. I remember
> lying in bed at night
> touching the soft, digressive breasts,
> touching, at fifteen,
> the interfering flesh
> that I would sacrifice
> until the limbs were free
> of blossom and subterfuge: I felt
> what I feel now, aligning these words—
> it is the same need to perfect,
> of which death is the mere byproduct. (*Descending* 32)

The speaker here acknowledges that the body is a grave, yet the remembered girl seems also compelled to deny that knowledge: she is motivated by the "fear of death." Her self-protective removal of her own "interfering flesh" thus subverts death even as—insofar as the speaker is dedicating herself to hunger, to self-starvation—it brings it closer. Part of what she willingly sacrifices is her body's eroticism, the "digressive" curves, the "blossom" that is also "subterfuge." To be without sexuality is to be "free"; it enables the speaker to write the poem itself. Writing too requires both self-destruction and self-rescue.

This poem culminates in a scene of writing in which the reader is not imagined. But *Ararat*'s "The Untrustworthy Speaker" (34–5), published ten years later, extends a similar aesthetic of refusal to the scene of readership. As "Dedication to Hunger" insists on perfection achieved through the erasure of the curves that might convert the body into an object of desire, "The Untrustworthy Speaker" interposes into the scene of reading a similar ambivalence about intimacy. The poem begins in negative apostrophe: "Don't listen to me." The reasons for this admonition, the speaker goes on to explain, are several. First, "my heart's been broken": having been hurt, she is compelled to hurt others, including, it seems, her sister, on whose arm she sees "bruises" she "can't account/ for." As a result, she can imagine only the dangers, rather than the rewards, of connection. But her demand that her listener not listen also recapitulates her own failure: she herself can't "see anything objectively"; only "when I'm quiet, [. . .] the truth emerges." As in other poems she keeps probing an eroticism she is insists is dangerous, here she does not relinquish address.

In very different ways, these poems emphasize the tension between the desire for connection and the need to challenge or undermine that desire. As the opposition between blossom and subterfuge suggests, much of the struggle of Glück's poems has always been tonal, a conflict between the particularity of the sensed world and the intellectual comfort of analytic categories, between ordinary and exalted language, and between the seductiveness of conventional lyric evasions—beauty, transcendence, happiness—and the need to resist them.[2] The apostrophe of *The Wild Iris,* read against the thematics of Glück's poems, seems less an anomaly than a kind of intensifier: her reliance on a rhetorical figure concerned with the problems of otherness allows her to enlarge and illuminate issues that have long preoccupied her.

The reading of *The Wild Iris* I am proposing situates Glück's poems in a different context than that in which they habitually have been placed. The ambivalence toward sexual union and the female body in Glück's poems has led many readers of her work to focus on their relationship to a range of notions of femininity.[3] Such readings are important, partly because they connect Glück's poems with the particular historical and cultural context in which she is writing. Yet her preoccupation with the dangers and allure of union—what Calvin Bedient has called in relation to her poems "the treacherous otherness that love reveals" ("Birth" 176)—also evokes an issue essential to all lyric. According to my reading of Northrop Frye, lyric involves a paradoxical relationship to otherness. It tends to operate through apostrophe—address to an other—while turning away from its always-concealed reader. Lyric utterance, insofar as it is personal and particular, is always concerned with identification, with the kinship between the speaker and what she describes and thus at least by implication with the relation to the reader; postmodern poems, as has often been noted, tend with particular urgency to interrogate the self as category. Thus my argument about *The Wild Iris* reveals Glück's intelligent preoccupation with questions central to the tradition and continued viability of the lyric.

More specifically, Glück focuses in *The Wild Iris* on disturbances in the self-other bond and in particular on the impossibility of representing an other who is truly distinct from the speaker describing him, issues several recent scholars have begun to consider.[4] These issues are central to what Glück in an essay published five years after *The Wild Iris* calls narcissism.[5] But while Glück's essay suggests narcissism to be an undesirable attribute of American poetry, *The Wild Iris* reveals narcissism to be essential to and productive for poetic utterance. Like Harold Bloom, who identifies "narcissistic self-regard" as "the center of the poetic self, of the speaking subject" (qtd. Li 8), *The Wild Iris* suggests that lyric is always concerned with problems of self-definition, autonomy, and desire central to narcissism. Glück's apostrophe also connects the seemingly narcissistic desire to coopt others with a different, elegiac desire to recover or animate absent others. In this way, even as *The Wild Iris* outlines the dangers of identification, it enacts the intensity of its speakers' longing for presence.

As its title suggests, Glück's 1997 essay "American Narcissism," on which I have based the claims about apostrophe with which I began this chapter, finds much recent American poetry narcissistic, even solipsistic. This poetry, Glück's essay claims, cannot let its others be other but transforms them instead into narcissistic images of the self, thereby obliterating the "independent reality [of] the world" (11). Narcissism may take various forms, including the "appropriation [. . .] of a *real* other" and the poet's "split [. . .] into two figures" (11), but Glück emphasizes that many recent poems rely on the pronoun "you"; they are structured around address or apostrophe. While these poems seem to speak to others, their addressee is for Glück little more than a projection or narcissistic image of the speaker. For this reason, Glück claims, narcissism's "dominant pronoun" is "you." Glück locates the source of what she calls the excessive American "taste for [this] pronoun" in the insistently apostrophic poems of Rainer Maria Rilke. Rilke's use of "you," Glück claims, tends to obliterate the otherness of the other:

> I cannot rid myself of the impression, in "Requiem," that [. . .] it suits Rilke exactly that Paula Becker died; dead she is his creature, a mirror, or adjunct of, the self. [. . .]
>
> When the poet says [. . .] "if you are still here with me," I cannot help but feel that Paula Becker is far more eagerly admitted into the poet's soul dead than she would have been alive: alive she was volatile, unreliable, separate in her will [. . . .] The seduction of this poetry is in part that nothing is not the self. (11–12)

For Glück, Rilke's poems reveal a paradox central to narcissism. Their "overriding impression of the autocratic or controlling" is achieved through a seemingly contradictory impulse: "In the place of the will or appetite imposing itself on the world, or [. . .] the soul seeking, Rilke postulated a void, an absence into which the world flooded. The self was entirely reactive" (11). Rilke's poems thus reveal a duplicity that Glück implies is central to narcissism: his posture of absolute passivity allows him to obliterate the otherness of his "you" and thus to aggrandize the position of the speaker/poet.

Glück establishes a different but analogous conflict in the description of Narcissus with which her essay begins.

> [Narcissus] *knows* what he's looking at [. . . .] He endures, until grief claims him, the knowledge of his passion's *impossibility* [. . . .] When Narcissus bends forward toward his image, the image manifests corresponding ardour. And the meticulousness of the correspondence illuminates the *impossibility* of the hunger. (10, emphasis added)

Glück's emphasis on impossibility foregrounds the tension between Narcissus's "knowledge" and his "passion": his desire for his reflected image to be other chafes in Glück's description of the scene against his realization that it is not other. Glück is here emphasizing a bodily enactment of what she later in the essay transforms into a metaphor for a literary predicament, yet her terms strongly evoke Jonathan Culler's assertion that apostrophe is characterized by "*impossible* imperatives"; it is "a fiction which *knows* its own fictive nature" (*Pursuit* 146, emphasis added) and thus is caught, like Glück's Narcissus, between knowledge and hunger. Apostrophe, that is, is compelled, as Glück's "Dedication to Hunger" suggests, to affirm the insatiability of its hunger.

That Glück's prose comments can be so easily read as a gloss on her poems reveals how overdetermined the question of otherness is for Glück: her self-doubling (in the essay she speaks as a reader-critic without reference to her poems or her identity as poet) evokes her notion of narcissism, in which the doubled self (the reflected image of Narcissus's actual face) is misidentified and understood to be not self but other.[6] Glück seems to be entering dangerous territory by insisting so forcefully in *The Wild Iris* on the pronoun "you," which her essay links directly with narcissism and in particular with the narcissistic tendency to disguise grandiosity with what seems to be humility. Her compulsion, a juxtaposition of the essay with the volume suggests, is to begin her poetic inquiry into the function of the lyric "you" at the site at which narcissism is most seductive; the risk she runs is that her own Rilkean impulse to use "you" as a disguised version of "I" will overcome the pragmatism and caution of the later essay. However forcefully the essay exposes the perils of narcissism, *The Wild Iris* reveals its seductiveness.

By emphasizing the gap between Glück's conception of narcissism in her essay and the self-referential apostrophe of *The Wild Iris*, I mean to be something other than perverse. I do not wish, that is, simply to argue that

Glück is guilty in her poems of the narcissism her essay condemns, although that is part of my claim. Rather, *The Wild Iris* proposes a notion of narcissism more nuanced, inclusive, and ultimately sympathetic than her essay. Narcissism, Glück's volume demonstrates, is both essential to and productive for poetic utterance. Glück's volume also helps clarify a more general conflict between poetics and psychoanalysis: *The Wild Iris* engages with psychoanalytic concepts while refusing to define them in fixed or stable ways. The resulting sense of resistance, which I have located in different ways in the poems of both Plath and Merrill, suggests a more general quality of postmodern poetry, although Glück's poems enact especially starkly the impulse both to invoke and undermine various forms of authority, retaining allegiance to what they are attempting to dismantle or remake.

The discrepancy between Glück's essay and *The Wild Iris* also suggests the narrowness of the essay's conception of narcissism. The essay draws solely on Ovid's version of the myth of Narcissus and emphasizes the familiar effects of narcissism—including self-absorption and a lack of interest in others. While Glück acknowledges that her reading of that text is itself partial and thus inaccurate (10), she never acknowledges the importance of this myth to postclassical thought. Particularly striking is her omission of the psychoanalytic notion of narcissism—introduced by Freud in "On Narcissism" (1914) and subsequently elaborated by Jacques Lacan and many others—although this notion complicates and even contradicts her own definition. Narcissism according to psychoanalytic theory involves a paradox that evokes, but ultimately inverts, Glück's description of Rilke: the narcissist seems inordinately self-involved, egotistical, and arrogant, yet these qualities imperfectly conceal an image of self so unstable and fragmented that the illusion of coherence cannot be attained without the mirroring, approving gaze of others.[7] Psychoanalysis thus emphasizes not so much the grandiosity on which Glück focuses as the vulnerability that underlies it. More exactly, narcissistic behavior alludes, according to psychoanalysis, to lost maternal intimacy; the narcissist's conception of self derives from and recapitulates childhood losses.[8] (Glück's assertion that Narcissus's story is "all psychology, no narrative, [. . .] a static image" [10] thus seems particularly inaccurate.) Narcissism thus recalls the projections, illusions, and denial of the fort/da game, which I discussed above: narcissism too derives from the recollection of a never-possessed, unobtainable intimacy.[9] It is also linked to melancholia, although distinct from it: both involve the internalization of attributes of the desired other.

The Wild Iris's preoccupation with loss is not surprising: Glück's poems have always both approached and denied elegy. Her early volumes, according to Bedient, focus on an "absent father" who can be neither approached nor abandoned ("Birth" 169–70). These features are intensified in *Ararat,* published just before *The Wild Iris:* that volume chronicles the speaker's family history, including the father's death, in a monotone that excludes both extremes of feeling and for the most part apostrophe. Helen Vendler's characterization of the volume as "some sort of self-chastisement" (*Soul* 17) testifies to its various exclusions—of tenderness as well as of an openness or invitation to the reader. Glück's turn to apostrophe in *The Wild Iris* and moreover to apostrophe addressed to a father who is at times "unreachable" (3) and at others a "dear friend/ dear trembling partner" (31) suggests that the volume at least partly reacts against *Ararat*'s refusal to mourn. One of Glück's central concerns in *The Wild Iris* is with ways of unmaking mortality; the buried flower bulbs that begin and end the volume are not dead but dormant, awaiting the time when they will once again blossom.[10] Such notions are conventional in elegy as well as in the religious meditation that elegy often evokes. Glück, though, permits such elegiac immediacy only by disguising elegy, displacing the actual father to a nonliteral realm, a gesture that recalls the narcissist's displacement of maternal loss.

I have until now been speaking generally about apostrophe, selfhood and otherness, and narcissism. In the remainder of this chapter, I will examine more closely several rhetorical strategies through which *The Wild Iris* explores these issues. Because Glück's volume is at once highly apostrophic and adamantly critical of apostrophe, it raises a series of questions: how are we as readers to make sense of a condemnation of apostrophe conveyed apostrophically? Is Glück as poet confined by a figure from which she is struggling to escape? Or is the volume a roundabout paean to apostrophe? Such questions overlap in Glück's volume with questions about narcissism: does *The Wild Iris,* in focusing so directly on the perils and temptations of narcissism, fall into the narcissism condemned by Glück's essay? To what extent does *The Wild Iris* redefine or even embrace narcissism?

The volume's structure insists on such questions. It is unified in place and time—all the poems are set in a single garden during a single season— yet its speakers as well as its addressees shift. The volume comprises three types of poems. In those entitled "Matins" and, after the solstice, "Vespers," a woman laboring in a garden addresses a divine other; in another group of poems, flowers address humans or God; in another, seasonal or natural entities address humans.[11] The poems are thus insistently apostrophic. Yet the structure also challenges the conventions of apostrophe: while each poem is uttered by a single speaker and the poems do not directly respond to one another, the presence of different speakers in the same place with often opposing claims implies a debate or conversation. The usually inanimate addressees of apostrophe—flowers, seasons—here not only speak but critique the human compulsion to address them in the first place.

To answer the questions I have posed above, I will look first at the volume's sustained conflict between metaphoric and metonymic models of understanding, a conflict enacted by the volume's different kinds of speakers. Glück seems to suggest an alternative to the human reliance on metaphor—on, that is, representing God through analogies with the familiar. Yet the metonymic model that seems to replace this mode of equivalence is, her volume makes clear, fundamentally flawed. This interplay helps clarify the volume's conflicted notions about voice and autonomy, which I will examine next. By giving voice to nonhuman entities, Glück offers an alternative to the solipsistic realm of human self-pity. Yet Glück also suggests this strategy to be merely a strategy—a way for the human voice to disguise itself. The volume's apparent personifications are, in the end, revealed to be nothing more than pathetic fallacy, the old poetic impulse to project human emotions onto the inanimate. Glück's resistance to narrative suggests both a cause for and a solution to such solipsism. By acknowledging the anachronism involved in relying on antiquated poetic modes and devices, Glück connects the volume's intersubjective failure—the failure to represent an other definitively outside the self—to an intertextual one. I will focus in the last part of this chapter on ways that the melancholic stubbornness of the volume's allegiance to the past—its speaker's willingness to be "bur[ied . . .] with the Romantics"—ultimately explains and redeems the volume's apostrophe and its narcissism: both for Glück mark absences too overwhelming to be easily relinquished.

There are, it could be argued, two central strategies for imagining God or any unfamiliar entity. The first seeks physical closeness, a site or position that brings the other near; the second, more analytic but also more emotional mode seeks similarity rather than proximity, attempting to locate some common element through which the unknown can be made familiar. In rhetorical terms, the first strategy is metonymic, the second metaphoric. Such impulses are in many ways distinct, even antithetical: the metonymic is concerned with what is apparent, contiguous, and therefore random; the metaphoric tends toward both stasis and depth.[12] Lyric contains elements of both: its impulse is often to convert what is accidentally juxtaposed into a pattern of signification. (Perhaps for this reason, it is often difficult to distinguish the metonymic from the metaphoric in particular cases. A single image in a poem often functions in several ways, and nature poems tend to blur the two more definitively; a described natural scene represents both a synecdochal miniature of the wider landscape and something that metaphorically illuminates the human condition.) Glück's poems, as I have suggested, often juxtapose these two realms: a longing for an end to solitude and in particular for sexual union (essentially metonymic impulses) tends to oppose a cooler, anticorporeal, metaphoric impulse to discern and distinguish likeness and difference.

In *The Wild Iris,* Glück directly opposes these two modes of identification to reveal the inadequacy of both. The human speaker's failure to find a metaphor or natural analogy for God testifies ultimately to God's evasiveness: he continually frustrates her attempts to know and speak to him.[13] Yet the metonymic model put forth by the flowers and seasonal entities is no better; their insistent synecdoche, in which "self" is merely an element of a greater whole, seems both strident and simplistic. To imagine an other metaphorically, as similar to the self, is in the terms of "American Narcissism" to lurch toward narcissism, yet Glück's attempt to imagine an alternative ultimately intensifies our sympathy with this metaphoric mode.

That different modes of identification will be central to the volume is made clear early on, in its second poem, the first of several entitled "Matins" (2). Glück's descriptive opening reveals the blurring of the metonymic with the metaphoric:

> The sun shines; by the mailbox, leaves
> of the divided birch tree folded, pleated like fins.
> Underneath, hollow stems of the white daffodils,
>   Ice Wings, Cantatrice; dark
> leaves of the wild violet [. . . .]

The scene is metaphorically unified: the finlike quality of the leaves is echoed and inverted by the daffodils' name, Ice Wings; the vertical hollow stems recall the dividedness of the birch trunk. These metaphoric connections underlie the metonymic relations between the objects in the scene. The speaker carefully juxtaposes the leaves of the birch with those of the nearby (and syntactically parallel) violet; the description emphasizes the contiguity of the lit exterior and the dimmer, more concealed underlayer.[14]

The relation between the metaphoric and metonymic in the opening description is central to the poem's thematics. The speaker enters the poem in an oppositional mode, attempting to defend herself against Noah's attacks:

> [. . .] Noah says
> depressives hate the spring, imbalance
> between the inner and the outer world. I make
> another case—being depressed, yes, but in a sense passionately
> attached to the living tree, my body
> actually curled in the split trunk, almost at peace,
> > in the evening rain
> almost able to feel
> sap frothing and rising [. . .]

Noah emphasizes difference, implying that the disjunction between springtime's external manifestation of hopefulness and the despair of the depressive prevents the depressive from loving or identifying with the spring. Yet the speaker's response eradicates the difference between metonymic and metaphoric connections through a kind a pun. She is, she claims, "*actually* curled in the split trunk": she is physically curled up inside the tree and so "attached" to it. The image suggests that through her proximity she becomes a near-tree, like Daphne. Yet her attachment is also metaphoric, hence provisional, "*in a sense* passionate": her contiguity with the tree allows her to become the tree, or nearly, "almost able to feel/sap frothing and rising" and thus "almost at peace."

The image is powerful, partly because it is so directly yet hesitantly described; the qualifier "almost" recurs. Yet the poem's structure, like Noah's early vision, is oppositional, and the poem allows Noah to have the final word:

> [. . .] Noah says this is
> an error of depressives, identifying
> with a tree, whereas the happy heart
> wanders the garden like a falling leaf, a figure for
> the part, not the whole.

Here, Noah's argumentative strategy shifts. The problem is not so much that identification is impossible for the depressive as that the depressive's identification is inaccurate. Her insistence on identifying with the tree, which somewhat obscurely stands for "the whole," is, it seems, strained and grandiose in contrast to the happy person (represented synecdochally by "heart"), who is content with a more evanescent, modest, partial identification with the falling leaf. Noah's vocabulary of part and whole proposes—though it imperfectly extends—a distinction between the totalizing, absolutist realm of metaphoric identification and a simile, which is also a metonymy, emphasizing part (the leaf, the heart) rather than whole (the garden, the self).[15] Though Noah's distinction is incomplete, this early poem emphasizes the question of how to represent or find "a figure for" identification, an issue central to the volume.

While the speaker of "Matins" (2) insists on the inextricability of metaphoric and metonymic attachment, much of the volume distinguishes these modes of identification fairly stringently. It is the human speaker who generally insists on metaphor, while the nonhuman ones more often emphasize synecdoche. The human speaker keeps trying to imagine God in terms of various earthly entities, but that process reveals qualities in her similar to those that enrage Noah: she keeps on identifying with the wrong thing. Her efforts also reveal her self-absorption or what Glück's essay calls narcissism. Although her analogies link God to the garden, her metaphor-making allows her to demand that God pay attention to her. Perhaps for this reason, her attempts at defining God metaphorically always fail. Sometimes the problem is that the metaphor itself is inaccurate or partial:

> What is my heart to you
> that you must break it over and over
> like a plantsman testing
> his new species? Practice
> on something else: how can I live
> in colonies, as you prefer, if you impose
> a quarantine of affliction, dividing me
> from healthy members of
> my own tribe: you do not do this
> in the garden, segregate
> the sick rose; you let it wave its sociable
> infested leaves in
> the faces of the other roses, and the tiny aphids
> leap from plant to plant [. . . .] ("Matins" 26)

Here the initial simile (you are like a plantsman) is undermined: the ailing human specimen is not treated by God the way the plantsman treats the sick flower. The speaker's desire to understand this disjunction makes her attempt to follow out the metaphoric logic: God's unwillingness to allow the speaker to live among afflicted others "prov[es] yet again/ I am the lowest of your creatures." Then the speaker abandons metaphor and address altogether and adopts another mode of explanation, in which a tentative series of conjectures, linked by "or," enables her to gain proximity not to the addressee but to the illusions that informed her own "mistaken childhood," where

> [. . .] I was
> sound and whole [. . .]
> or if not then, under the light weight
> of my mother's heart, or if not then,
> in dream, first
> being that would never die.

That the breakdown or abandonment of metaphor comes at the moment the speaker acknowledges her isolation or more exactly her inability to live "in colonies" is not accidental. It is her awareness of her own isolation, her failure to find proximity to God, that forces her to abandon the attempt to make metaphors.

Elsewhere, the human speaker more directly acknowledges that metaphor itself marks not what God is but what he exceeds or resists. Another poem entitled "Matins" (12) begins with questions:

> [. . .] are you like the hawthorn tree,
> always the same thing in the same place,
> or are you more the foxglove, inconsistent, first springing up
> a pink spike on the slope behind the daisies,
> and the next year, purple in the rose garden? [. . .]

But then the failure of metaphor—the speaker's inability to settle on one or another way of representing the addressee—becomes the point. At first, the tone is condemnatory: God's refusal to be pinned down leaves humans "to think/ you couldn't possibly exist." Then the logic shifts:

> [. . .] Is this
> what you mean us to think, does this explain
> the silence of the morning,
> the crickets not yet rubbing their wings, the cats
> not fighting in the yard?

A realm antithetical to the visibility of hawthorne and foxglove, one constituted by withheld sound and suspended action, is here not a metaphor for God. Rather, his refusal to be represented affirms, paradoxically, his existence.

God's nature, as this poem defines it, is to be unrepresentable; his otherness exceeds the human impulse to contain him.

Both these poems shift midway through, like many of Glück's poems, as if a second voice had entered them, mucking up their neat analogies with a less dramatic version of the annoyed irritation with which Noah interrupts the non-apostrophic "Matins" (2). The poems thus keep enacting the failure of the human narrator's attempts to justify her vision in metaphoric terms; in this way they dramatize the narcissism inherent in this mode of imagination. The volume's nonhuman narrators more directly critique this model, at times by drawing attention to human delusions, which include both the obsession with inwardness or what the field flowers cynically refer to as "the soul! the soul!" (28) and also an excessive reliance on what clear morning calls "vehicles" and the related inability to grasp pure concepts (7). These speakers are also openly contemptuous of the human impulse to find metaphors between God, self, and garden as well as of the human tendency to believe in human uniqueness, to insist, as April mockingly echoes, that *"No one's despair is like my despair—"* (20). Glück ultimately suggests, though, that a metonymic model—in which the individual is significant only through inclusion in a larger whole—is no better.

The scilla directly assert that solitude and autonomy are ineffectual: "to be one thing/ is to be next to nothing" (14). (Here, as in all the poems spoken by nonhumans, the poem's title identifies its speaker.) The scilla's image is metonymic. These flowers are "next to"—in proximity to—each other, and this position makes them unable to distinguish the individuals they address:

> Not I, you idiot, not self, but we, we—
> [. . . . .]
> . . .] *You are all the same to us,*
> solitary, standing above us, planning
> your silly lives [. . . .] (14, emphasis added)

Similarly, April makes sense of human grief first by locating it in many humans and then by asserting that it exists not for the benefit of humans but for April itself:

> grief is distributed
> *between you, among all your kind, for me*
> *to know you,* as deep blue
> marks the wild scilla, white
> the wood violet. (20, emphasis added)

Here even the simile of the scilla affirms April's synecdochic vision. Elsewhere the synecdochic notion of the inclusion of the individual in some larger entity is more direct. The ipomoea's meditation on sorrow implies, like April's, that some agent oversees all grievers, although the poem contains no reference to the human and also no bitterness:

> Source of my suffering, why
> have you drawn from me
> these flowers like the sky, *except*
> *to mark me as a part*
> *of my master* [. . . .] (48, emphasis added)

The suffering derives from the master and allows the sufferer to be "a part" not of a community of sufferers but of him. Yet—the line break emphasizes the pun—the speaker also remains apart from the master she longs to join.

What links many of the poems spoken by flowers, as the examples I have cited reveal, is their contempt, often expressed through sarcasm, for the solipsism and self-aggrandizement of the human. In the process, these speakers express dissatisfaction with the valorization of longing and grief toward which much lyric tends. These poems seem in some ways to articulate Glück's own frustrations with both the human and the lyric, but their effect, paradoxically, is to affirm the richness of human feeling. The voices of these speakers are ultimately both too glib and too absolutist to be sympathetic or even plausible; they leave the reader wishing for the subtler, more self-questioning voice of the human protagonist.

The poem's different voices undermine the apparent authority (or, in the terms of Glück's essay, the narcissism) of the human: the human speaker's account keeps being interrupted, and for this reason it is demonstrated to be one of several possible versions. They also unmake the solitude that I have been arguing apostrophe ultimately affirms. Glück's decision to allow these rebuttals into her volume converts the conventionally silent other of apostrophe into an actual other and helps unmake the self-pity and solipsism that Glück's essay condemns in much lyric.

Glück's volume, though, stops short—as Merrill's epic does not—of dialogue. The sequence's many voices compete rather than converse, and the non-human voices are often too weak or embittered to garner our sympathy. Their shrillness reminds us of the provenance of such voices: they are, in the end, like Merrill's ouija board companions, projections of the human poet rather than autonomous characters. The personification of inanimate entities, as I argued in relation to Plath, closely resembles apostrophe: to apostrophize an inanimate object assumes that object's capacity to understand human speech. But Glück goes further: by allowing these others not merely to listen but to speak, Glück reminds us of the ridiculousness of prosopopeia or the granting of voice to the inanimate. All prosopopeia is ultimately pathetic fallacy, defined by John Ruskin as the "imbu[ing of] the natural world with human feeling" (qtd. Preminger 889): it projects the human onto the inanimate. Glück's speaking flowers and seasons, as the fantasies of the speaker/poet, thus confirm rather than undermine her narcissism. More directly and more viciously than Merrill's, Glück's volume reveals that what at first resembles drama is, in the end, a version of self-address.

"Daisies" (39) reveals such issues by considering the dramatic and emotional effects of its apparently autonomous voices. In what is one of the volume's more direct considerations of the subgenre of flower poems, the poet's doubts about her undertaking are rendered safe by being set into the extremist voice of an other. The poem thus creates a tension between the fully realized, distinctively nonhuman voice and the reader's realization that this disguise allows Glück herself as author to speak; the poem functions both as dramatic monologue and ars poetica.

Spoken by a group of flowers, "Daisies" seems, like many of the volume's poems, to challenge narcissism; the daisies are directly contemptuous of the human addressee. They demand from their first words something analogous to what many human apostrophizers desire, that their addressee speak: the poem begins, "Go ahead: say what you're thinking." Yet the human addressee is exhorted to utter not exalted or timeless words but rather to enumerate her doubts about the daisies themselves.

> [. . .] The garden
> is not the real world. Machines
> are the real world. Say frankly what any fool
> could read in your face: it makes sense
> to avoid us, to resist
> nostalgia [. . . .]

The conventions of lyric address are here confused: the speaking daisies urge the mute human addressee to speak. Moreover, it is not clear that the daisies are competent readers of the speaker's thoughts, since it is they, not the speaker, who insist that they should be avoided. In fact, as the daisies soon acknowledge, the human addressee refuses such avoidance, "cautiously/ approaching the meadow's border in early morning" to hear them.

The poem begins, then, by emphasizing the daisies' projection of themselves onto the human: the addressee's silence allows them to articulate their self-hatred. But then it complicates that pairing, introducing a third figure, a contemptuous listener/reader to whom the poem's "you" is imagined speaking:

> [. . .] No one wants to hear
> impressions of the natural world: you will be
> laughed at again; scorn will be piled on you.

The entry of this additional listener (significantly, it is represented indirectly, through negative and impersonal passive constructions) mitigates the daisies' initial insistence that their addressee speak: speaking—at least about nature—is now seen as dangerous. The daisies' cajoling of the addressee is thus displaced onto another scene of speech and hearing, to which negative reception or "scorn" is also central. This imagining of audience ridicule coincides with another shift: while the daisies began with a chronological argument (they are not modern; they are allied with a compulsion toward nostalgia or looking backward), they turn to a generic one. For the first time, the addressee is imagined to be a writer. It is the fact that the addressee will offer "*impressions of the natural world*," that she will convert her observations into poems, that makes her speech dangerous.

Throughout "Daisies," then, questions of agency and projection—concerning who is actually speaking, who is listening, who is condemning whom—are implicit. Within the poem's frame, as in other poems I have examined, the human addressee remains distinct from the speaking daisies. It is not until the last lines that the daisies are revealed to be personae through which the poet articulates her doubts about her poetic undertaking.

> As for what you're actually
> hearing this morning: think twice
> before you tell anyone what was said in this field
> and by whom.

The daisies' final assertion is in some ways consistent with everything they have said before, but these last lines also slip out of that fiction: by emphasizing the dubiousness of the scene of "actually/ hearing" and in particular of "who[. . .]" is doing the speaking, the daisies remind us that they are not "actually" speaking at all and so dissolve as protagonists. Rather, "Daisies," like the other poems in the volume, enables the poet to articulate her not-implausible concern that her work is anachronistic and will thus be seen as an irrelevant group of "impressions of the natural world," not least because of its reliance on the implausible notion that flowers can actually speak. (In fact, Vendler has characterized the volume as "pre-Raphaelite, theatrical, staged, [. . .] posed [. . . and] affected" [*Soul* 22].) The daisies, despite their explicit contempt for the human, end up affirming the inescapability of narcissism, of the human projection of fears and desires onto others. The daisies ultimately function, in the terms of Glück's essay, as a thinly veiled version of self.

"Daisies," by exposing the fiction on which prosopopeia relies, complicates the apparent distinction of self from other implied by the poem's address. Its emphasis on nostalgia also illuminates related issues of memory and narrative. The daisies are allied with the out-of-date; their anachronism and in particular their association with an obsolete mode of writing engender the poem's various scenes of mockery. Yet the addressee refuses to "resist/ nostalgia." She stubbornly embraces this anachronism, standing at the edge of that field and uttering her impressions. The poem thus insists on flower poems while acknowledging their obsolescence, and the addressee depicts herself in a position of trying to resuscitate what the daisies imply ought to be abandoned.

That the relation between the static and the recollected, the transcendent and the out-of-date is central to Glück's volume is unsurprising. All lyric, in Sharon Cameron's formulation, is caught between a proclivity toward self-obliterating stasis and an insistence on narrative that threatens to undermine its lyricality (23). Lyric sequences intensify these questions by alluding to a chronological narrative while refusing the coherence of epic or drama. By recounting a season in the garden, *The Wild Iris* opposes nature's ever-continuing "circular" cycles (15) to the permanence of human death.

In suggesting that the addressee of "Daisies" stubbornly refuses to relinquish the dead or moribund genre of flower poems, I mean to imply that Glück enacts a melancholic relation to the poetic tradition, something like Plath's relation to Romantic apostrophe.[16] Glück's insistence on both flower poems and apostrophe, that is, resembles the griever's refusal to abandon the dead and in this way recalls the psychoanalytic notion of narcissism as a similarly endless, always displaced attempt to recapture proximity to the lost maternal body. The melancholic elements of *The Wild Iris* may derive from *Ararat*'s refusal to mourn the father's death, but they also articulate Glück's ambivalent relation to lyric in ways that strongly recall *Ariel,* whose recurrent apostrophe reveals both Plath's devotion to apostrophe and her conviction that it is archaic, limited, and inadequate.

Glück's preoccupation is not only with the antiquated elements of the flower poem but also with the relation between her own apostrophe and that of the Romantics, as another poem entitled "Matins" (13) makes particularly clear. A reading of "Daisies" in terms of psychoanalytic dynamics might emphasize the initial sense of collusion between daisies and addressee, an intimacy interrupted by the entrance of a third figure, that of the hardly visible but hypercritical audience. "Matins" (13) involves similar terms, but here the narrative is reversed: fluid, dyadic relations replace a relationship constituted by a paternal prohibition of intimacy. Here is the poem's opening:

> I see it is with you as with the birches.
> I am not to speak to you
> in the personal way [. . .]

The speaker's realization that her addressee has prohibited this kind of "personal" speech first causes her to question her assumption of their past intimacy and then to blame herself for her addressee's indifference:

> [. . .] Much
>   has passed between us. Or
> was it always only
> on the one side? I am
> at fault, at fault, I asked you
>   to be human [. . .]

In Romantic poetry, the silence of the addressee seldom impels the apostrophizer to cease apostrophizing; rather, the indifference of nightingale or skylark makes the speaker ever more ardent. Here, though, the failure of intimacy impels the speaker to shift to a nonapostrophic consideration of the past. She attempts to recapture this past, although to do so risks a particularly literary annihilation:

> [. . .] I might as well go on
> addressing the birches,
> as in my former life: let them
> do their worst, let them
> bury me with the Romantics,
> their pointed yellow leaves
> falling and covering me.

Here the speaker's insistence that the birch leaves cover her links her metonymically with the Romantics, who did not hesitate to apostrophize trees. Yet the poem does not address the birches. Instead, the near-imperative ("let them") emphasizes her passivity; the birches possess an agency that ultimately annihilates the speaker. In insisting that the leaves "cover" her, she is unmaking her isolation (the Romantics are with her under the birch leaves), yet this sense of community is achieved only through her burial. The poem begins with the speaker's attempt to establish intimacy with her addressee, yet in the end death is what links the autumnally yellow birches, long-dead Romantics, and the speaker. This is the archetype of melancholia, according to psychoanalysis: because the speaker refuses to abandon her desire for intimacy with an unobtainable other, she remains in the end caught in and paralyzed by this desire.

"Matins" (13) chronicles several connected losses: the speaker acknowledges the inaccuracy of her former belief in the possibility of "personal" speech; she relinquishes apostrophe; and she gives up agency by submitting to a burial beneath the birch leaves. Perhaps most centrally, the notion of forward movement is undermined: the speaker has no choice but to return to the "former life" the poem implies she once believed she had outgrown. She cannot convert the Romantics' unthinking, narcissistic apostrophizing into something more "personal" and thus pertinent. Yet her refusal of narrative also seems to provide comfort, paradoxically, through something like metonymy or her proximity to literary tradition, the fact that her body is beside those of earlier poets.

I have been arguing that Glück's volume expresses melancholia—an impulse both to cling to what is gone and to acknowledge its absence—beneath and through its struggles with narcissism. In this way, *The Wild Iris* reveals an understanding of and sympathy with narcissism not acknowledged in Glück's essay. This melancholia, as "Matins" (13) indicates, pertains not only to the possibility of physical proximity to God but also to lyric itself. The sequence is inflected by and perhaps longs for narrative and drama. But despite its implication that lyric is obsolete, self-absorbed, and narrow, *The Wild Iris* affirms—partly through its retention of and insistence on apostrophe—the possibilities of a lyric that, drawing on these other modes, nonetheless remains lyric. Glück sticks with lyric, although her speakers remain ambivalent about that decision.

I do not mean to imply that Glück's volume is merely or wholly an example of narcissistic melancholia or any other condition. Instead, the sequence—both structurally and because of the restlessness and suspicion of its human speaker—resists models of all kinds. Glück's poems, like those of Plath and Merrill, are rendered more complex and engaging through their challenges to received wisdom. Like Merrill, Glück thematizes her suspicion of orthodoxies of all kinds (the other great orthodoxy she resists is the Judeo-Christian one) by representing her speakers as readers and insisting on scenes of reading and rereading. Such scenes set her speakers, sometimes surprisingly, outside the events they recount. They also free her actual readers from the risks that often come—as the responses of readers of Plath's poems perhaps most directly reveal—from excessive identification.

Detachment has always been celebrated by Glück's poems, as the examples with which I began make clear. Glück's speakers seek among other things to be disentangled from their bodies ("free/ of blossom and subterfuge") and from the compulsion to please ("Don't listen to me"). *Ararat's* interior spaces often include three characters, allowing the speaker to consider her father indirectly, by means of a mediating figure (the mother, a dead sister). Threesomes are if anything more crucial to *The Wild Iris:* the volume's structure—with its three "kinds" of speakers who partly recall the Christian trinity—insists on scenarios of exclusion, and in many poems a seemingly indifferent figure (sometimes human, sometimes a seasonal entity) mediates between two others.

"The Garden" (16–17) stages such a situation while directly considering the temptations and dangers of detachment. By detailing a scene not only of looking but "overlooking," the speaking garden helps to resolve questions raised by the volume about the relations between speaker, observed scene, and reader. Glück's explicit wish in her discussion of "Lady Lazarus" was to be invited into the poem. But "The Garden" reveals the difficulty of such a task. Detachment, exclusion, and isolation are, the poem suggests, inevitable in lyric, although these qualities do not necessarily prevent the reader from gaining access to the poem.

That problems of vision will be central to "The Garden" is made clear by the first lines, in which the speaking garden, who resembles God surveying Eden, asserts his wish not to look, along with his compulsion to do so:[17]

> I couldn't do it again,
> I can hardly bear to *look* at it—
>
> in the garden, in light rain
> the young couple planting
> a row of peas [. . .
> . . . .]
> *Look* at her, touching his cheek
> to make a truce [. . .] (emphasis added)

The members of the couple "cannot see themselves," but the speaker can. He sets them into "perspective" partly by seeing himself (the couple are "in the garden") and so converts their gestures to "image[s]"; he does not merely look but interprets. This capacity comes partly through the garden's sense of history: he can recall things that the humans do not. The couple in the garden erroneously believe that "no one has ever done this before." Yet, as the first line makes clear, the speaker both recalls and regrets "do[ing] it." (The unnamed antecedent of "it" may be the act of creating the couple or allowing them to argue or to inhabit the garden; "this" in the previous citation is similarly undefined but also seems linked to both love and argument.) The discrepancy between the garden's position as remembering, interpreting observer and the humans' lack of self-regard leads in the poem's final image to an indirect assertion of the "sadness" implicit in the speaker's interpretive seeing:

> and they think
> they are free to overlook
> this sadness.

The garden, these lines make clear, knows, as the couple do not, that they are not free; their sadness cannot be overlooked. Paradoxically, by "overlook[ing]" or looking from a distance on the scene, the garden reveals that he resembles the humans: he too is not "free."

This vision is ambivalent—the speaker's physical detachment does not allow psychological detachment or indifference—but it avoids the anatomization of self of a poem like *Ararat*'s "The Untrustworthy Speaker." That earlier poem described the speaker's inability to "see myself." The garden's preoccupation with "do[ing] it again" in relation to looking recalls and revises this earlier situation as well as the opening of Plath's "Lady Lazarus," "I have done it again." "The Garden," while sad, is serene; it is a poem to which apostrophe is unnecessary. But while the garden does not try to speak to the witnessed couple, his sympathetic watching helps convert their failure to see themselves into an aesthetic object, the poem itself:

> Look at her, touching his cheek
> to make a truce, her fingers
> cool with spring rain;
> in thin grass, bursts of purple crocus—

As a father figure, the garden may be inadequate—he cannot save his children or reverse whatever his initial mistake was—yet unlike the mostly mute, emotionally inept father of *Ararat,* he not only speaks but considers a paradox central to Glück's poetics: the ability to overlook, to analyze, to watch from a distance does not eradicate the pathos, the powerlessness of looking.

The garden interprets or reads what he sees; he empathizes but cannot intervene. Northrop Frye has imagined the reader of lyric in broadly similar terms, although his metaphor differs slightly. For Frye, lyric is by definition overheard by its readers, who are excluded from the scene of the poem's utterance. Like the garden, Frye's reader (to mix Frye's aural with Glück's visual image) is a kind of voyeur, seeming to spy on what, insofar as poems require readers, he is meant to witness. That such a position might result in a heightened sense of pathos is suggested by Herbert Tucker's notion that "overhearing" lyric involves excessive hearing, a sensitivity in particular to the poetic voices that have come before.[18] This notion jars against Glück's claim in relation to Plath that "to overhear [a poem] is to experience exclusion" ("Invitation" 115) and that more successful poems "invite" their readers in as "coauthors" (123). In the context of *The Wild Iris*, such a claim seems dangerous. If poems address their readers directly and allow them to participate in writing them, Glück's volume argues, their speakers risk narcissistically coopting these readers, eradicating their autonomy and resistance. In places, as I have been arguing, Glück's sequence allows its human speaker to yield at least briefly to the temptations of narcissism, to project herself onto some outside entity and thus incorporate that other into herself. But "The Garden," which depends on its speaker's refusal to intervene, presents a clearer model for *The Wild Iris* as a whole. The sequence's difficulties—the volume's refusal to cohere into narrative or dialogue, its tone shifts, its strident and unlikable speakers, its insistence on pushing at the limits of our willingness to suspend disbelief—impel us to struggle to make sense of it. In exiling us from its vision, they leave us "free" to judge it. From this position of exclusion, paradoxically, we are able, like the garden, to reverse the human speaker's failures of vision: our separateness grants us the perspective she lacks and so unmakes the volume's apparent narcissism.[19] "The Garden" thus suggests something startling: the exclusions of lyric and of apostrophe can also function as invitations; the tendency of lyric to dwell on the problems of self-regard or narcissism can allow actual readers into the realm of the poem. This connection is not based on identification. We do not become either speaker or addressee, according to Glück's austere model. Instead, we overlook (or overhear) the poems from far away, imbuing them with our own opinions, irritations, resistances. This detachment is not, as it is not for the garden, desolate. Rather, it grants us the power to notice, to judge, and to make sense of both problems and felicities of which the speaker remains ignorant.

Chapter Four

Homo Faber: Frank Bidart's *Desire*

Apostrophe expresses desire, and in particular the desire to unmake isolation. The strictures of lyric, however, prevent this desire's fulfillment: insisting on a unitary voice, lyric prevents the speaker from confirming that her words have been heard. The effort of affirming the other's presence in the face of the seemingly overwhelming evidence of absence, as I have been arguing, often renders the speakers of postmodern poems frenetic, sad, or bitter. Yet apostrophe persists, and its persistence at times creates a kind of antidote to the frustration inherent in apostrophe itself. The poem itself, by rendering the calling-out of apostrophe permanent, offers a partial if pathetic substitute for the always-evasive other. The act of making, the labor of writing poems, in this way makes desire manageable. Such is something of the argument of Frank Bidart's 1997 *Desire*. Deeply preoccupied with the pathos—a term that recurs in critical discussions of Bidart's work—that derives from the distance between speaker and addressee, these poems also find in the articulation of this distance the possibility of connection.[1]

The term *desire,* while not often used by Plath, Merrill, or Glück, is nonetheless central to the impulses that underlie address in their poems; these poems often struggle between the desire for presence and the knowledge of absence. The bravado with which these poems will the other to appear and with which they speak to the other as if it is already there, though, tends to convert this desire into something that can be, at least for the space of the poem, fulfilled and thus eradicated. The poems of Plath, Merrill, and Glück often work to overcome or displace their apostrophic desire by converting desire into revulsion, contempt, or mockery, by embracing the fiction of reciprocity, or by turning away from desire altogether. Even in Merrill's poems, the desire associated with lyric itself emerges only indirectly, a product of the force with which it has been suppressed. To be stuck in yearning, it seems, is paralyzing, painful, and poetically useless. It brings the speaker perilously close to the kind of obliteration that apostrophe seeks to deny.

Desire, though, reimagines the nature and function of desire. The volume discusses directly, at length, and in a range of formats and contexts what is temporary or fragmentary in many other apostrophic poems. In the process, Bidart's poems reconfigure desire not by subjecting it to a range of lyric tricks but by refusing to forsake it: these poems do not attempt to evade or unmake their origin in abandonment or bereavement, a state often informed by the larger losses of AIDS.[2] In a way that recalls the negations essential to Lacanian thinking about desire, desire is associated with irrevocable loss.[3] But within desire, within a process of grieving that foregrounds erasure and negation, Bidart reveals that the dead can appear, not as they were in life but in a form defined by the desire that animated them. Although Bidart's poems have been seldom discussed by scholars, *Desire* in this way sets forth a sustained if not always consistent argument about the connection between lyric, grief, and memory.[4] Converting loss itself into something like the antithesis of loss, reconfiguring the relation of the material to the ineffable in ways consistent with the different meanings of the term "desire" itself, Bidart's poems gesture toward a poetics of recovery that involves not evasion but a refusal to cede or budge.[5] It is perhaps unsurprising that Bidart's poems move differently from the poems I have been examining: rather than progressing or changing, they tend to repeat themselves, to circle back, to emphasize the failure of forward progress. In the process they offer up a model of lyric that is almost painfully pure.

Bidart's poems are, far more directly than even those of Plath, elegiac: several directly address particular dead others, especially Bidart's friend the artist Joe Brainard, and others consider mortality and mourning in other contexts.[6] They do not, as do Plath's, pretend that the other is actually alive and capable of hearing. Instead, Bidart's elegiac apostrophe reiterates absence and grief. The adherence of these poems to both the dead and to desire is quite different from what Peter Sacks identifies as traditional elegy's "movement from loss to consolation," which he claims involves not an articulation but a "deflection of desire" (*English* 7); desire for Sacks is associated with death and self-obliteration. Jahan Ramazani's revisionary reading of modern elegy refuses the consolation central to Sacks's notion of elegy in favor of what he calls melancholic mourning or the retention rather than severing of connection to the dead (*Poetry* 4–5); his interest is in poems, like Bidart's, that do not forsake the dead. Yet Ramazani, like Sacks, emphasizes the ways that elegiac desire is transformed and ultimately undermined through the process of grieving. Bidart's poems, though, redeem elegiac desire, revealing it to be not only necessary but productive.

Homo Faber

Bidart's earlier poems are less ascetic, less defiantly lyric than those of *Desire,* but they examine desire, sometimes incompletely or haltingly, in ways that the later volume elaborates. Bidart's 1968–69 apostrophic "Golden State" (*Western* 149–63) is concerned, like *Desire,* with the wish for the other to appear and speak and with the sacrifices required by that wish's fulfillment. Here, as in *Desire,* the dead addressee is made present only through a series of refusals, both on the part of the speaker and of the addressee himself.

The poem's first nine sections attempt through a series of described scenes to define the speaker's relation to his dead father. In the final section (162–3), the speaker pulls back from this effort, describing instead the illusions and sacrifices required by the poem itself. "When I began this poem," he asserts,

> I sensed I had to become not merely
> a speaker, the "eye," but a character . . .
>
> And you had to become a character: with a past,
> with a sense of internal contradictions and necessities
> which if I could *once* define, would at least
> begin to release us from each other . . . (emphasis Bidart's)

Writing the poem involves fictionalization, the speaker admits, the imposition of a gap both between the father in the poem and the actual father and between the son and the poet. Yet the "freedom" he hopes will result from this splitting does not come, nor does the knowledge of "necessity" that he claims must precede the freedom: "of course, no such knowledge is possible;—"

The rhetoric of refusal and failure here, though, is partly unmade in the poem's final lines; in fact, the speaker's dismantling of the illusion of presence he has just laid out seems necessary for the poem's final movement toward a qualified mode of transcendence. The speaker demonstrates the limitations of his own position as " 'eye,' " but he claims that several photographs of his father that lie before him as he writes are capable of seeing, although what they reveal is disappointing: "they *stare back at me/* with the dazzling, impenetrable, glitter of mere life" (emphasis added). In fact, these personified photos do at least partly restore the father to life, as the present-tense description of one photo reveals: "*you seem* [. . .] happy/ to be surprising; unknowable; unpossessable . . ." (emphasis added). The image leads to another paradox: the speaker's acknowledgment of the dead father's unpossessableness allows the father to appear and speak, like the mother at the end of Lowell's "During Fever," in the present moment of the poem. In the process, the father clarifies the notion of "freedom" that earlier evaded the speaker: "You say it's what you always understood by freedom." The poem's multiple refusals—of the consolations afforded by "character," of vision, of animation—in this way enable the speaker to animate the father and thus gain access to him, although the access remains qualified: the father's words are merely overheard by the son, and they emphasize evasion.

The conflicted, dense mode of "Golden State" is very different from the minimalism of *Desire,* although *Desire* too connects embodiment with erasure and desire with repudiation. Another, somewhat later poem probes similar issues not by turning not away from "character" but by systematically considering the ramifications of becoming someone else. "Ellen West," published four years after "Golden State," is both a sustained dramatic monologue—the twelve-page poem is spoken mostly by Ellen—and an exploration of the limits and function of dramatic monologue itself. The removal of self permitted by dramatic monologue, Bidart implies, can resolve problems—here about the possibility of speaking autobiographically—that seem irresolvable within the poem. In the process, the poem splits body from voice in a way that anticipates *Desire*'s discovery that the body is dispensable.

"Ellen West," perhaps the best known and, some argue, the most successful of Bidart's dramatic monologues, is narrated by a young female anorexic, the subject of an actual case history by Ludwig Binswanger. Ellen begins by distinguishing her "true self," which is "thin" and whose "body is the image of her soul," from her actual body, which, because it "love[s] sweets" and constantly desires food, is itself "meat" (109). Hunger—a kind of desire—is thus something from which Ellen seeks but fails to be free; in the poem's first twelve lines (109), the adversative "but" recurs three times in different contexts, suggesting that the conflict between what is "true" and what is "love[d]" cannot be resolved, only reiterated. (The opposition of these notions persists in *Desire.*) Bidart's decision to undermine the integrity of Ellen's voice in the poem, most obviously through the repeated interruptions of her first-person account by a doctor's case notes, enacts a somewhat analogous textual split: Ellen's essentially lyric account of her thoughts and impressions—her soul—contrasts with the doctor's narrativizing, prose chronicle of her diminishing weight—her body—in ways that evoke Ellen's divided consciousness itself.

The poem's more drastic fracturing of its narrative coherence is less direct: Bidart affirms the possibility that he himself can persist in the poem as pure voice, unencumbered by body. The gesture converts the sense of victory at the end of "Golden State" into explicitly textual form. Bidart, that is, exists in the poem within but concealed by the character he has created and through which he speaks; here, the creation of "character" offers a protected mode through which the poet himself, obliterated as a character, can be made present. A similar paradox is central to *Desire:* the requirement that the speaker be eradicated by his efforts to reach the dead is not a cause for grief but rather permits the possibility of contact.

The poem elaborates this dynamic through a several-times layered description of autobiography. Ellen has been considering the paradox of the opera singer's Maria Callas's infamous weight loss: it liberated an "extraordinarily/ mercurial; fragile; masterly creature" previously concealed by her body but destroyed her formerly "huge voice" (114). Ellen then describes a performance in which she heard a thin Callas sing Tosca, imagining that Callas is articulating this paradox through the words she sings:

> —I know that in *Tosca,* in the second act,
> when, humiliated, hounded by Scarpia,
> she sang *Vissi d'arte*
>   —"I lived for art"—
>
> and in torment, bewilderment, at the end she asks,
> with a voice reaching
>   harrowingly for the notes,
>
> "Art has *repaid* me LIKE THIS?"
>
>   I felt I was watching
> autobiography—
>   an art; skill;
> virtuosity
>
> miles distant from the usual soprano's
> athleticism,—
>   the usual musician's dream
> of virtuosity *without* content . . . (115)

Ellen's claim "I felt I was watching/ autobiography" refers primarily to the fact that art has repaid Callas in much the same way it has Tosca, the character she is playing: the boundaries between performer and character have here dissolved. But the idea of autobiography is more devastating. Ellen allows us to understand that she resembles the figure she is watching, not least physically, and so in watching Callas, she is watching her own life.[7] More profoundly, the connection between art, self-disguise, and autobiography invites us to question the poem's essential fiction: if Callas's attempt at concealing herself by pretending to be Tosca fails, mustn't the poem's dramatic monologue—Bidart's attempt to disguise himself as or speak through Ellen—similarly fail? If watching art is watching autobiography, who else can we be watching in "Ellen West" but Bidart, the poet, himself?[8]

This moment links Ellen's desire to exist while dispensing with her body with the central desire of dramatic monologue, in which the poet speaks while remaining concealed, a voice unencumbered by body. Ellen's account confirms the impossibility of fulfilling this wish. Callas's voice, unsupported by bodily bulk, is painful to hear, and Ellen's refusal to "give up/ [the] ideal" (109) of thinness causes her death at the end of the poem. Yet Bidart as poet in fact achieves the bodily erasure Ellen is so relentlessly seeking—something like what he accomplishes at the end of "Golden State"—without eradicating his voice. In fact, the erasure here is more complete; here, the first-person "I" is not necessary.

Desire explores similar concerns with more sustained attention: the entire volume focuses both on physical absence and on voice. Bidart's earlier poems repeatedly considered the nature of performance, but *Desire* dispenses with many of the devices—the credible speakers and fully elaborated dramatic and narrative situations—that affirm the illusion of presence. *Desire*'s poems are shorter and less formally exuberant than those in Bidart's earlier volumes. While Bidart's earlier poems contained idiosyncratic typography, lineation, punctuation, italics, and capitalization, many of the poems in *Desire* look conventional, with lines that begin regularly at the left margin, of relatively consistent length; some even look like sonnets. Bidart's interest has shifted from representing the intonations of actual speech to what in *Desire* he repeatedly calls "formal question[s]" and in particular questions that draw attention to distinctively lyric and elegiac concerns with temporality, closure, and the obstacles to chronology.[9] This movement away from dramatic monologue into a sparer and also more conventional lyric in some ways inverts Merrill's poetic development. While Merrill came to the loose, dialogue-filled narrative mode of *The Changing Light at Sandover* relatively late, Bidart has returned to lyric and to apostrophe.

Bidart distinguishes these poems from the ordinary, chronological realm by explicitly describing the impossibility of forward motion:

> *Four steps forward then*
> *one back, then three*
> *back, then four forward:—* (*Desire* 40)

This repetitive, nonprogressive mode undermines both Bidart's earlier impulse to tell stories and the ordinary temporal sequence that ends in death. Narrative or tale-telling attempts, as Bidart's discussion of Ovid suggests, to transform or master bereavement. While Sacks exemplified his narrative conception of elegy by analyzing several tales from Ovid, Bidart emphasizes the source of Ovid's tales.[10] Orpheus' "litany of tales"

> filled the cruel silence after Eurydice
> had been sucked back down into the underworld
> cruelly and he driven back cruelly
> from descending into it again to save her . . . (32)

The impulse to tell tales, according to Bidart, "fill[s] the [. . .] silence" of bereavement: it derives from, expresses, and expands the narrator's grief rather than, as Sacks suggests, accomplishing that grief's dispersal.

Bidart's "The Yoke" (14), the most cogent articulation of the problem of apostrophic elegy in *Desire*, links the problem of presence to that of forward motion. Apostrophe, the poem's first lines acknowledge, desires the other's embodiment but also is nourished by the continued frustration of that desire:

> *don't worry   I know you're dead*
> *but tonight*
>
> *turn your face again*
> *toward me*[.]

Like Ellen West, Bidart links his sentence's clauses with "but"; here too desire and knowledge coexist. The speaker begins by acknowledging what elegists and apostrophizers often deny: their elegies cannot impel their addressees back to life. Yet as the soothing "*don't worry*" implies that the addressee might otherwise have cause to worry, the speaker's acknowledgment of what he "know[s]" does not eradicate his yearning but rather heightens a wholly conventional desire for the other to appear. The speaker insists that his desire is temporary (he wishes to be turned toward only "tonight"), minor (he wishes merely for the repetition of something that has already occurred), and imprecise (his wish is not for the beloved's direct gaze but merely to be "turn[ed . . .] toward"). Yet for all the modesty with which this wish is expressed, its implications are radical. The desire for the other to be made present persists not despite but because of the speaker's knowledge that his invocation cannot succeed.

The poem begins in a logic-defying affirmation, inviting the addressee to turn toward a speaker who turns, himself, away from his knowledge that this addressee is dead. But the speaker is far less certain of the other's presence than these lines suggest. The following couplet shifts yet again, away from its initial faith in the bodily presence of the other:

> *when I hear your voice there is now*
> *no direction in which to turn*

The addressee's voice is audible to the speaker, yet he emphasizes its invisibility: it seems to come from no location. The early request that the other turn toward the speaker thus seems to have failed, or been inverted, since the speaker cannot turn toward the other. This gesture of relinquishment evokes Sacks's notion of elegiac narrative: here the speaker seems to approach the dead, acknowledge that the dead is not there, and move away. The imagery of turning also recalls the gap between speaker and poet in a way that undermines the poem's fiction of direct speech and recalls the displacement of autobiography in "Ellen West": the poet is able to accomplish linguistic turns that dissociate him from his immobilized speaker.

The poem's turning away from its addressee, though, is undermined by the addressee's continued presence. The speaker cannot see the addressee, but the poem affirms that he exists since he can be heard, a state of sensory disjunction that evokes among other scenes the speaker's seat in "embalmed darkness" (206) in Keats's Nightingale Ode, which intensifies rather than diminishes the beauty of the heard song. Bidart also makes it clear that it is not the speaker who is turning away from the heard voice, but the opposite: the speaker desires the addressee to turn toward him, but the addressee turns away or fails to become visible. The speaker is thus portrayed as powerless, characterized wholly in terms of his longing, while the addressee remains evasive and yearned for. The speaker's acknowledgment of his addressee's absence—which seems to diminish the addressee's power—thus paradoxically affirms both the addressee's power and the speaker's near-erasure as an autonomous being in ways that recall the imagery of self-erasure in "Golden State" and "Ellen West." The poem's revision of conventional elegiac paradigms of renunciation is also emphasized by its lack of closure: the speaker repeats throughout the poem his initial wish to be turned toward, undeterred by the other's invisibility. The rhetoric of turning away recalls, as does Glück's "The Garden," Northrop Frye's notion that the lyric poet turns away from his reader. But where Glück's poem affirms Frye's edict, the persistence of the speaker's desire to be turned toward in "The Yoke" contrasts with Frye's diffident, powerful poet. Instead, Bidart's speaker's desire undermines his authority as the voice, the maker of the poem.

The opposition of desire to knowledge in the apostrophe of "The Yoke" ultimately affirms desire: the other is present, if incompletely, in the poem. But desire is far less benevolent in Bidart's non-apostrophic translation of Catullus's two-line "Odi et Amo," one of the best known of classical attempts to define the suffering inherent in desire. In contrast to Bidart's earlier translation of this poem, published in 1983, his version in *Desire* asserts that desire obliterates the beloved. The poem is not about death, yet Bidart insists on connecting desire with bereavement.

Catullus's poem represents erotic desire through paradox, as a literal translation makes clear:

> I hate and love. Why do I do it? Perhaps you ask.
> I don't know; but I feel it and I'm tortured.

Both of Bidart's translations convert the direct, somewhat clumsy assertion "I feel it and I'm tortured" into an image: they enact the torture and in the process reveal the particular ways that desire enslaves the desirer. While "The Yoke" emphasizes a presence that cannot be located or seen, Bidart's first version, "*Catullus: Odi et Amo*," depicts the disjunction between seeing and being able to obtain:

> I hate *and* love. Ignorant fish, who even
> wants the fly while writhing. (*Western* 52)

Bidart mocks the desiring subject by representing it as other, in the third person rather than the first. The desirer is himself the fish "ignorant" of the fact that the fly it has caught has already caught him; his desire will end only when the fish capitulates to the hook on which it writhes. The fish's ignorance is compounded by its inability to acknowledge the realities of chronology: it still desires what has already been possessed or rather been revealed to be illusory. Writhing on the hook, it continues to want a fly it cannot understand does not exist.

Bidart's reworking of the poem in *Desire* emphasizes the incompleteness of his first translation in ways that recall the writing practices of his mentor Robert Lowell.[11] It also emphasizes the excruciation—the last word of Catullus's original is "excrucior" and the title of his second translation is "*Catullus: Excrucior*"—that accompanies the simultaneity of hate and love:

> *I hate and—love.* The sleepless body hammering a nail nails
> itself, hanging crucified. (8)

The paradox of desiring is clear from the first phrase, which sets off love as something removed from hatred (the dash indicates hesitation) and also a necessary complement to it: after "love," the poem moves out of painfully heightened, italicized speech. This sense of anguish is intensified and explained by the second sentence. Bidart's metaphoric representation of the speaker's state of desire, like his earlier translation, emphasizes bodily entrapment: the image of the body hanging crucified from a series of nails evokes the fish similarly caught on the hook. In the earlier poem, the fish is still writhing—it resists and is conscious. But here the persistence of movement in the midst of bodily paralysis reveals not resistance but capitulation to desire's demands. The body—its sleeplessness partly recalls the speaker ceaselessly turning in "The Yoke"—inflicts on itself more and more bodily torture.

In this difference lies the most profound shift in Bidart's notion of desire's excruciation. Whereas the pairing of fish and fly affirms that the speaker's hate-love has an object (the literal translation also imagines an at-least potential listener to the speaker's outcry), here desire involves isolation. The body may be hammering a nail, but it can only "nail [. . .]/ itself": it is set by its desire into a state of self-referentiality emphasized by the awkwardness of the reflexive. The confusion of agency implicit in the noun-verb pair "a nail nails" also defies the possibility of real action: the verb merely reiterates the subject. The poem's strained syntax enacts the subject's difficulty in defining an object, a *you* distinct from its speaker. Desire is thus solipsistic; in Bidart's revision of the Christian tableau of crucifixion, no soul is freed to render meaningful the body's sufferings and no witness interprets its significance. The vision is thus far bleaker than the consideration of body and soul in "Ellen West"; soul here has been excised from the conflict. Desire unmakes or prohibits the possibility of the beloved's representation, and death is its only possible outcome. This vision is more extreme than that of "The Yoke," yet its suffering extends that poem's inability to allow the other to appear.

In different ways, "*Catullus: Excrucior*" and "The Yoke" connect desire with isolation. The speakers of both poems cannot incarnate their desired others; both physically paralyze their speaker, implying that desire, because it cannot be fulfilled, prohibits temporal change. These poems refuse to tell a story. As the double narration of "Ellen West" makes clear, the vexed relationship of narrative to lyric has long been of interest to Bidart. The doctor's chronological account contrasts with Ellen's temporally unmoored musings; Ellen speaks most of its lines, yet the poem tells a story that ends with her death. That Bidart would turn more definitively to lyric in *Desire* is not surprising: elegy is, despite Sacks's insistence on its embedded narrative of consolation, a lyric mode. But elegy's consciousness of death tends to lead to a kind of double bind. A pure lyric freed from all reference to time's passage offers sanctuary from death's inevitability. But such a lyric also risks becoming a kind of tomb: without action or change, it is like death itself.

These contradictory and untenable impulses toward both narrative and stasis tend to inflect discussions of elegiac refrain. Because it staves off narrative, sequence, and closure, refrain affirms, in Sacks's terms, the poet's ability to create "a sense of continuity, of an unbroken pattern [. . .] oppose[d] to the extreme discontinuity of death." By affirming the elegist's freedom from conventional chronology, that is, refrain enables his grief to be resolved (*English* 23). Sacks also connects repetition to a reiteration of the loss which, while rendering it real, also helps "retroactively [. . .] create [a] kind of protective barrier [. . . against] the disruptive shock." Finally, repetition can help "conjure [. . .] forth and exorcise" grief, helping to naturalize it by setting it into a larger, natural cycle (23–4). But because refrain also establishes its own temporal rhythms, it establishes, in John Hollander's terms, "a dialectic of memory and anticipation" (139) that may recall real-life memories, real-life anticipations: even as it attempts to deny death, it evokes death. Thus, for example, the repeated "Weep no more" of Milton's "Lycidas" asserts a rupture with a temporal realm in which weeping is necessary and affirms an alternate world that is closed and reassuring; similarly, the "Nevermore" of Poe's "The Raven" allows the speaker directly to fend off the threatened return of the dead. Both refrains defy the need for "more" or repetition, but both also operate through reiteration and thus accrual.

Refrain in this way recalls psychoanalytic models of loss and compensation.[12] It also resembles apostrophe: as the act of summoning up an absent other recalls the fact of the absence, elegiac refrain cannot help alluding to the realm of death it attempts to deny. Yet for both Sacks and Hollander, poetic refrain also functions in a different and ultimately more constructive way. As Hollander suggests, refrains not only evoke their own earlier iterations within a particular poem but gesture toward a poetic tradition that is itself filled with echoes (77). To use echo, Sacks suggests, is to externalize loss (*English* 24–5) and thus to affirm a world beyond the consciousness of the griever. Because the use of refrain and the particulars of each refrain evoke the continuity of the lyric tradition, refrain succeeds in fulfilling the central wish of elegy: it brings the past close, makes it accessible, and imbues it with new life. In Sacks's terms, "the elegy takes comfort from its self-insertion into a longstanding convention of grief" (*English* 23). While within a poem refrain may emphasize the loneliness of bereavement, in which the speaker can only repeat his own earlier words, the refrain's allusion to the tradition evokes a different, narrativizing echo. This double function of echo recalls Ovid's account of Echo and Narcissus. Though neither Glück nor Freud discuss her, Echo is an important character in the Narcissus tale. Compelled to mimic Narcissus's words, she is able to articulate through them her own feelings and intentions. This, then, is the elegist's burden: constrained to echo both earlier elegies and her own earlier words, she must fashion from these familiar sounds her own poem.

By relying so heavily on echo and refrain in many of these poems, Bidart clarifies these paradoxes. His attempt directly to revive the dead seems destined to fail. Yet, by reviving antique or seemingly dead texts, including those by Catullus, Ovid, and others, he effects a more successful, if less direct, reincarnation. Bidart's intertextual poetic animations thus fulfill an impulse similar to his less successful efforts at intersubjective animation. As Bidart has commented of the poetic impulse to return to past texts, "Artists, poets ransack the world's art for ways that art has been made, to increase their imagination of the forms that-which-is-within-them can begin to inhabit." Past forms offer "containers" for "the thing-that-is-struggling-into-existence" within the poet's consciousness and thus ensure its transformation into art ("Pre-existing" 115).

I noted earlier that "The Yoke" chronicles the failure of its initial request to be turned toward, a failure enacted by the speaker himself, who is similarly unable to turn. The poem's form does something similar: its apparent dialogue disguises a series of echoes that reveal the failure of the other to materialize. As I mentioned above, Bidart's earlier poems often use italics for emphasis, to indicate the range and intensity of actual speech. In a few cases, most notably in the 1983 "Confessional," two voices in different typefaces converse. In *Desire* Bidart tends to italicize whole passages rather than individual words or phrases and in this way suggests the presence of multiple voices or modes of speech. "The Yoke" alternates italicized and Roman passages. Here is the entire poem:

> *don't worry*   I know you're dead
> *but tonight*

> *turn your face again*
> *toward me*
>
> *when I hear your voice there is now*
> *no direction in which to turn*
>
> I sleep and wake and sleep and wake and sleep and wake and
>
> but tonight
> turn your face again
>
> toward me
>
> *see   upon my shoulders is a yoke*
> *that is not a yoke*
>
> don't worry   I know you're dead
> but tonight
>
> turn your face again

Visually, this alternation resembles dialogue. Yet the poem's two apparent voices do not converse; the poem contains none of the interaction, development, or closure that characterize dialogue. Instead, the second, Roman-type text mostly echoes, partially, the poem's initial statement, as in a song, or perhaps more exactly, as the title of a subsequent poem of Bidart's makes clear, a "little fugue" (*Music* 13). In this way, Bidart enacts formally what his speaker refuses directly to acknowledge within the poem: the second voice is actually the first, and the pair is reduced to singularity.[13]

The poem's setting at night, its repeated, lulling phrases, and its lack of closure evoke lullaby, which, somewhat like elegy, both affirms and denies the proximity of sleep to death. The poem attempts to get its speaker to sleep even as it expresses his frustration with the ceaseless cycle of "sleep[ing] and wak[ing]." This analogy too affirms the solitude of Bidart's speaker. Lullabies are usually sung to a particular listener. Even W. H. Auden's "Lay your sleeping head, my love," whose simple language, forthright presentation of paradox, and repeated allusion to death "The Yoke" recalls, contains an actual addressee, even if, already asleep, he cannot hear the song addressed to him. But Bidart's speaker is entirely alone: he is both his lullaby's comforter and its comforted. The poem nevertheless lulls. Its creation of verbal patterns, of repetition, even of a desire that cannot be fulfilled, is, it intimates, inherently consoling.

"A Coin for Joe, with the Image of a Horse; c. 350–325 BC" (23), an elegy for Joe Brainard, explores in more detail the nature of textual recovery. The poem focuses on a recovered object that stands at least partly for Joe himself, although here what is recovered and reanimated is an antique coin rather than a text:

COIN

    chip of the closed,—L O S T world, toward whose unseen grasses

this long-necked emissary horse

                          eagerly still
                          stretches, to graze

       *

                              World; Grass;

stretching Horse;—ripe with hunger, bright circle
of appetite, risen to feed and famish us, from exile underground . . . for

you   chip of the incommensurate
closed world   *A n g e l*

The coin is an artifact from a "*L O S T world.*" Its recovery—it was presumably dug up from some underground site—evokes the speaker's wish for the dead friend to be unearthed, to "rise [. . .] from exile underground" and thus to free the speaker from his own "exile" from him. The coin thus suggests the possibility of rendering present and alive what is absent. The wish of the poem is that, though the coin remains a "*chip of the closed,—L O S T world,*" the addressee can undermine this loss: he is a "chip of the incommensurate/ closed world" an "*A n g e l,*" the elided syntax of the last lines suggests, to which the poet can gain access.

    The speaker's exploration of the metaphoric significance of the coin ultimately affirms not the triumph of the poet's act of reanimation but, as in "The Yoke," the persistence of stillness, exclusion, and loss. Like Keats's Grecian urn, the coin represents a world that is permanently immobilized although it portrays motion. And like Keats's speaker, Bidart's works throughout the poem to release the figures on the coin from stillness. He affirms that the horse "still/ stretches" (the pun on "still" recalls Keats's "still unravish'd bride of quietness" [207]) toward grasses that, while "unseen," also seem alive. Moreover, the speaker claims that the horse, and by extension the coin itself, is an "emissary." Yet the poem also acknowledges, like "Ode on a Grecian Urn" and "The Yoke," that its affirmations are themselves strained. Thus, the image of the horse not only "feed[s]" but "famish[es]" and the world on the coin remains "*closed—L O S T.*"

The speaker's ambiguous relation to the addressee intensifies this sense of loss. Although the title's reference to Joe seems clear (the coin is or was a gift for Joe), the poem's late, incomplete repetition "for// you" is less so. By the poem's end, it is not clear whether "for" marks a simple gift (the coin is here given or imagined being given to Joe) or something closer to a metaphor: the coin, that is, substitutes for Joe, representing him in his absence. More emphatically, it may offer a currency with which the speaker can buy Joe back: the poem, that is, proffers the coin "for Joe" while acknowledging the failure of this offer before a world that, "incommensurate," resists measurement or valuation. By addressing Joe, the poem reveals its wish—like that of "The Yoke"—to restore or reanimate him. Yet, here too, he remains unembodied, absent from the poem until the penultimate line. The poem seems to want to satisfy its hunger, to remove its desire. Yet like the youth on Keats's urn eternally straining toward his beloved who "can [. . .] not leave/ Thy song," who "never, never can [. . .] kiss,/ Though winning near the goal" (208), the horse itself is caught just before its hunger is satisfied. The poet, in terms of the analogy set up by the poem, is similarly caught. Ellen West's desire is to transcend hunger, to renounce her appetite, but here the "circle/ of appetite" is itself "bright": the state of desiring offers beauty when the effort at animation fails and no other consolation is available.

In a sense, then, "A Coin for Joe" cannot overcome the conflict inherent in its central image. The coin's value lies partly in its represented scene, which renders permanent the fleeting world, but also partly in its function as a coin, to be used for transaction. Standing both for what endures and what vanishes, for reanimation and its failure, for aesthetics and commercial exchange, it compels its possessor both to retain it and to give it away. Like all poems, it could be argued, "A Coin for Joe" does both, permitting through language the dispersal that its speaker resists. Yet the issue remains not fully resolved within the poem, which emphasizes, among other things, the difficulty of distinguishing the pleasure of art from its utility. Bidart's interest in performance is here pertinent. Elegy's parameters provide—as Sacks and others have claimed—an artificial, "ceremonial" frame for mourning; elegy itself "develops the effect [. . .] of a performance" (Sacks, *English*

19). Elegy is thus for Sacks both performed and performative: in its staging of grief, it attempts to resolve grief.

"A Coin for Joe" and *Desire* more generally propose a different notion, offering the static, permanent realm of art as an alternative to the often fleeting gesturings of performance. In the process, Bidart does not affirm, as elegy conventionally does, the solitary poet as vanquisher of death. Rather, he emphasizes the resemblance between death and the artistic process in that art annihilates individuality. To create art in the vicinity of death, Bidart implies in ways that recall "Golden State," requires that the artist eradicate himself and in the process abandon the fiction of selfhood.

Bidart elaborates these notions most directly in a series of poems in the middle of *Desire*'s first section, which consider the extent to which art can redeem or unmake death and the extent to which self-erasure can intensify the illusion of the dead's return. These poems emphasize the permanence of art more than the reanimation of the dead. Yet apostrophe persists in at least some of these poems.

Like "*Catullus: Excrucior,*" the prose poem "Borges and I" (9–11) remakes an earlier text, Jorge Luis Borges's short story of the same title, but here the process of revision is an explicit theme of the poem, as the first sentence makes clear: "We fill pre-existing forms and when we fill them we change and are changed." Bidart begins by explaining that Borges' story concerns a struggle between two elements of the self, the narrator or "I," and the third-person "Borges," called by Borges "the other one" (324) and by Bidart "the self who makes literature." But Bidart's speaker objects to Borges' distinction between actual and writing selves, and in the process he challenges the hierarchy implied by Borges' self-division, in which what Bidart calls "an essential self" who seeks "to remain unchanged" underlies the "inauthentic" public self. That Bidart's attack on Borges is based on a misreading of Borges only heightens the sense that Bidart is not only responding to Borges but reconsidering his own earlier preoccupation—in a poem like "Ellen West"—with the possibility of authentic selfhood.[14]

Borges' piece, included in a collection of his fiction, seems to be a story, while the placement of Bidart's similar account in a poetry volume makes it a prose poem. This apparently incidental issue of placement highlights the ways Bidart changes the "form" of Borges' story. Borges represents a power struggle between "Borges" and "I," two seemingly autonomous characters. But Bidart's imitation refuses this dramatic structure; his version contains neither dialogue nor multiple characters. By beginning a series of one-sentence paragraphs with the phrase "Frank had the illusion that," Bidart transforms Borges' interpersonal conflict into a psychological one. Borges' account chronicles a change—"I" gradually realizes that Borges has mastered him. Although Bidart's repeated phrase implies a disjunction between the past and the subsequent moment when the illusion is recognized, the repetition undermines narrative or development. Instead, his highly subordinated sentences establish a realm of reversals and contradictions in which, as he says, "the opposite of [any assertion] seems to me to be true, as true" as the assertion itself.

This complex syntax is evident in the poem's consideration of the process of artistic creation. In an image that evokes the end of "Golden State," where the speaker's obliteration of himself as "the 'eye' " impels the photographs to "stare back" at him, the poem here ultimately compels the poet to obey its logic:

> Frank had the illusion that though the universe of one of his poems seemed so close to what seemed his own universe at the second of writing it that he wasn't sure how they differed [. . .], after he had written it its universe was never exactly his universe, and so, soon, it disgusted him a little, the mirror was dirty and cracked.
>
> Secretly he was glad it was dirty and cracked, because [. . .] only when he had come to despise [a book he had written] a little, [. . .] only then could he write more. (10)

Poem-making requires first that the poet imagine that the poem represents "his own universe" or selfhood and then that he acknowledge the inaccuracy of this notion. While Borges' "I" is in thrall to the false and opportunistic artist-self, here the artist is forced to obey the absolutist, self-contradicting dictates of the artwork itself. Bidart's insistence on the gap between personal experience and art's representation of it minimizes the self, and in the process evokes the analogous, if less embittered unmaking of selfhood in "The Yoke," in which the speaker's longing ultimately undermines his autonomy and power.

If "Borges and I" indirectly evokes *Desire*'s more explicitly elegiac poems, the next poem in the collection, "Homo Faber," examines the relationship between art-making and death more directly. In "Borges and I," the conflict between the poem and the poet's illusions about his experience is played out through dialogue, as the title makes clear; here, the opposition is transposed to a realm from which both self and other have been nearly effaced. Here is the entire poem:

> Whatever lies still uncarried from the abyss within
> me as I die dies with me. (12)

Because the poem moves toward, culminates in, and reiterates death, it suggests that man as maker cannot transcend death. The syntactic equivalence of what is "within/ me" and what "dies with me" suggests an equivalence between the poem's two implied levels of imagery: the residue remaining inside a partially excavated pit converts the self into a tomb for all that is caught, "uncarried," within itself. Yet the poem also affirms the artist's act of defiance. The title defines man as maker, and the poem's implied double negative of "uncarried [. . .] dies" partly affirms that position: the artist, after all, does manage to carry some things out from the abyss. More subtly, Bidart's midphrase line break suggests something antithetical to the apparent syntactic and narrative affirmation of death's ultimate triumph. The chiasmus in the last line—"me-die-dies-me"—affirms, like the self-nailing nail of "Catullus: Excrucior," an anti-logical mode marked by reflexivity, reversals, and confusion about agency. Thus, death enables as it obliterates art: the speaker becomes a maker by attempting to beat death in the race to carry out what he can despite his knowledge that death will triumph. Yet Bidart refuses to exalt art as a mode of immortality. What endures is not the speaker himself but "whatever" he manages to carry out from himself; the poem stubbornly, awkwardly focuses on the unnamed things that are salvaged.

In emphasizing the dependence of art on death and in moving from the title's affirmation of art to the last line's affirmation of death, "Homo Faber" implies that art is suffused with death; it cannot help being elegiac. As the title makes clear, "In Memory of Joe Brainard" (13), the volume's next poem, elegizes a particular person. But it does so by describing and considering an artwork, a collage by Brainard. Whereas the stark "Homo Faber" insists that art derives from the futile attempt to outrun death, here Bidart considers the more consoling possibility that making art can overcome death.

Somewhat like the various attempts to capture the father in "Golden State," the poem self-consciously chronicles the speaker's attempts to define an elegiac mode that will capture or represent Brainard. After an attempt, in italics, to describe what is unique in Brainard, the speaker self-consciously insists on the importance of interpretation, conflating Brainard's artwork with the man himself:

> When I tried to find words for the moral sense that unifies
> and sweetens the country voices in your collage *The Friendly Way*,
>
> you said *It's a code.*

> You were a code
> I yearned to decipher.—

The speaker here depicts himself in the process of attempting to articulate ("find words for") and "decipher" or use language analytically and representationally, having apparently forgotten the insistence of "Borges and I" that language can never represent experience exactly.

The next section abandons this clumsy effort at equating the "code[s]" of Brainard's life and his art. Here the speaker attempts another strategy for representing Joe Brainard, one that, as "Borges and I" more directly affirms, embraces contradiction:

> In the end, the plague that full swift runs by
> took you, broke you;—
>
> > *in the end, could not*
> > *take you, did not break you—*
>
> you had somehow erased within you not only
> meanness, but anger, the desire to punish
> the universe for everything
>
> *not* achieved, *not* tasted, seen again, touched—;
>
> . . . the undecipherable
> code unbroken even as the soul
>
> learns once again the body it loves and hates is
> made of earth, and will betray it.

The opposition between a plague that "took you, broke you" and that "*could not/ take you, did not break you*" is not explained, but the poem insists on the gap between and juxtaposition of the two versions, the first perhaps representing the actual or accepted version—what is, in the terms of "The Yoke," "know[n]"—and the second the more tenuous realm of desire. Joe has, the speaker suggests, achieved a double erasure. His ability to erase "anger, the desire to punish/ the universe" is a natural response to a universe that itself withholds achievements and tastes, yet this capacity also allows him not only to see but "see [. . .] again." This interplay between erasure and abundance, refusal and persistence allows the speaker to reimagine the code in new, paradoxical terms: because the code resists being deciphered, it remains "unbroken" and so, by implication, helps to affirm the plague's inability to "break you." The final, complex opposition of soul and body, love and hatred, devotion and betrayal haltingly contrasts an enduring soul to the mutable body and suggests indirectly that art may mitigate death's compulsion to break and betray. While the convoluted syntax of "Borges and I" reveals the difficulties of trying to argue with a literary precursor while resisting the illusion of dialogue, "In Memory of Joe Brainard" offers a more positive example of artistic influence. Brainard's collage allows the speaker to free himself from his compulsion to "decipher"; more importantly, it enables a poetic mode that is itself collage-like, relying on juxtaposition, overlap, and omission, enabling the griever to articulate the simultaneous, contradictory attempt to possess while relinquishing the dead other.

While the poems I have been examining repudiate many of the dramatic tendencies of earlier volumes, *Desire* remains preoccupied with performance: to forgo performance, as "A Coin for Joe," "Borges and I," and "Homo Faber" imply in different ways, would be to create a poem that replicated the stasis of death. Bidart's repeated insistence on "pre-existing" forms, which allow us to "fill them" and thereby to "change and [. . . be] changed" connects performance with the bestowing of form: as Bidart's poems re-write or "fill" the texts or "forms" of earlier writers, they re-perform them. This tendency is most richly enacted in "The Second Hour of the Night," the long poem that constitutes the second half of *Desire*. The poem meditates on a different kind of form-changing: Bidart connects bodily metamorphosis with bodily desire while emphasizing the ways that metamorphosis enacts the elegiac desire to undermine or unmake death.

"The Second Hour," unlike the short lyrics of *Desire*'s first half, uses many of the techniques of Bidart's earlier poems: the poem includes multiple narrators, dialogue, and three separate stories, two of them revisions of earlier written texts. Yet the poem does not reiterate or mimic Bidart's earlier long poems. Instead, it clarifies the connection between Bidart's impulse to dramatize or perform in his poems and the elegiac impulse to animate the other. Like the poems in which Bidart directly connects art, revision, death, and elegy, "The Second Hour" associates the urge to tell or perform stories not with an autobiographical urge—as in "Ellen West"—but with an unmaking of self that is necessary for the other's embodiment.

"The Second Hour of the Night" is a sequel to "The First Hour of the Night" (*Western* 183–219), the elegy that ended Bidart's *Collected Poems*. "The First Hour" is a sustained meditation, occasioned by the return of the speaker to the house of a recently dead friend, on the speaker's grief and the extent to which various philosophical models can explain death and offer consolation for it. Through the recounting of four allegorical dreams which the dreamer, like the pilgrim of Dante's *Inferno,* helplessly witnesses, the poem moves haltingly toward resolution. The poem considers through a study of the profound, "passionate" intellectual bond between the "*SOUL[S]*" of the speaker and his dead friend a more general kind of love which, the speaker affirms, "ha[s] never betrayed me" (190). The only exception to love's trustworthiness, he notes, is his experience of erotic love, in which the need for "the *RECIPROCATION* of *EROTIC* DESIRE" has "bewildered" feeling (190).

"The Second Hour" (*Desire* 27–59) begins here, in the bewildering, unreliable realm of erotic desire that is, except for this single reference, excluded from "The First Hour." I indicated above that Sacks cites Ovid in support of his claim that desire and mourning are antithetical. The central section of "The Second Hour" also relies on Ovid to set forth a more precarious connection. By emphasizing Ovid's alliance between desire and what Bidart calls "transformation [. . .]/ [. . .] to an inhuman, un-/ riven state" (33), Bidart implies that desire requires a self-sacrifice that, undoing humanity and rivenness, approaches death. Metamorphosis involves a similar bodily relinquishment: the transformed one is, in the terms of Bidart's version of Ovid's tale of Myrrha and Cinyras in the second section of "The Second Hour," "*not alive, not dead*" (54). This intermediate state dramatically fulfills the wish proposed in "The Yoke" and other poems that death be unmade, that the dead be allowed to inhabit a region beyond both life and death.

In "Ellen West," Ellen's description of Callas's performance revealed the poem's wish to undermine conventional distinctions between performance and real life. In the first section of "The Second Hour," Bidart more directly and devastatingly connects performance and personal life. The account, drawn from Berlioz's description in his autobiography of his wife's death, emphasizes an intrusion of the personal into the wife's acting career so radical that it compels her to end her career:

Her accident.

*(Just before a benefit
performance designed to lessen, if not
erase her debts, a broken leg left her
NOT—as the doctors feared—lame, but visibly
robbed of confidence and ease of movement.)*

> Her humiliating
> return to the Paris stage.
>
> *(After Ophelia's
> death, which a few years earlier at her debut
> harrowed the heart of Paris, the cruel
> audience did not recall her to the stage
> once, though it accorded others an ovation.)*
>
> Her decision, made voluntarily but forever
> mourned, to give up her art. (29)

Art, according to this model, cannot redeem the individual or even enable coded autobiographical speech: rather, it is hindered by an autobiography that is both mundane (the accident is precipitated by the wife's financial troubles) and mysterious (although her physical injury is not permanent, its psychological effects are). This scene anticipates a connection between the characters reenacting Ovid's familiar tale in the second section and the direct, apparently autobiographical speech in the third. It also affirms the ubiquitousness of mourning. The wife's mourning for her lost career reiterates and perhaps displaces Berlioz's mourning at her death; the poem's speaker indicates that he first read Berlioz's account just after learning that his own mother was dying.

Bidart's account of the incestuous relationship between Myrrha and her father, Cinyras, in the poem's long second section reimagines the connection between performance, autobiography, and retold stories. As the speaker of the first section recounted Berlioz's recollections in the context of his own attempt to make sense of his mother's illness, Bidart uses Ovid to explore in detail the contradictions of desire that recur in many of the earlier poems in *Desire*. As such, Bidart's revision of Ovid is also an appropriation; he compels Myrrha to enact or perform the questions that preoccupy him as elegist.

Bidart's account emphasizes from the outset the contradictory nature of Myrrha's desire. This contradiction is introduced as an alternation of bodily sensations felt by the young Myrrha in the presence of her father:

> once, as a child, she had in
> glee leapt upon him surrounded by
> soldiers and he, then, pretending to be overwhelmed

> by a superior force fell backwards with
> her body clasped in his arms as they rolled
> body over body down the long slope
> laughing and that peculiar sensation of his weight
> full upon her and then
> not, then full upon her, then not,—
>
> until at the bottom for a half-
> second his full weight rested upon her, then not,—(39)

As Bidart's revision of "Borges and I" converted its narrative conflict into a psychological state in which opposing sensations coexisted, Myrrha's subsequent desire also converts this temporal alteration into a terrible and negative simultaneity: "drawn down the dark corridor toward her father," Myrrha is "not free not to desire" and is "draw[n . . .] forward" by "neither COMPULSION nor FREEWILL:—" (46).

This physical sensation of being caught between mutually exclusive alternatives also characterizes Myrrha's attempt to describe her desire. Pregnant with her father's child and banished from his house, Myrrha compulsively retells her own story to her unborn child. The story keeps changing, and finally her autobiographical chronicle becomes address, a prayer to the gods:

> *Make me nothing*
> *human: not alive, not dead.*
>
> *Whether I deny what is not in my*
> *power to deny, or by deception*
>
> *seize it, I am damned.*
>
> *I shall not rest until what has been*
> *lodged in me is neither*
>
> *lodged in me,—nor NOT lodged in me.*
>
> *Betrayed, bewildered eyes*
> *wait for me in death.*
>
> *You are gods. Release me, somehow, from both*
> *life and death.* (54)

The self-contradicting terms of Myrrha's request emphasize the inexorability of desire: even in trying to evade it through transformation, Myrrha can only reiterate its contradictions, its status as neither-nor. Desire, this prayer suggests, cannot be escaped, and so it is not surprising that the myrrh tree Myrrha metamorphoses into affirms the paradoxes that defined her desire, including the inextricability of sweetness and bitterness, love and death, mortality and immortality:

> *Aphrodisiac. Embalmers' oil. (Insistence of*
> *sex, faint insistent sweetness of the dead undead.)*
> *Sacred anointment oil: with wine an*
> *anodyne. Precious earth-*
> *fruit, gift fit for the birth and death of*
>
> *prophets:*—no sweet thing without
> the trace of what is bitter
> within its opposite:—
>
> . . . MYRRH, *sweet-smelling*
> *bitter resin.* (55)

Myrrh, according to Bidart, evokes death, but it also unmakes death by keeping the body from deteriorating even as its everflowing sap evokes the tears of grievers. Myrrha's transformation does not allow her to remain *"alive,"* but in persisting outside the binarism of death and life, she recalls the elegiac wish for the dead beloved similarly to transcend both categories, to occupy some other realm. All elegy to some extent ensures a similarly partial, ambivalent reincarnation: the dead other lives within elegy itself. Bidart extends this elegiac conceit; even after she is freed from mortality, Myrrha is not allowed relief from grief. She thus evokes not only the dead beloved of elegy but also its captive, grieving elegist. This enduring grief is the cost of fulfilling elegy's wish. Myrrha's ambivalent reincarnation also allows Bidart to reconcile the two kinds of form-changing central to the poem. Myrrha is not wholly released from suffering, and Bidart's version of Ovid's dead text similarly revives the story but cannot change its desolation.

Up to this point in the poem, the connection between bodily transformation and elegy is implied, but the poem's final section makes it explicit. Here Bidart shifts—far more directly than in "Ellen West"—to autobiography:

> *on such a night,*
> > *at such an hour*
>
> . . . grace is the dream, half-
> dream, half-
>
> light, when you appear and do not answer the question
>
> that I have asked you, but courteously
> ask (because you are dead) if you can briefly
>
> borrow, inhabit my body.
>
> When I look I can see my body
> away from me, sleeping.
>
> I say *Yes.* Then you enter it
>
> like a shudder as if eager again to know
> what it is to move within arms and legs.
>
> I thought, *I know that he will return it.*
>
> I trusted in that none
> earlier, none other. (58)

The scene strongly evokes the similarly first-person, nighttime, apostrophic account of "The Yoke." But where that poem's speaker was insomniac, here the speaker is asleep or inhabits a "half-/ dream, half-// light" that unmakes the earlier, absolute opposition between knowledge and desire. While the fantasy of presence in "The Yoke" involved the speaker's turning away from his "*know[ledge] that you're dead,*" here the other makes his courteous request "because you are dead." While "The Yoke" insisted on the addressee's invisibility or failure to occupy a known location, here the addressee's request concerns visibility and is affirmed by the speaker's own vision of his body's separateness from himself. The dreams of "The First Hour of the Night" affirmed death's power and so allowed the griever to relinquish his dead friend. But here the dream unmakes death.

As the passage fulfills what "The Yoke" left incomplete, it revises the Myrrha account by releasing desire from suffering. The poem is preoccupied with the possibility of being inhabited by another. Myrrha's pregnancy undermined her bodily distinctness in a way that recalled her father's sexual union with her. But here the state of being occupied by another is both more complete and less hindered by eroticism. The speaker's body is given up entirely to the addressee, a state to which the speaker entirely acquiesces ("I say *Yes*") and which also seems to satisfy the addressee, who enters the body with a "shudder."[15] But the speaker's relinquishment of his body is also temporary and so removes the punishment, the suffering from bodily joining. (The gesture evokes Bidart's ability to inhabit, then let go of Ovid's text.)

This intimacy also requires something more drastic than reciprocated sexual merging: the speaker must give up his body. The other is embodied by unmaking the speaker's integrity; he persists not alongside but through the living friend. The passage in this way recalls Ellen West, who also wished to persist without a body, to sacrifice her body for a purer realm of soul. Yet the speaker's self-sacrifice here is temporary, a gift rather than a lonely affirmation of an ideal, and it allows the speaker to go on speaking. The poem is thus poignant because it is so ambivalent; it achieves belatedly, at great cost, the consolation that has mostly evaded the volume's speaker.[16] This consolation is achieved, paradoxically, both through Bidart's patient exploration of apostrophe's refusal of consolation and through his speaker's willingness, in the end, to sacrifice self, autobiography, and verisimilitude.

The paradox with which I am ending this chapter thus evokes the paradoxes about desire with which I began. Bidart's poems find solace in desire by allowing the other to possess the self and thus to eradicate it, if temporarily. The unmaking of mortality in Bidart's poems thus comes only through the speaker's willingness to sacrifice his autonomy; the isolation of lyric can be dismantled only through the dismantling of the lyric speaker. The pathos others have identified in Bidart's poems recalls, therefore, something evoked in different ways by Plath, Merrill, and Glück, but Bidart's version is more tender: what Glück has called the "premise of union" can be fulfilled only at great cost to the self. Yet the poems persist, perhaps less vulnerable than this nearly-dissolved self, recalling even as they alter the forms that preexisted them.

Conclusion
"A dream of this room": Self-Effacement and Lyric Space

I have in the preceding chapters connected the lyric figure of apostrophe to a series of emotional and thematic issues. Postmodern address, I have been arguing, emphasizes both isolation and the yearning for companionship, both mortality and the possibility of circumventing it. A focus on lyric address in this way illuminates the nature of lyric subjectivity: the attitude of speaking to an absent other allows the postmodern lyric subject to be defined at least partly by the yearning to unmake an isolation fundamental to lyric, which cannot, in the end, be unmade.

In focusing on the nature of lyric subjectivity in this final chapter, I mean both to examine more directly the bond between the poems of Plath, Merrill, Glück, and Bidart and to consider the more general repercussions of poetic address. Not all the poems I consider in this final chapter are apostrophic, but even in those poems in which there is no address, a central question recurs: how can the self persist given the irreducibly alien quality of the world outside the self? The differences among the poets I have been examining make the similarity of their answers in some ways surprising: the self, they repeatedly assert, does not preexist the poem or even validate its existence; the poem does not represent the articulation of a preexisting or fixed speaker. Rather selfhood is a concept to be manipulated and even dispensed with, something approaching a lyric device or trope. More crucially, this manipulation or, in the recurrent term of several poems, "effacement" of the self is often directly linked to—it results from or leads to—the other's embodiment.

That lyric subjectivity is inherently oxymoronic has been argued by several critics. In Vernon Shetley's cogent terms, lyric contains a "problem at [its] very root [. . .], that of embodying subjectivity in the impersonal and resistant medium of language" (8). A similar but more acute conflict between subjectivity and language is often noted in the more experimental strand of contemporary poetry.[1] Such a tension derives in Paul de Man's terms from the nature of figuration itself. For de Man, poetic figure—and in particular prosopopeia, which as I indicated above is for him both "the trope of autobiography" (*Rhetoric* 76) and essentially indistinguishable from apostrophe (78)—corresponds to a "defacement" or mutilation of the possibility of coherent selfhood. Attempting to "confer a mask or a face" (76) on that which is inanimate, prosopopeia ends up affirming (or even exaggerating) the death and disfigurement that it attempts to conceal. Prosopopeia thus articulates the impossibility of coherently representing subjectivity. De Man's notions are, as I argued at more length above, pertinent to my own. Yet his notion of defacement remains quite different from the effacement I have located in postmodern lyric. Affect is not excised from postmodern poems by any means; rather, these poems scrutinize the possibility of identification with various others. As the term "effacement" implies, any erasure of the lyric subject is both temporary and textual.[2] The mild, even salutary quality of self-effacement derives at least partly from its function as a strategy to effect union, an impulse that is often explicitly represented as a way to move the poem forward. Rather than eradicating the speaker as voice, self-effacement allows the poem's articulation.

The recurrence of self-effacement in postmodern poetry also helps clarify the nature of the pathos that I have been arguing inheres in the scene of lyric overhearing.[3] Postmodern lyric repeatedly stages exclusions—of the addressee and also at times of the reader—that ultimately emphasize the irreducible isolation of the lyric speaker. The notion of self-effacement intensifies this pathos by rendering the speaker as well as the addressee unfixed. In such a situation, union is rendered even less likely, relying as it does on multiple illusions of coherence and presence. Yet self-effacement also paradoxically permits the creation of a distinctive space, negative and often explicitly represented as illusory, in which this isolation can in some ways be alleviated. Effaced, the speaker resembles the addressee, who is similarly imaginary, a projection or product of the speaker's yearning. I will examine one configuration of such a space at the end of this chapter, through a reading of the ways that multiple effacements in John Ashbery's "This Room" suggest lyric to be neither an entity to be desired nor an ordinary, actual space but rather a dreamed space, adjacent to and inexactly replicating the actual.

The connection between self-sacrifice and textual integrity, which the term "effacement" itself implies, is central to Louise Glück's non-apostrophic "The Deviation," a poem I examined in more detail above. Body and text

"A dream of this room"

here share an aesthetic of reduction or what Glück explicitly terms a willingness to "sacrifice":

> [. . .] I remember
> lying in bed at night
> touching the soft, digressive breasts,
> touching, at fifteen,
> the interfering flesh
> that I would sacrifice
> [. . . . .
> . . .] : I felt
> what I feel now, aligning these words— (*Descending* 32)

Glück's poem is startling partly because it transposes familiar critical terms: the body is not, as de Man's notion of defacement suggests, the metaphor's vehicle, to which the fact of prosopopeia (the tenor, the entity with which de Man is most concerned) refers. Rather, more frighteningly, Glück suggests that the female body is the tenor: these lines refer to the actual sacrifice of actual flesh. Frightening though this bodily sacrifice is, it is partly naturalized by the reference to the process of writing: the sacrifice seems nearly a means by which the poet attains her identity as poet. (Plath's late letter claiming that her poems will make her name similarly if less directly associates poetic identity with bodily annihilation.) For Glück, the paring down of flesh clearly resembles, and perhaps enables, the creation of poems.

Yet the connection between body and text is also inexact: the two are never described as analogous. The experience of writing the poem postdates the bodily experience, and the speaker does not claim that one experience enabled or even resembles the other; she merely "felt" something similar during the two different situations. Moreover, although her impulse is to be rid of "the interfering flesh," that impulse fails, and her claim that she "would" make such a sacrifice suggests it to be a hypothetical or at least subsequent occurrence. The description of her body also emphasizes its substantiality. Although its curves are "digressive," they are also "soft"; the touching is both violation and caress. The passage, for all its ferocity, evokes autoerotism, even a kind of self-comforting. As a result, the obliteration is at most partial. The body of the speaker may be pared down, but it is not eradicated: the speaker persists, drawing attention to her ability not only to write poems, but to write "these words," the very words we are now reading. The immediacy of the image helps us, ironically, to see the act of bodily self-erasure as merely figurative, as tenor rather than vehicle, after all: we recognize it as a kind of poetic ploy, something meant to draw us in and keep us reading. As a way to move the poem forward, to force the poem to its climax, it seems, for all its physicality, like a mostly rhetorical gesture.

In this way, self-effacement seems partly a stage of devotion, a way to articulate the speaker's desire for her lines' alignment. Glück's poem contains no addressee; its only dialogue is an implied one between the self desiring erasure and the resistant body. Yet, as other poems by Plath, Merrill, and Bidart more explicitly reveal, the representation of self-effacement permits postmodern lyric to imagine and stage an alternative to separation, even to mortality. Glück's poem suggests an analogy between bodily thinness and the careful alignment and minimalism of the poem's lines. Other poems expand this analogy, linking the deliberate dismantling of the speaker to a kind of verbal proliferation, an affirmation, paradoxically, of lyric itself. Repeatedly, these poems insist on a space in which lyric desire can be fulfilled through the dislocation of the lyric subject itself.

Both Plath and Merrill articulate this impulse toward self-effacement directly. That Plath would do so is perhaps unsurprising; self-destruction in her poems often becomes, as I argued above, a kind of aesthetic strategy. Nor is it surprising that this notion is enacted in relation to the speaker's body, by means of a scene that like Glück's involves a woman alone in bed, one who like Glück's speaker is preoccupied with her physical position. "Tulips" begins by describing facelessness in seemingly literal terms, in terms, that is, of seeing and being seen:

> Nobody watched me before, now I am watched.
> The tulips turn to me, and the window behind me
> Where once a day the light slowly widens and slowly thins,
> And I see myself, flat, ridiculous, a cut-paper shadow
> Between the eye of the sun and the eyes of the tulips.
> *And I have no face, I have wanted to efface myself.*
> (*Collected* 161, emphasis added)

The bodily in Merrill's "The Book of Ephraim," is generally associated with intellectual rather than physical puzzles. Yet in Section Y, JM imagines a somewhat analogous bodily fragmentation:

> And here was I, or what was left of me.
> Feared and rejoiced in, chafed against, held cheap,
> A strangeness that was us, and was not, had
> All the same allowed for its description,

> And so brought at least me *these spells of odd,*
> *Self-effacing balance.* Better to stop
> While we still can. Already I take up
> Less emotional space than a snowdrop.
> My father in his last illness complained
> Of the effect of medication on
> His real self—today Bluebeard, tomorrow
> Babbitt. Young chameleon, I used to
> Ask how on earth one got sufficiently
> Imbued with otherness. And now I see. (*Changing* 89, emphasis added)

Attempting to define a primarily "emotional space" rather than a physical one, JM locates in self-effacement not so much the cataclysmic dismantling evoked by Plath but something milder: self-effacement here is grammatically subordinate to "balance."

Both passages, though, imagine a similar, mysterious origin to self-effacement. For JM, it arrives unexpectedly, by way of a "strangeness" difficult to define or locate. Plath's speaker connects her current physical condition ("I have no face") with what seems a desire for something more existential ("I have wanted to efface myself") but does not spell out the exact relation. More strikingly, both passages suggest that the impulse to efface the self derives from the incursion of others into the self's apparently private realm, although the poems represent this incursion differently. The tulips threaten to overcome and annihilate Plath's speaker (they "eat my oxygen"). Their personification, that is, corresponds directly to her diminishment into an object in ways that recall Barbara Johnson's connection of animation with deanimation and death. JM also names and partly personifies the strangeness, although the emphasis of his passage remains more positive.

Both passages in this way emphasize self-effacement as a product of the breakdown of distinctions between self and other. In "Tulips," this dynamic is enacted through an "I"/ "eye" pun similar to that which I explored above in "Ariel." The situation of "now" being "watched," Plath's speaker asserts, is not entirely negative: it enables her to take on a kind of reciprocal vision, to "see myself." The equivalence of "I" to "eye" blurs the difference between the "I" as subject and as object of a gaze: "*I* see myself [. . .]/ Between the *eye* of the sun and the *eyes* of the tulips." Yet as in "Ariel," the multiplied gaze that results leads not to an affirmation of self as either gazed-on object or autonomous subject; rather, it seems that the conflation of these terms impels the speaker toward the desire for self-effacement.

JM similarly derives self-effacement from the confusion of self and other. He first dismantles his integrity ("here was I, *or what was left of me*"), then defines himself as part of the larger entity comprising himself and DJ ("us"). More crucially, JM abandons self-description to attempt, haltingly, to define first the strangeness, whose relation to him and DJ remains unclear (it "was us, or was not"), then an otherness that, in multiplying identities (the father is "today Bluebeard, tomorrow/ Babbitt") reveals directly the limitations of the concept of "real self." This incursion of otherness, which as in "Tulips" seems caught between affirming and eradicating self, leads for JM to a similar outcome. While the self-effacement here is less frightening, it nonetheless hints at annihilation. Rendered by it as small as a snowdrop—a flower very different from the tulips of Plath's poem, which resemble "dangerous animals"—JM pulls back from a more absolute diminishment: "Better to stop/ While we still can."

Self-effacement in these poems responds to an otherness that is both compelling and threatening. Yet self-effacement, like Glück's bodily sacrifice, remains for Merrill and Plath an answer to a problem engendered in and represented through poetry. Glück's sacrifice is temporary; her poem enacts the illusion of erasure while affirming the speaker's bodily continuance and more crucially her empowerment as a maker of poems. Similarly, for both Merrill and Plath, self-effacement is a figurative rather than a literal or bodily strategy: it enables the poem to continue. JM's emphasis on the series of compensations enabled by self-effacement removes this position from anything resembling actual bodily destruction. While "Tulips" is more psychically acute, its self-effacement remains more clearly hypothetical: Plath's use of the present perfect ("I *have wanted* to efface myself") places self-effacement in the realm of desire rather than actuality. This temporal distance anticipates her subsequent turn toward what she later, in an act of self-diagnosis that recalls the title of Glück's "The Deviation," calls "health" (*Collected* 162).

A reluctance wholly to embrace the fiction of the other's presence, these poems suggest, leads to a pulling back from the more extreme manifestations of self-effacement: the power of the tulips diminishes as Plath's poem progresses, and JM's description of otherness is framed by Ephraim's absence. The late autobiographical passage of Bidart's "The Second Hour of the Night," a poem I discussed at more length above, suggests something similar, but here the holding-back is absent: the speaker's self-effacement permits him to gain access to the absent other. That Bidart's poem, unlike those I have been examining this far, is apostrophic intensifies the sense of proximity. The speaker of "The Second Hour of the Night" near the poem's end emphasizes the act of "*seeking to be allowed to S U B M I T*"

(*Desire* 59). The phrase links submission to the mastery or power of others (here unnamed), emphasizing a progressive act of prostration: submission must be "allowed," and the allowance itself must be sought. The implication of this assertion—that submission requires the presence, even the permission of the other—is more fully elaborated in the passage just preceding this one, in which the speaker recounts the dead addressee's request to "briefly// borrow, inhabit my body" and the speaker acquiesces to this request (58). Here, more directly than in the poems of Glück, Plath, or Merrill, the speaker's act of bodily self-sacrifice permits the dead other's embodiment: "I say *Yes*. Then you enter [my body]// like a shudder" (58). The shudder, like Glück's self-touching, accommodates both pleasure and pain. It involves the bequeathing of body but paradoxically affirms the speaker's own bodily continuance: he is able to perceive the other's entry. Moreover, the speaker's giving up of his body is temporary (the speaker is secure in the knowledge "*that he will return it*"), mutual, and erotic. Rather than defacing the autonomous body of the speaker (or the poem that it engenders), the gesture animates and completes them both, permitting the speaker to marvel, by witnessing the addressee possess his body, at "what it is to move within arms and legs."

The connection between self-erasure and erotic merging is familiar to elegy: to speak to the beloved dead has for poets at least since Orpheus involved approaching or entering their realm, and elegy often melancholically invites death. "The Second Hour" is typical of postmodern poems in its refusal to pull back from this approach to death. Yet, more poignantly than Glück's bodily sacrifice, the annihilation remains fictive. The possession of the speaker's body by the dead beloved marks not an actual event but the intensity of the speaker's desire for presence and thus his loneliness. Bidart's speaker, by addressing an actual human other (rather than describing, as do Plath and Merrill, an object or abstract concept), excises the fear that both Plath and Merrill associate with otherness. But the desire enacted by the scene remains, no less than in the other poems I have been examining, a marker of distance and of the pathos involved in trying to dismantle this distance.

I observed above that the term "effacement" involves a particularly textual erasure, one that alludes in poems to the poems themselves. "The Deviation" somewhat awkwardly points to a connection between bodily sacrifice and the poem's continuance. Self-effacement in all these poems implies something similar: it enacts the ferocity of its speaker's yearning as it advances the poem. This connection between self-effacement and poetic production is elaborated most directly by Merrill. Self-effacement becomes in his terms a strategy through which the poem can come into being. In the passage I cited above, JM marvels not at strangeness in general but at the quality of the strangeness that "allowed for its description": what enables the spells of self-effacing balance seems partly to be the possibility that JM can describe their origin. A similar connection is more directly expressed in the last lines of Merrill's "Lost in Translation," a poem originally published in the same volume as "The Book of Ephraim." Here, self-effacement permits an explicitly linguistic restitution:

> But nothing's lost. Or else: all is translation
> And every bit of us is lost in it
> (Or found—I wander through the ruin of S
> Now and then, wondering at the peacefulness)
> And in that loss, *a self-effacing tree,*
> Color of context, imperceptibly
> Rustling with its angel, turns the waste
> To shade and fiber, milk and memory. (*Divine* 10; emphasis added)

The landscape is here in "ruin[s]," identified with a place itself so sketchily evoked (by the abbreviated "S") that it suggests an imagined rather than an actual scene. In this setting, the self-effacement of the tree is unsurprising. Metonymically located "in [. . .] loss," the tree partakes of the loss. Yet the speaker's perception that it is the "color of *context*" undermines the loss by establishing its literary, rather than bodily, identity. The passage's final gesture of restitution—the transformation of "waste" into the variously useful "shade and fiber, milk and memory"—derives partly from the conversion of the physical tree into a wholly textual one. The tree occupies a realm in which puns bridge the gap between the physical (rustling trees) and the metaphysical (wrestling with an angel). The tree's self-effacement, that is, is less an erasure than a stage in its transformation into poetic prop: it links the actual peaceful landscape of S to the possibility of restitution through language itself.

More crucially, Merrill's consideration of self-effacement here emphasizes not mortality, as does the description of JM's father's "last illness" in "The Book of Ephraim," but translation, the imperfect transformation of one language into another. The tree itself exists only in a poem, Paul Valéry's "Palme," and—in a further displacement—in that poem's recalled but missing German translation (*Divine* 9). Yet this linguistic distancing renders Merrill's tree, like the myrrh tree described by Bidart at the end of "The Second Hour," powerful: the tree can transform or translate one kind of entity

"*A dream of this room*" 129

into another. Caught in "loss," it is also capable of transformations or "turns." As in "The Second Hour," this process of metamorphosis delineates and makes visible the space between being lost and being found.

In turning in the last part of this chapter away from the work of the four central poets of my study, I am entering a realm in which self-effacement is ambient rather than explicit. I do not intend to argue that John Ashbery's "This Room" (3) can or should be made similar to the already dissimilar poems I have been discussing. Rather, the idiosyncrasy of Ashbery's poetic vision illuminates the ways I have been reading lyric address and lyric more generally throughout this book. More exactly, Ashbery's emphasis on space, and a space associated with lyric itself, redefines and clarifies many of the issues related to postmodern lyric address, subjectivity, animation, and identification that I have been examining. The poem defines a space something like Merrill's ruined S, which in that poem blurs loss and recovery. Caught between the actual and the imaginary or "dream[ed]," the room of Ashbery's poem enables effacements and deanimations of various kinds. Although Ashbery never identifies the room or its dream as anything but itself, it becomes in the context of my earlier discussion an accurate and powerful model for postmodern lyric itself.

"This Room" articulates a paradox that I have located in numerous poems. Here is the entire poem:

> The room I entered was a dream of this room.
> Surely all those feet on the sofa were mine.
> The oval portrait
> of a dog was me at an early age.
> Something shimmers, something is hushed up.
>
> We had macaroni for lunch every day
> except Sunday, when a small quail was induced
> to be served to us. Why do I tell you these things?
> You are not even here.

The abrupt turn in the penultimate line from description to address recalls Bidart's similarly condensed, present-tense opening to "The Yoke":

> *don't worry   I know you're dead*
> *but tonight*

turn your face again
toward me. (Desire 14)

For Ashbery as for Bidart the pathos of lyric utterance is central: we persist in address while knowing the act of address to be useless. If anything, though, Ashbery's view is bleaker. Where Bidart ends with an articulation of the speaker's desire for presence, Ashbery ends with an assertion of absence; even his admission that he is "tell[ing] you these things" is enclosed within a question. And because these lines disrupt and end the poem rather than, as in "The Yoke" serving as a refrain, the refusal of presence is more absolute.

I have been arguing throughout this chapter that an acknowledgment of self-effacement often permits or marks proximity to an other, even if this proximity is ultimately revealed to be illusory. Ashbery's last line emphasizes the absence of this other, yet the first eight lines of the poem evoke a series of connections enabled, paradoxically, by effacement or deanimation. The predominance of absence, erasure, and removal in this way permits the partial breakdown of the distinction between self and other.

"This Room" begins by defining a pair of spaces that nearly, but inexactly, reflect each other: "The room I entered was a dream of this room." This first line equates two rooms (the sentence's subject "was" its object). Yet it also confuses these two realms, or our ability to perceive and delineate them. The confusion derives partly from the juxtaposition of the immediate "this room" with the more distant, past-tense "was" and from a simultaneous foregrounding and distancing of the entered room: the line begins with the entered room, but defines it as a dream of this, a more immediate, room. The first line can thus be read at least two ways: a recently entered room is compared to a remembered one whose vividness the speaker expresses though the direct pronoun "this." Or this room exists in the present, and evokes a dreamed or dreamlike other room, which was entered in the past. In this way, the poem, from its first line, both affirms and refuses equivalence: we are left off kilter. This situation in some way resembles the conflicting gestures of the poem's last lines, which at once invoke the "you" and acknowledge its absence.

This intact but unreal space recalls similar spaces in the poems I have been examining. The ballroom at Sandover, setting for Merrill's "Coda," is opulent and vivid partly because it is imaginary: the actual ballroom of JM's childhood has long since been lost to him (*Changing* 556-7). The room exists only through and within the poem, as Merrill's recurrent pun on "stanza"—the word means "room" in Italian—makes clear. The fire-lit room in which son and mother "with unadulterated joy/ [. . .] bent" (79) in

Lowell's "During Fever" is similar, vividly recalled but absent. Glück's garden and the poor black shoe of "Daddy" offer containers which the speakers of these poems inhabit and from which they speak, although the speakers also chafe against these spaces, begging for more cover (in Glück's case) or attempting to burst forth (in Plath's). Ashbery's poem exposes both the artificiality of such spaces and the necessity of delineating their parameters.

Within the space of the dreamed room, a room both immediate (it is "this") and unreal (it is a "dream of" an actual room), Ashbery emphasizes problems that in some ways derive from the room's ambiguous status: questions recur about what is real and what is imagined, what is alive and what is not. The poem's final address is at least partly an animation. The addressee may be "not [. . .] here" but it seems, nonetheless, to exist; the poem has effectively brought it into being out of the solitary space of the first part of the poem. Yet this final, provisional animation is effected, paradoxically, via a series of deanimations, through which the living are at least partially stilled.

Perhaps the most direct and also quirky manipulation of agency and animation relates to the quail, which the speaker endows with a will in order for it to sacrifice itself as sentient being: "a small quail *was induced/ to be served* to us." The awkward passive both evokes the quail's existence as a bird—it can be "induced" to act and thus is alive—and affirms its obliteration into an entrée. The speaker inhabits a similarly nebulous realm. He struggles to enter a room (this room) to which he cannot gain access (he enters only "a dream of" it, what seems to be another room altogether). He is in the first line identified as the poem's protagonist, yet the rest of the stanza dismantles his agency. At first he is associated with the "feet on the sofa," all of which are "mine"; he is defined through what he possesses. The next line intensifies his deanimation. "The oval portrait/ of a dog" that "was me" stands in for the speaker. Moreover, it is a portrait not of a boy but of a dog, a further distancing. The allusion to Dylan Thomas's *Self-Portrait of the Artist as a Young Dog*, itself a corruption of James Joyce, further distances the scene from conventional notions of representation while recalling and mocking the problems of autobiography or self-portraiture: not only has the portrait effaced the humanity of the speaker, it has set him into a realm of already-recycled allusions. After such deanimations, the speaker remains altogether absent from the poem (although he is included in the nonspecific "we" of the second stanza) until the penultimate line, when he is identified by his capacity to "tell [. . .] things," by his articulation of the poem itself. In some ways, then, the poem enacts a narrative similar to those I examined earlier in this chapter: the effacement of the speaker enables him to emerge as the maker of the poem.

Within the dreamed room, a multiplication of identities also occurs. The once singular speaker becomes a collection of feet; the solitude of the room becomes a space in which the "you" is imagined if not embodied. Perhaps most crucially, the "you" is not merely or wholly the conventional addressee of apostrophe, an absent but particular other who exists only within the poem's frame. Instead, partly by remaining unidentified, partly by entering the poem so suddenly, partly by being addressed with such colloquial intimacy, the "you" invites a different, perhaps more radical kind of identification: more directly than in any poem I have thus far considered, it represents the poem's actual reader.[4] Yet this reader remains, like the "you" of apostrophe, inaccessible and mute. The poem thus calls to its actual readers, insisting that its words are for us. It also acknowledges, in ways that evoke the analogy I have been suggesting between lyric readers and apostrophized others, that these readers cannot be embodied, that they exist only at the level of desire.

In this way, "This Room" grants us a space within its frame by putting us into or nearly into the dreamed room. And here the notion of the room as a dream of a room rather than an actual room is particularly crucial. It is only within the imagined space established by lyric, that patently artificial but for this reason capacious space, that the lyric wish to end its speaker's isolation can come close to being fulfilled. I claimed above that in Merrill's *Sandover* the embodiment of the addressee required a violation of lyric itself. Ashbery's solution is more economical. Speaking directly to the reader is possible but only within a lyric space explicitly distinguished from actual, familiar spaces.

And so, through the force of its logic, "This Room" undermines distinctions that sometimes seem essential to lyric. In particular, its chain of deanimations—the analogies between quail, speaker, and addressee—permits, oddly, the possibility of identifications often prohibited by lyric. Lyric identification is here linked to what I have called the pathos of overhearing. That notion implies isolation: the speaker cannot become one with the addressee, and the reader remains excluded from the lyric frame. Yet Ashbery's poem implies that a kind of bonus can come from effacement. Because the speaker's dismantling resembles the addressee's, the two come to seem similar, perhaps versions of the same being. In this way, Ashbery's poem recalls Culler's notion that apostrophe is a form of projection, that the other is ultimately a version of self. I have been refuting Culler's model throughout these chapters, suggesting that the lyric addressee remains for the most part resolutely other. Ashbery's poem suggests something different, but in a way far more negative than Culler's model. Culler imagines a stable speaker who through apostrophe externalizes some part of himself. But Ashbery blurs speaker, addressee, and reader through less direct means. If Ashbery's poem permits identification, it is wholly negative: the speaker's resemblance to the other requires the dissolution or effacement of both figures. Insofar as the poem permits us to enter its frame, it does so with the stipulation that we be absent, not "here" at all. The pathos of overhearing, I suggested in the Introduction, involves a simultaneous impulse toward and a refusal of identification. Ashbery recovers identification as a lyric model even as he insists, in ways that recall the ways that Plath's excluded readers resemble her poems' lonely speakers, that this identification derives from erasure and absence.

"This Room" thus enacts, for all its hiddenness, a vision of lyric that is in many ways simpler and also more optimistic than that put forth by the other poets I have examined. Lyric is a space in which desire and doubt can coexist without canceling each other out; amid the deanimation, animation is also possible, not in contradiction to effacement but as an outgrowth of it. But I have ended with "This Room" not because I mean to cast it as anomolous or even extreme. Rather, the poem reveals an answer to the more general paradox of lyric subjectivity that I have been examining, and more exactly to the problem of inventing a speaker to inhabit the poem and keep it moving. The space offered by "This Room" to its readers is, in the end, multiple in yet another way. More explicitly than any other poem I have examined, "This Room" offers us as readers a range of ways into the poem. We are, as the ambiguity of the pronoun "you" suggests, figures who might be confused with the "you" of apostrophe. But we also resemble the speaker himself.

In this way, "This Room" does not limit the possibilities of lyric identification but rather creates a space in which identifications can flourish. In so carefully defining both room and dreamed room and in insisting on the particular and intangible space of the dreamed room, Ashbery is reminding us that such identifications can only persist within an uninhabitable space, one that seems to affirm what really happened while imagining what isn't even there. Lyric, Ashbery suggests, impels the self to be disassembled or effaced so that the lyric, the illusion or dream of selfhood, can persist. This is part of the surprise of lyric, even postmodern lyric: it represents as whole what it seems already to have unmade.

The multiple identifications of "This Room" affirm, then, that identification need not be complete, positive, or consistent. It is not that we must identify only or wholly with the poem's "you" or with its "I," but that we identify partly, fleetingly with both. I alluded above to Helen Vendler's claim that lyric proposes "a twinship between writer and reader" (*Poems* xliii) and that our identification as readers of lyric is always with the speaker,[5] a claim that modifies Vendler's earlier implication that lyric equates addressee with reader ("Quarter" 4). Ashbery's ambiguous "you" embodies in this way the paradox of all lyric address. It enables us to identify with the lyric speaker; in Vendler's terms, when we read the poem aloud, its "I" becomes our own (*Poems* xliii). Yet we also identify with the addressee, the reader who seems to be us. The pathos of overhearing, Ashbery suggests, thus inheres not so much in a refusal as in an excess of identification. Lyric compels us to shift identifications: our connection, in the end, is not only with the absent, mute addressee but also, perhaps more strongly, with the poet's recognition of his essential loneliness, which resembles our own. To recall the terms of Glück's discussion of Plath, postmodern poems of address both invite and exclude us; they set us simultaneously into the position of participant and judge, object and subject. We can do nothing but equivocate, turn away, and in the process perhaps, like JM, find some "balance." We believe, we don't; we are spoken to and abandoned. By enabling us to take on all these roles at once, poems that use address come to seem profoundly uncertain. This, then, is the kind of identification that postmodern poems invite: seeing ourselves as peripheral, we come to feel nearly effaced. Yet the awareness of our own insignificance renders the poems, or our reading of them, poignant, even elegiac. What we identify with is the lyric speaker's effort, always frustrated, to assert equivalence, connection, identification. And so we read on, attempting to suspend disbelief at least within the space of our reading, helped by the poems themselves, which keep inscribing the difficulty of defining what it is, in the end, that language forfeits or reclaims.

Notes

NOTES TO THE INTRODUCTION

1. The conflict I am outlining between Romantic apostrophe and postwar recollections of that apostrophe is partly one between antinarrative and narrative notions of apostrophe. In this context, it is worth mentioning Neil Roberts's suggestion that V. N. Voloshinov's concept of "addressivity" provides a useful alternative to Culler's concept of apostrophe in at least one important way: "addressivity inaugurates narrative by establishing a relation to the addressee" (3).
2. According to Culler's "Deconstruction and the Lyric," apostrophe includes both "address to apparently inanimate objects" and "address to the beloved" (44). Yet, as William Waters points out, lyric address may include, in addition to "prototypical apostrophe," "prototypical reader address[, . . .] address to a contemporary," "address to God[, . . .] and to the poet's self" ("Answerable" 130). Poems addressing a muse may also constitute a distinct category.
3. Several critics of contemporary American poetry mention the figure in passing. Perhaps most explicit is Charles Molesworth, who notes that many postwar poets rely on an "interlocutor" (8). Both James McCorkle and Nathan Scott emphasize the centrality of what McCorkle calls "interconnection" in contemporary poetry, which involves, in Scott's terms, "approach[ing] a given reality out of a sense of its having the character of a *Thou*" (2). William Waters emphasizes the centrality of address not only to lyric but to discourse, although his focus is not on postmodern or American poetry (*Poetry's*). Vernon Shetley, Timothy Bahti, and others are more generally concerned with audience in postwar American poetry. Among critics who discuss apostrophe in relation to specific poems are Lesley Wheeler, who reads Gwendolyn Brooks's apostrophe as a political strategy, and Barbara Johnson, whose essay on poems apostrophizing aborted children includes several American poems written since the 1950s, which I discuss below.

4. Perloff argues that postmodern poems blur "theory" and "poetry" in a way consistent with poststructuralist theory: "the texts [. . . are] always already [. . .] 'both/and' " ("Postmodernism" 201). For a detailed summary of critical definitions of the term "postmodern" in relation to American poetry, see Blasing 3.

5. Gray contrasts the confessional to the postmodern: "At the other pole [from language poetry] is a flat disavowal of theory, in the form of a persistent confessionalism which regards the poem as a verbal device meant to reproduce the poet's emotion in the reader" (714). The term "postconfessional" is sometimes used to define poetry in the confessional tradition written after the mid-1960s. Stan Rubin claims that for postconfessional, as opposed to confessional, poets, "the 'I' is cast into suspicion." While "highly personal experience" often impels these poems, their "general thrust is nearly always [. . .] toward something sensed to be larger" (17).

6. Several recent studies of postmodern American poetry defend subjectivity in contemporary poetry, often in explicit reaction to Charles Altieri's 1984 condemnation of the "scenic style" in recent poetry, in which a seemingly sincere speaker suggests the relevance and utility of the personal, often by depicting a scenario of loss (10). Thus, Alan Williamson argues for the importance of a tradition of "introspection" in contemporary American poetry, while James McCorkle argues that this poetry emphasizes a self that is "always provisional, splintered, impoverished, but also copious" (4). For Helen Vendler, lyric by definition emphasizes the self or more exactly "what Matthew Arnold called 'the dialogue of the mind with itself'" (*Poems* 93). Perloff is among the few critics directly to challenge the notion that postmodern American poems are concerned with issues of subjectivity, although her emphasis on "undecidability" (*Poetics* 44) reflects the concerns of numerous other critics.

7. As Blasing has cogently argued, critics tend to see postmodernism as either consistent with or divergent from modernism: "The consensus is that the history of American poetry since World War II represents a contest between a formalist academic consolidation of early modernism's experimental impulse and an antiformalist revolt" (1). Although Blasing challenges this division (2), most readers tend to adhere to one or the other of the two strands of thought Blasing identifies.

8. Culler's focus is on the "post-Enlightenment" lyric in general (*Pursuit* 143), with examples drawn primarily from Romantic and post-Romantic poets (including Charles Baudelaire and W. B. Yeats); Paul de Man (*Rhetoric*) focuses on Baudelaire and Wordsworth; John Hollander's account is generally ahistorical, though he does at times discuss modernist references to and revisions of earlier "poetic imperatives." W. R. Johnson is one of the few critics to consider postmodern poems of address in a historically inflected framework, although he considers what he calls "I-you poem[s]," poems,

that is, addressing an other meant to be present within the poetic frame rather than (as in apostrophe) one known to be absent. This seemingly minor difference leads Johnson to a radically different conclusion from my own. Recent poems, he claims, reveal a decline in address to an other meant to be present within the lyric space itself; they affirm "the isolation of the lyric I and the virtual disappearance of the lyric You" (8).

9. My definition of lyric is supported by Cameron's claim that "the lyric voice is solitary" (*Lyric* 23); my notion that lyric both resists and is drawn toward narrative is suggested in slightly different terms by Culler, who notes that narrative is both antithetical to and at one extreme of lyric (*Pursuit* 149). Bahti's assertion, by way of Plato, that lyric involves "the poet speaking in his own voice" (9) supports my distinction of lyric from dramatic monologue against the New Critical tendency to read the former as if it were the latter.

Among the readers who have claimed that lyric address and apostrophe articulate a version of dialogue is Michael Macovski, who in a study of Romantic lyric claims "literary discourse," including lyric, to be "a composite of voices, interactive personae" (3) extending from the poem itself outward to engage "with other discourses [. . .]—political, religious, and historical" (4). Paul Friedrich similarly argues that "all lyric poetry is dialogical because the poet, no matter how solipsistic he intends or claims to be, is actually engaging or attempting to engage someone else, an interlocutor." Apostrophe is for Friedrich a version of dialogue "that is implicit, subliminal, or even unconscious" (79). Zofia Burr's recent study of contemporary American women's poetry, like Macovski's, draws on Bakhtin's notion of the dialogic and emphasizes the "cultural work of poetic address," and "how poetry functions as communicative utterance and not only as self-expression" (4). Yet Burr also acknowledges the limitations of a strictly dialogical model. Contemporary lyric, she claims, emphasizes "the asymmetries of address rather than the mutualities of dialogue" (10), mutualities which are themselves "idealized fictions" (11). Nonetheless, Burr like Macovski emphasizes the capacity of poetry to communicate directly with the reader: the poets she examines, she claims, "us[e] poetry to engage audiences in the task of changing the world" (16). In contrast, Waters defines poetry as "not so much a stable communicative situation as a chronic hesitation, a faltering, between monologue and dialogue, between 'talking about' and 'talking to,' third and second person, indifference to interlocutors and the yearning to have one" (*Poetry's* 8).

10. Loeffelholz notes that Dickinson's poems often include the speaker, a beloved, and "the third—the father, God" (60), a scenario, that is, in which a dyad is interrupted by a prohibiting third figure. This situation, she claims, reiterates the psychoanalytic model of development, in which the child's intimate, exclusive relation with the mother is interrupted by the father.

While I do not intend to lay out in great detail the analogies between apostrophe and Lacanian theory, the Lacanian emphasis on the dependence of "you" on "I" evokes my claim that apostrophe reveals the extent to which the lyric self is defined by its invocation of others. For Lacan the terms "I" and "you" are unstable, partly because they shift according to who speaks them in what context (298–99). Similarly, apostrophe reveals that "I" and "you" are ultimately constructs not merely of language but of lyric itself. The "you," like the misperceived mother in Lacan's mirror stage, ultimately reveals the absence of an actual other occupying that position. Lyric subjectivity involves the articulation of a wholeness that resembles what Lacan calls the "necessary fiction of wholeness" (71) informing the child's sense of self: the lyric subject does not exist independent of its articulation.

11. Culler calls apostrophe "a fiction which knows its own fictive nature" (*Pursuit* 146); Barbara Johnson asserts that lyric "manipulates the I/thou structure of direct address in an indirect, *fictionalized* way" (185, emphasis added).
12. The first of these claims might have been implied by a literal-minded reader of Barbara Johnson's observations about the kinship between apostrophe and Lacanian notions of speech. Susan and Leslie Brisman ingeniously but somewhat implausibly devise and rank three kinds of lyric address corresponding to Lacan's three phases of development (40). According to Peter Sacks, elegy evokes the loss implicit in the oedipal narrative, in which the illusion of oneness with the mother is replaced by the acceptance of castration (*English* 8).
13. I am partly challenging Culler's assertion that apostrophe is always a way of referring to the status of lyric itself: "invocation is a figure of vocation" (*Pursuit* 142) and apostrophe "is the pure embodiment of poetic pretension" (143).
14. More exactly, Tucker defines the intersubjective in terms of a concern with the possibility of a coherent, "fictive" speaker within the poem and thus with a "confirmation of the self" (242), notions Tucker links to New Critical methods of reading. The intertextual, which he links to deconstructive reading, emphasizes the idea "that textuality is all and that the play of the signifier usurps the recreative illusion of character" (243).
15. W. R. Johnson has argued that "the person addressed [in lyric . . .] is a metaphor for readers of the poem and becomes a symbolic mediator, a conductor between the poet and each of his readers and listeners" (3), but he also claims of ancient Greek lyric that "the listener can identify either with the *ego* ('I') or with the *tu* ('you') of the song, or he can identify with both almost simultaneously" (72). Vendler emphasizes the lyric reader's identification with the speaker rather than the reader's with the addressee: "a lyric is meant to be spoken by its reader as if the reader were the one uttering the words. A

lyric poem is a script for performance by its reader [. . . .] It construct[s] a twinship between writer and reader" (*Poems* xlii–xliii).

16. Although Frye does not acknowledge it, apostrophe in classical rhetoric is an "*aversio*" or turning away from the actual, present audience to some other, absent entity: in oratory, L. M. Findlay points out, "what is heard apostrophically [. . .] is also overheard by the remainder of the exordium's original audience [. . .] The *turning away from* the judge is not a rejection of him but a specially deferential act of rhetorical inclusion" (338, emphasis Findlay's).

17. The OED defines "pathos" as the quality in a work of art "which excites a feeling of pity or sadness." While "pathetic" is the adjectival form of "pathos," it also contains a nearly opposed meaning: "miserably inadequate; so poor as to be ridiculous." David Gervais's taxonomy of pathos helps link these notions: sometimes pathos or pity arises because of our distance from what we observe; at others, "pathos invites callousness" (21).

18. Lowell's *Life Studies* was published in 1959; Frye's *Anatomy of Criticism* in 1957.

19. My reading is quite different from that of Lawrence Kramer, one of very few readers to comment at length on Lowell's apostrophe, who claims that "During Fever" and other poems from the same volume, *Life Studies,* blur oedipal with apostrophic desires: the speaker's desire sexually to possess the mother while she was alive mirrors his desire to reanimate her now that she is dead.

20. Kramer faults Lowell's apostrophe for obfuscating what he claims ought to be simple reader address, arguing that the apostrophe in the poems of *Life Studies* is instead "chimerical, regressive [and] distracting" (83).

21. Deborah Nelson sees in this juxtaposition a representation of "a generational decline in patriarchal power": the mother's father "invade[s . . .] other people's privacy" while the speaker's father is "the subject of inspection and exposure" (60–1). Nelson associates the poem's preoccupation with "voyeurism" and "the gaze" with tensions between the public and private during the time Lowell was writing (52).

22. Waters claims for this reason that "a lyric addressing the absent and unhearing is [. . .] just the converse of a letter[. . . .] If contact is made [in a lyric], then this occurs not at some later time of receipt (there is none) but exactly in the moment of composition" (*Poetry's* 48).

23. In suggesting an analogy between reading and hearing, I am perpetuating an old metaphor for lyric used by Mill, Frye, Tucker, and many other theorists of lyric, whose claim that the audience hears rather than silently reads the lyric poem recalls the historical fact that lyric poetry was once sung in public. Yet as Bahti argues, the lyric "has become a genre whose 'public' or 'audience' is readers"; by privileging "silent reading," lyric emphasizes the "individual and private" (6). The disparity between what is heard and silent

in Brock-Broido's poem may evoke the ongoing tension within lyric between the requirement that it be music and text.

24. The fact that two are women and two are gay men may partly explain this sensitivity to the position of the other, although because of the numerous theoretical problems raised by such an explanation, I have chosen not to elaborate on it.

NOTES TO CHAPTER ONE

1. That Glück's poems are influenced by Plath's seems inarguable, though no critic has fully explored the connection. Glück's assertion that poems like Plath's force their readers into "the repetitions of mimicry, which are mechanical and stationary, which lead nowhere, that is, which lead solely to the poem they echo" ("Invitation" 123) implies that she as poet has expended energy trying to imitate such poems.

    Several authors, including Jacqueline Rose (*Haunting* 12), Jon Rosenblatt (148), and Christina Britzolakis (106–7), mention in passing the importance of address or the silent other in Plath's poems. Silvianne Blosser (103–21) uses the term apostrophe, but she does not elaborate on its significance. The most sustained study of Plath's apostrophe is the chapter devoted to Plath in Neil Roberts's study of mostly British postwar poets. Drawing on both Jonathan Culler's apostrophe essay and on Bakhtin's notion of "addressivity," Roberts emphasizes the "'voiced,' even [. . .] *performed*" (23) aspect of Plath's late poems. As I discuss below, Jahan Ramazani also discusses the apostrophe of "Daddy" in relation to the elegiac tradition.

2. Apostrophe is central both to the 1966 edition of *Ariel*, edited by Ted Hughes, and to Plath's own ordering of the volume, published as *Ariel: The Restored Edition* in 2004. More than half the poems in both editions include a "you," a figure at times unidentified, but also ranging from father to romantic partner to, less often, mother, child, literary character, or personified object. Of the twelve poems Hughes deleted from Plath's version, seven contain apostrophe; of the thirteen he added, seven are apostrophic.

3. I am in this catalog including the four central groups of readers of Plath, although they cannot always be so absolutely distinguished. Readers who emphasize Plath's poems as biographical articulations include David Holbrook, Edward Butscher, and, to some extent, Stephen Axelrod and Diane Middlebrook (*Her Husband*); the reader who has most fully argued for the mythological element of Plath's poems is Judith Kroll, although Hughes and Rosenblatt have made related claims; among feminist readers who have emphasized the importance of Plath's struggles with the notions of femininity, authorship, and wifehood are Suzanne Juhasz, Sandra Gilbert ("Fine"), and Lynda Bundtzen, as well as, more recently, Susan van Dyne and Joanne

Feit Diehl (*Women*). Readers emphasizing the cultural and political framework of Plath's poems include Margaret Dickie Uroff, Robin Peel, and Tracy Brain. In Mary Lynn Broe's useful if somewhat dated summary,

> Critics have split between the speculative and the biographical; the craft followers and the cult devotees; the mythmakers and the demythologists; those Gradgrindians who praise the cast-iron discipline of her prosody and the necrophiliacs who probe the poems for sufficient pain and suffering to require a deadly consummation; the crowd that hears her literary ventriloquism and the one that watches her stage-direct her own Gothic romance. (ix)

The most sustained critique of previous readings of Plath and in particular of their emphasis on the biographical remains Rose's 1991 *The Haunting of Sylvia Plath*. Rose has subsequently affirmed in relation to the reception of that book the difficulty of escaping biographical readings of Plath (*Not* 49–63).

4. The poem also emphasizes the identity between the crowd and Lady Lazarus, as a pun on the word "charge" makes clear: the audience must pay a fee, but also receives a thrill from observing this spectacle, a thrill also, the impersonal construction suggests, felt by the speaker herself.

5. In the strip-tease scene, the third-person, indicative description of the crowd ("The peanut-crunching crowd/ Shoves in to see") shifts to address ("Gentlemen, ladies,/ These are my hands,/ My knees"). The poem's addressee also changes. Lady Lazarus begins by apostrophizing a singular addressee: "Peel off the napkin/ O my enemy." Then she abandons this addressee for the gentlemen and ladies, returning in the last stanzas to the address of a singular other, a version or perhaps multiplication of the poem's original addressee, now called Herr Doktor, Herr Enemy, Herr God, and Herr Lucifer.

6. Despite his insistence in several essays that Plath's poems represented "mythic" ("Sylvia" 474) or "ritual[ized]" (480) versions of her biography, Hughes repeatedly refers to Plath's father as "Daddy" in *Birthday Letters,* his apostrophic volume of poems about his relationship to Plath, implying that the character in the poem is equivalent to Plath's biographical father. This notion contradicts Plath's assertion in an introduction to a BBC reading of "Daddy" that the speaker's father was "a Nazi and her mother very possibly part Jewish" (*Collected* 293), a lineage distinct from Plath's. Britzolakis claims that "only a very determined misreading [of "Daddy"] could identify the speaker with the biographical Sylvia Plath" (123).

Rose and van Dyne have noted the tendency of readers who emphasize both the biographical and the mythological sources of Plath's poems to affirm "poetry as the expression of a transcendent selfhood" (Rose, *Haunting* 8). They and other critics have argued, in contrast, that Plath's poems undermine consistent, stable, and isolated selfhood. For Rose, Plath's poems, including "Daddy," emphasize "a fundamental reversability of agency that confounds active and passive and then dramatises, through that confounding, the question of who is agent, who is victim, who (or what) suffers and who (or what) kills" (*Haunting* 132); for van Dyne, they reveal a "highly theatricalized performance of the feminine victim" (5).

7. Axelrod views Daddy as a part of the speaker (223). In contrast, Diehl asserts that the other in Plath's poems is always an actual "oppressor," albeit one on whom the speaker feels "total dependence" (*Women* 133). Pamela Annas sees Daddy as a "figure who represents the patriarchal society [Plath] lives in" (143).

8. The line suggests at least three distinct, even opposed readings: that the speaker has finally gotten through to where Daddy is (a sense emphasized by the earlier line "The voices just can't worm through"); that she is through with or has vanquished Daddy; and that she herself is through or finished. These different readings are all anticipated by the ambiguous earlier line "So Daddy, I'm finally through."

9. Annas, for example, affirms that "Daddy" ends with a "frenzied communal ritual of exorcism" (141), albeit one that is "violent and, perhaps, provisional" (143), while for Broe, it is "a mock poetic exorcism of an event that has already happened" (172).

10. Ramazani's notion of melancholia is somewhat different from Freud's in "Mourning and Melancholia" (1917). Here Freud claims that while melancholia and mourning share many features, including "a profoundly painful dejection, cessation of interest in the outside world, [and] loss of the capacity to love" (244), melancholia involves "a disturbance of self-regard" not found in mourning (245). For Ramazani, melancholia involves "a fierce resistance to solace" as well as "intense criticism and self-criticism" (*Poetry* 4). R. Clifton Spargo also connects elegy with address: "The elegist tries to compensate for her loss through a wishful fiction of intimacy, which would retain and contain the lost other." Because, for Spargo, Plath "contests [this] rhetoric of intimacy," her poems are for him "anti-elegy" (143).

11. For Anthony Easthope, this repetition affirms the stability of Plath's conception of selfhood and the continuity of her poems with Romantic precursors; Gilbert, though, reads the repetition of "I" as a marker of the speaker's struggle to locate and define a self ("My Name").

12. Ramazani similarly notes that while Plath's earlier poems allowed the father to occupy the position of subject, she here "grammatically demot[es] the father from sovereign agent to passive target" ("Daddy" 1153).

13. For an elaboration of the significant differences between these tropological modes, see Rose, *Haunting* 228.

14. Earlier critics have most often discussed the influence on Plath's poems of contemporaries including Theodore Roethke, Robert Lowell, Hughes, and Anne Sexton; of earlier female authors including Dickinson, the Brontës,

and Christina Rossetti; and, less often, of modernist poets including T. S. Eliot and W. B. Yeats. Diehl has most fully elaborated Plath's kinship with the British and American traditions of the sublime. She claims that Plath's poems both evoke and revise a Wordsworthian prototype (*Women* 121); faced with a post-Romantic nature that is "self-sufficien[t and . . .] retreating from the self, Plath focuses upon her own body as a source of nature's rejection" (126).

15. All previous definitions of confessional poetry share an emphasis on self-revelation and a lack of concern with the position of the lyric confession in relation to the auditor or the addressee, despite the prevalence of apostrophe in the poems of Lowell, Anne Sexton, W. R. Snodgrass, Plath, and their peers. M. L. Rosenthal asserted in 1967 that Plath's poems are "genuinely confessional" in that "they put the speaker himself [*sic*] at the center of the poem in such a way as to make his psychological vulnerability and shame an embodiment of his civilization" (79); Middlebrook's more recent discussion of confessional poetry contains an essentially similar definition, although Middlebrook emphasizes the poet's simultaneous "nonconformism to American ideals" and "faith [. . .] in Freudian, secular, and critical" values consistent with contemporary American culture ("What" 648). The continuing power over Plath studies of these ideas can be measured in the frequency with which recent critics continue to allude to them. For a detailed critique of the suppositions underlying the notion of confessional poetry, see Travisano 32–66.

16. DeSales Harrison reads this phrase as even more radically distinct from address: " 'God's lioness' appears at first to be Plath's term for the horse, [. . .] but rider and horse are never separate enough to establish a stable polarity of master and servant, rider and ridden. 'God's lioness' refers more properly to the compound beast they form together, woman and horse combined in one kinetic element" (147).

17. Perloff has subsequently "retract[ed]" this notion about Plath's poems as inaccurate in the light of subsequent published volumes of Plath's poems, most of them composed before those in *Ariel* ("Sylvia" 177, n. 24). But similar observations about the abundance of animation or personification in Plath's poems have been made by several more recent critics, including Britzolakis (104–110) and Bedient ("Oh Plath!" 279) as well as, in different contexts, Susan Gubar, who emphasizes the ways that Plath's poems speak in the voices of the dead, and Amy Hungerford, who claims that recent readers of Plath's poems have imbued them with the characteristics and agency of people (24–45).

18. Although personification and prosopopeia are generally not seen as identical, they are closely linked. Prosopopeia generally involves the imbuing of something inanimate with the characteristics of the living and thus is similar (but not always identical) to personification; Alex Preminger claims that prosopopeia is "the speech of an imaginary person" (994). Gubar defines it

broadly as "the impersonation of an absent speaker or a personification" (191) but her focus in Plath's poems is on the "reanimation of the dead" or an adoption of "the posthumous voice" (192). For de Man, prosopopeia is "the trope of apostrophe" (*Rhetoric* 44) or more exactly "the fiction of an apostrophe to an absent, deceased, or voiceless entity" (*Rhetoric* 75). Others, though, including Waters (who calls de Man's definition a "muddl[ing]" of terms ["Poetic," 199n.]), J. Douglas Kneale (who claims that apostrophe, unlike prosopopeia, involves a "turning from an original [implicit or explicit] addressee to a different addressee, from the proper or intended hearer to another" [147]), and Diana Fuss (who distinguishes "corpse poems" which employ prosopopeia and "giv[e] voice to the voiceless cadaver" [1], from "the elegy's poetics of apostrophe," which "in maintaining a clear distance between the living and the dead [. . .] obscure[s] the dead" [22]) distinguish apostrophe from prosopopeia.

19. Britzolakis, however, does distinguish "two successive movements or phases" in the poem, one "earthbound and horizontal" and the other "phallic, solar, and vertical" (184–5). Harrison locates two kinds of movement. "The first is a linear vector, pure trajectory and pure transformation [. . .]—an arrow into dew into the sun. The other movement is a countervailing pull, back toward the dark center of the poem, toward the dark center of the body" (148).

20. The explicitly erotic quality of the speaker's union with Ariel—which involves being "haul[ed] through air," "unpeel[ing]," and "Foam[ing] to wheat, a glitter of seas"—leads not to a defiance of death but to the dew's suicidal flight; oneness with Ariel leads to oneness with suicide.

21. Unlike many of the poems in *Ariel* but like earlier poems such as "Blackberrying" (*Collected* 168–9) the speaker of "Ariel" passes through a carefully delineated landscape: she first passes the tor, then the furrow, then the blackberries, then a field of wheat and view of the sea. Like much Romantic lyric, this experience prompts her to consider her relation to a natural world that remains in the most absolute sense distinct from her. If anything, the poem coheres more fully than "Ode to a Nightingale," whose narrative is unclear, as is evident from the perhaps apocryphal account of its composition a stanza at a time on scraps of paper that were scrambled and then reassembled.

22. Axelrod, for example, emphasizes the poem's imagery of destruction: "in Plath's drama, the inner being has been denied for so long that when it rises out of the ash it has virtually no being to be [. . . .] It becomes a figure of revenge or, conversely, of self-annihilation" (233). For Janice Markey, in contrast, the end of "Ariel" is "suicidal only in the sense that there is an escape [. . .] into the feeling of being at one with the world" (30).

23. My reading evokes Perloff's assertion that at the end of "Ariel" "the 'I' and the 'eye' merge." Perloff associates this merging with "joy" ("Angst" 117) for Plath's speaker. My claim, though, is that it reveals the speaker's solitude.

24. The lack of critical attention "Cut" has received may be due to the opacity of several of the poem's images, to the almost nauseating vividness of its description, or to its relative simplicity of execution. Or it may derive from its tone: the poem treats its injury with a lightness and hilarity absent from many of Plath's later explorations of self-inflicted violence.
25. Perloff answers this question by linking Plath's practice to one strand of the lyric tradition, although she does not explain why Plath might be drawn to this tradition.
26. The preoccupation of de Man and those influenced by him with statues, mirrors, and windows reveals an impulse to read descriptive textual details metaphorically, even prosopopeiacally, as comments on the status of the text. One of the more dramatic critiques of de Man's reading method is suggested by Neil Hertz's observation that de Man's writing is itself filled with imagery of dismemberment and murder, imagery he links to the death of de Man's mother. Other critics, including Lehman (*Signs*), have connected this feature of de Man's writing to his Nazi sympathies.
27. The poem's dedication complicates its notion of address. The poem is "for" an actual other, but the relation of the dedicatee to the poet is never made clear. Perhaps Susan O'Neill Roe—she was a friend of Plath's—was the poem's actual protagonist, or she has some knowledge of the real-life events that the poem recounts, or she suggested the topic to Plath or helped with revisions.
28. Several recent critics have focused on the question of the extent to which Plath represents femininity as essential or socially constructed. Another influential strand of feminist criticism associates Plath's writing with the subversive possibilities enabled by traditionally female roles, especially that of the hysteric. Plath's writings, according to Elisabeth Bronfen, demonstrate "the hysteric's concern with keeping the question of identity undecided, oscillating between various self-fashionings, celebrating each, but as constructions" (*Sylvia* 53).

NOTES TO CHAPTER TWO

1. Plath was born in 1932; Merrill in 1926. Plath was in psychoanalysis several times (in 1953 and 1958–9 [Stevenson 47–8, 144–5]); Merrill's analysis in Rome is chronicled in his prose memoir *A Different Person (Collected* 457–683). One of the only critics to discuss the resemblances between these poets is Helen Sword, who focuses on their poems about ouija boards in the context of a more general discussion of spiritualism in modern and contemporary American poetry.
2. According to one definition, narrative poetry involves "a verbal presentation of a sequence of events or facts [. . .] whose disposition in time implies causal connection and point" (Preminger 814). My notion of narrative poetry here

emphasizes, as do many definitions, its concern with representations of temporality, although I am also aware of the problems of defining it as a coherent "genre."

3. Brian McHale, for example, calls the ouija board "the great embarrassment of *The Changing Light*" because it directly raises the questions "how seriously are we expected to take this? How *can* we take it seriously?" McHale locates the source of the embarrassment in its status as "a 'dictated' poem" which challenges our sense of "authority" and authorial autonomy (40). Merrill himself has commented that that "the mechanics of the board" do "embarrass the sort of reader who can't bear to face the random or trivial elements that coalesce, among others, to produce an 'elevated' thought" (*Collected* 110).

4. Harold Bloom admits his uncertainty about the poem's premise: "It would comfort me to say that the central trope of *The Changing Light at Sandover* is the Ouija board, and that Merrill's spooks [. . .] have come to bring him metaphors for poetry. Unhappily this is not so" ("Introduction" 6). But Vendler is content to put forth an essentially metaphoric reading, arguing that "the 'machinery'—[. . .] the ghosts of dead friends and other revenants" must be "accepted as a mode of imagination" ("Divine" 137). This response evokes Culler's readers of apostrophe; Merrill's readers similarly tend to avoid the issue of verisimilitude, converting the poem into a more normative and thus praiseworthy allegory in which Merrill's otherworldly conversations are viewed not as real but rather as elaborately encoded meditations on the nature of language, mortality, poetic creation, or faith. Although Merrill has expressed his sympathy for readers to whom the message of the trilogy's last two poems do not appeal (*Collected* 86), neither Merrill's interviews and essays nor Jackson's comments have dispelled the illusion that the ouija board sessions actually occurred, although Jackson has emphasized the extensive changes made by Merrill to the original transcribed conversations (298–305).

5. Ramazani notes that elegiac apostrophe "convert[s] the [. . .] relation to the dead from 'I-It' to 'I-Thou.'" (*Poetry* 281). For Culler, elegiac apostrophe defies narrative and "substitute[s] a temporality of discourse for a referential temporality" and thus a model in which "poetic power" rather than "time" predominates (*Pursuit* 150).

6. Claiming that "the long poems of this century grow out of lyric modes" (127), Kalstone examines the recasting of a number of early lyrics in sections of *The Changing Light at Sandover*, arguing that Merrill's revisions of his early lyrics "naturalize" what were once "exotic and secretive image[s]" even as their new placement associates these images with "decomposition and the impersonal processes of change" (137).

7. Sacks (in "Divine") is most direct in characterizing *The Changing Light at Sandover* as an elegy. JM and DJ, he notes, tend to bring out the ouija board

after a death, and Ephraim allows them to locate dead friends and relatives and hear them speak. While Sacks's emphasis is on the later books of the trilogy, where this tendency is more marked, it applies as well to "The Book of Ephraim": JM's father's death occurs midway through (in section K), and the poem emphasizes the future permanent separation through death of JM and DJ (section G), which even the poem's promise of reincarnation cannot unmake.

8. Sacks notes that Merrill's trilogy, unlike many other modern long poems, is "triumphantly consoling" ("Divine" 159), but for other readers, this emphasis on consolation distinguishes the poem from elegy. According to Bloom, Merrill "is *not* an elegiac poet" because "for Merrill, trauma and grief do become precisely poetic gains" ("Introduction" 5).

9. Merrill, as well as virtually all readers of the sequence, have found "The Book of Ephraim" and the final section, "The Ballroom at Sandover," in the "Coda" more "lyric" than the trilogy's two later books, partly because JM's voice here predominates, partly because these sections are more "shaped" and crafted: "The Book of Ephraim" took Merrill "twenty/ Years in a cool dark place [. . .]/ [. . .] to be palatable wine," as JM claims, while the trilogy's second volume, "Mirabell's Book of Numbers," is "by contrast, immature, supine, / Still kick[ing] against its archetypal cradle" (261).

10. Earlier psychoanalytically informed readings of *Sandover* have focused on Jungian archetypes (Timothy Materer), paranoia (D. L. MacDonald), and Kristeva's notions of love (Eric Selinger). Richard Saez emphasizes the oedipal themes of Merrill's early lyrics ("Oedipal") but emphasizes different issues in a discussion of *The Changing Light at Sandover* ("Salon"). Sacks argues that Freud's notion of mourning is consistent with his notion of the Oedipus complex (*English* 7–8). Just as the child must renounce his desire for his mother when he enters the oedipal phase, elegy according to Sacks reenacts the child's acceptance of his own castration (*English* 14–6): the elegist must renounce his connection with the dead beloved.

11. Typical is Bruce Bawer's description of Ephraim as a "defense mechanism"; Tom's reading, he claims, "hits the nail right on the head" (41); Willard Spiegelman unironically adapts JM's own vocabulary in acknowledging Tom's analysis to be "insightful" (*Didactic* 19); Alison Lurie echoes Tom in calling Merrill and Jackson's preoccupation with the ouija board evidence of their "*folie à deux*" (108). Other critics, though, are more skeptical, including Yenser, who calls Tom's reading "at best a fractional truth" (*Consuming* 233) and Vendler, who associates this scene with Merrill's "self-protective irony" ("Divine" 137).

12. The section begins with JM's confirmation of his need to delve into material with which he feels uncomfortable: "I'd rather skip this part, but courage—/ What we dream up must be lived down, I think."

13. My reading of the anti-narrative component of the game seems nearly opposite to Peter Brooks's claim, derived from a reading of *Beyond the Pleasure Principle*, that "narrative always makes the implicit claim to be in a state of repetition" partly to forestall death (97). However, Brooks also acknowledges that repetition is antithetical to narrative's purely chronological, forward-driving tendencies (91). Culler sets forth a similar opposition between the eternal present of apostrophe and conventional notions of history or chronology (*Pursuit* 149).
14. Sacks argues that the fort/da game derives it own consolation for its (temporary) loss from (primitive) language: the child "learns to *represent* absence, and to make the absent present, by means of a substitutive figure accompanied by an elementary language" (*English* 11). In this way, the game represents a primitive form of elegy, which finds consolation in the poem itself.
15. For Jacques Lacan, the game is associated with the losses implicit in the entry into language; it is, in Elisabeth Bronfen's summary, "a trope for the fading [. . .] of the subject before and within the process of signification" (*Over* 26).
16. My reading challenges the common critical distinction between metaphors and puns, one that has been applied to Merrill by Mutlu Blasing. Blasing reads Merrill's puns as an assertion of a nonhierarchical simultaneity reminiscent of the child's "pre-Oedipal language before the intervention of the third party, the father" (174). Although Blasing acknowledges that puns themselves are often hierarchical (174), her argument relies on an opposition between the simultaneity of puns and what she characterizes as an oedipal triangularity enacted by metaphor (173). In contrast, Walter Redfern emphasizes the general similarities between metaphors and puns: like pun, "metaphor incites us to think, see and hear on more than one level concurrently, or at least with only a slight time-lag, the time needed to seek the connection." Puns like metaphors locate "deeper affinities" in apparently distinct things or concepts (97).
17. Merrill suggests oedipal notions themselves to be historically and culturally relative: its legend of mother-son desire is "quaint" because its pre-Freudian characters are not aware of the forbiddenness of mother-son kisses. JM's later suggestion that his mother is not only the rescued maiden but "my dragon" reveals more directly his need to complicate or even invert the oedipal narrative in relation to himself.
18. For example, puns also connect the next verse paragraphs. The much-maligned dam in his lost novel, JM explains at the end of the second verse paragraph, has a positive influence as well, announced in a corny pun: "On the *bright* side, it means a *power* station,/ *Light* all through the valley." The next verse paragraph's opening converts these terms into a way of talking about the self, emphasizing JM's own "power" to speak and "the naked current" of language itself. Here, in contrast to the previous example, it is the

visible (the power station) that enables the psychological (the speaker's own internal power). JM's attempt to recover what is lost—both by retelling his lost novel and by discerning in its losses a "bright side"—allows him, by speaking of feelings that evade his poetic "power," to "grasp" them.

19. "The Book of Ephraim" is cowritten with Jackson, who is present at all the ouija board sessions; DJ is, in the ouija board's terms, the "HAND" to JM's "SCRIBE." The inclusion of increasingly long passages of ouija board text also confuses the sense that JM is the poem's author; while he resents the "insinuation" that the poem is "ghostwritten" (72), he himself complains late in *Sandover* that his poem is "all by someone else!" (261).

20. Deborah Forbes also discusses Merrill's embrace of Keatsian "negative capability," especially in relation to the stance of the reader, although her emphasis is not on *Sandover* (177).

NOTES TO CHAPTER THREE

1. That prayer is related, though not identical, to apostrophe, has been argued by Waters ("Answerable" 130), among others. In a discussion of *The Wild Iris,* Linda Gregerson suggests that both lyric and prayer address a similar inaccessible or nonexistent other: "The spectral possibility that gives lyric its urgency is not that the beloved isn't listening, but that the beloved doesn't exist. Prayer takes place at the edge of a similar abyss" (141).

2. The persistence of seemingly unbridgeable splits in Glück's work has been much commented on, in somewhat varying terms, by earlier readers. Lynne McMahon notes the "uncrossable chasm between Eros and art" (333); Lynn Keller observes a conflict between "language and life, between spoken language and body language, between man and woman, [. . .] between woman and her body" (126), although she notes that these conflicts have diminished in Glück's more recent volumes. Elizabeth Dodd observes that Glück "imbeds the personal in the mythic" (189), while Lee Upton notes the "war between flesh and spirit" in her poems (119). Nick Halpern sees her poems as achieving a "hybrid speech genre" (*Everyday* 239) informed by both "everyday" and "prophetic" language.

3. Both Keller and McMahon situate their discussions of Glück in the context of questions central to feminism: McMahon begins by posing a general question about the difference between writing by men and women (333), while Keller situates her discussion of Glück's poems in a more general discussion of the "dilemma of being at once poet and woman" (120), a conflict that has long been important to feminist criticism. Both these readers attempt to discern in what Keller calls Glück's "often extremely negative sense of womanhood" (120) distinctly female, even feminist concerns. Elizabeth Dodd reads Glück's poems alongside those of other twentieth-century American women poets, setting her into a female tradition of "personal clas-

sicism." Lee Upton emphasizes Glück's preoccupation with and resistance to conventional notions about femininity (119–20).

4. Most notable is a 2004 MLA special session entitled "Lyric Utterance and the Reader: Overheard, Performed, or Addressed?" which focused on Glück's poems and included papers by E. Jane Hedley, Willard Spiegelman, and Nick Halpern considering, respectively, Glück's address of the reader, the ambiguous position of Glück's speakers, and the way the poems invite the reader to identify with the speaker. Spiegelman's "Repetition" also considers Glück's "you" and her use of dialogue (151–3). Gregerson examines the function of "I," "you," and "we" in *The Wild Iris*. Diehl's Introduction to a 2005 collection of essays on Glück's poetry considers audience, reception, and what she calls "the fiction of dialogue" (*On Louise* 13) as well as Glück's relation to the lyric tradition.

5. Several other readers have discussed narcissism in relation to Glück's poems. For Ira Sadoff, Glück's poetic speaker "appears mercilessly conscious of her narcissism while at the same time distancing herself—with gestures of irony, self-mockery, and diminishment—from a recognition of the damaging cultural imperatives that contribute to an agonizing narcissistic paralysis" (89). While this claim is similar to my own notion that Glück's critique of narcissism is complicated by her poems, Sadoff's emphasis is on Glück's reinterpretation of Romantic notions of transcendence and the sublime. His focus is on her poems in general; he discusses *The Wild Iris* only briefly (83–4).

6. The issue of self-division and self-doubling is complicated further by Glück's tendency in *The Wild Iris* to speak through a variety of voices; "American Narcissism" may represent yet another form of ventriloquism or strategy for concealing the self by multiplying its voices. This, of course, is what Glück condemns in the essay; the disembodied authoritative tone of the essay thus paradoxically draws attention to the difficulty of evading the multiplied, disguised, ultimately treacherous representation of self for which she excoriates Rilke. It is also worth noting that a reading could be proposed in which the later essay is read as a clarification, even a direct critique, of the earlier volume, whose narcissistic flaws only gradually became clear to Glück. While my reading prefers the multivoiced, self-contradictory mode of Glück's volume to the clearer, colder voice of "American Narcissism," the disjunction between these visions affirms the urgency of this issue to Glück, since she has spoken of it in different ways over time.

7. According to Otto Kernberg's detailed definition, narcissistic people reveal "an unusual degree of self-reference in their interactions with other people, a great need to be loved and admired by others, and a curious apparent contradiction between a very inflated concept of themselves and an inordinate need for tribute from others" (qtd. Berman 22). Narcissists "project [. . . their] grandiosity" onto others by idealizing them, although because the praise of these others is inadequate, the idealization often ends in repudiation (Berman

23). These conflicts are, according to Richard Boothby, essential to the Lacanian Imaginary, whose structure involves "fantasies of omnipotence and utter helplessness, mastery and victimization" (26).

8. As Jean Laplanche and J. B. Pontalis point out, Freud early on vacillated between various notions of narcissism (255) before distinguishing two kinds and phases: primary narcissism involves "a lack of differentiation between the ego and the id" (256) and derives from the normal infantile confusion of the boundaries of self with mother. In contrast, secondary narcissism occurs later in life and involves the pathological inability to see the object as other and to distinguish desires for others from the desire for self. Nearly all subsequent psychoanalytic theorists of narcissism have followed Freud's emphasis on the infantile sources of pathological adult narcissism and in particular on the origin of narcissism in the preoedipal mother-child relationship; most agree that pathological adult narcissism reiterates the normal infantile confusion of self with mother. For Lacan, this connection is particularly central: narcissism is the unavoidable outcome of the structure of the Imaginary bond between mother and child; Lacan's notion of the mirror stage itself evokes the Narcissus myth. Because the mirroring of the child by the mother is always illusory and incomplete, the ego is for Lacan "the monumental construct of narcissism" (qtd. Kochhar-Lindgren 39).

9. Jeffrey Berman's notion that Narcissus' "compulsive ritual in which he makes an object—himself—disappear and return" resembles the motion of the spool in the fort/da game (6–7) may be somewhat too literal (Narcissus' image remains constant in the water; it does not come and go), although Freud remarks that the child engaged in the fort/da game plays a similar game with his own mirror reflection (*Beyond* 9 n. 1).

10. The wild iris, in the volume's opening poem, describes itself "surviv[ing]/ as consciousness/ buried in the dark earth" and insists that " whatever/ returns from oblivion returns/ to find a voice" (1). Burial is more directly redemptive in the volume's last lines, spoken by the white lilies: "Hush, beloved. It doesn't matter to me/ how many summers I live to return:/ this one summer we have entered eternity./ I felt your two hands/ bury me to release its splendor" (63).

11. The titles of this last group of poems, which identify their speakers, vary from "Clear Morning" to "Retreating Wind" to "Love in Moonlight" to "Harvest" to "Lullaby."

12. These generalizations are based, as are most discussions of these terms, on the distinction first laid out by Roman Jakobson between discourse that, emphasizing similarity, is metaphoric and discourse that, developing through contiguity, is metonymic (129). Jakobson associates Romanticism with metaphor and Realism with metonymy and adds a generic distinction: "The principle of similarity underlies poetry. [. . .] Prose, on the contrary is forwarded essentially by contiguity. Thus for poetry metaphor—and for

prose, metonymy" (132–3). Paul de Man has noted, though, "numerous examples [. . .] of the metonymisation of apparently metaphorical structures" (*Resistance* 52, n. 18).

13. My emphasis in what follows is on the human speaker's analogies between God and the garden in which she is laboring. Yet such analogies are always implicitly triangular: the speaker is seeking through them to render God familiar, to discern his resemblance to herself (and her own to the garden through which he manifests himself). That these impulses underlie the speaker's attempt to represent God in terms of the garden is often made clear in the course of the poems.

14. The passage establishes other, aural analogies as well: the near-rhyme establishes the likeness of the fins to the daffodils, and assonance links *shin*ing sun, di*vi*ded birch, *Ice* Wings, and *wild vi*olet.

15. Noah cannot achieve the distinction he seeks: his conflation of tree with whole is synecdochal, while metaphor is central to his notion of the happy person, who ultimately resembles the depressive in attempting to define self through images borrowed from the natural world.

16. I am referring to melancholia primarily in Ramazani's sense, as discussed more fully in previous chapters.

17. Although the gender of the garden is not specified, I am using "he" rather than "it" to emphasize the garden's humanness, as well as the poem's allusion to *Genesis*'s scene of God observing Adam and Eve.

18. Tucker's notion of intertextual "overhearing" seems particularly pertinent in Glück's case: as I have been arguing, her sequence is preoccupied with the dangers deriving from her own belatedness. The intensity with which Glück's volume represents an overhearing of earlier lyric, it could be argued, derives partly from her unacknowledged reliance on Dickinson—to whom she refers in the narcissism essay—as well as Plath.

19. The argument I am making—that narcissism alleviates the otherness of the reader—differs from the claims of several studies of narcissism in fiction, most notably Linda Hutcheon's defense in *Narcissistic Narrative* of works of what she calls "metafiction" published in the 1960s and 1970s. Hutcheon claims that such texts "turn in on the reader, forcing him to face his responsibility for the text he is reading" (138). J. Brooks Bouson puts forth a similar but more generous notion of the narcissistic demands made by texts on their readers, arguing that readers always "re-enact" texts in the course of their interpretations (25).

NOTES TO CHAPTER FOUR

1. Jeffrey Gray argues that Bidart's poems "sustain what seems a figuration of pathos" while affirming "not the language of affect but [. . .] that of thought, abstraction, discussion" (718–9). Langdon Hammer refers to "the pathos of

Bidart's mad or violent speakers" who "refuse [. . .] contemporary poetic idioms" (76).
2. Bidart's volume has not been discussed by readers of AIDS elegy, although it alludes quite directly to "the plague that full swift runs by" (13) and includes a number of elegies for the artist Joe Brainard, who died of AIDS.
3. For Lacan, desire seeks what Richard Boothby calls "an original source of utter plenitude" that was "in fact never possessed" (31). The foreknowledge of death thus, in Henry Staten's terms, underlies all our desires: "mourning is the horizon of all desire" (xi).
4. Critical neglect of Bidart may derive from his small body of work and slow rate of composition. Bidart is also interested in seemingly outdated issues; he studied with Robert Lowell, whose *Collected Poems* he edited, and is often associated (somewhat inaccurately) with the confessional or postconfessional tradition. At the same time, Bidart's poems tend to be talky, abstract, and circuitous, or in Robert Pinsky's 1976 term "discursive" (134): he is thus largely uninterested in the linguistic devices associated with postmodernism. Nor do his poems—though concerned with homoerotic relations—take a particularly politicized or generalizing approach to this issue.
5. "Desire" evokes both bodily lust and spiritual or psychological yearning.
6. Bidart has explained, "Joe was someone who did not fit into the categories. We were never lovers, but it was more than a friendship. There was a sweetness of sprit in him that was very extraordinary, and I definitely was in love with him" (Rathmann 41). Dan Chiasson adds that Bidart met Brainard after Brainard's diagnosis with AIDS; in his terms, the poems about this relationship therefore possess "a strange blurriness," partly because the relationship itself, in Bidart's favored terms, had an "inward 'meaning' [that] never found fully happy instantiation in an outward 'form'" (128).
7. Like Callas, who performs before a crowd of spectators, Ellen has throughout the poem been under constant observation by her doctors. As Callas has lost, Ellen tells us "within/ four months, [. . .] at least sixty pounds" (104), Ellen, we can calculate, has lost even more. We know that Ellen now weighs ninety-two pounds (110), but once, she tells us, weighed "one hundred and sixty-five" (117).
8. Gray reads this moment similarly: "we feel we're watching autobiography as we read Bidart" (732).
9. In the essay "Pre-existing Forms: We Fill Them and When We Fill Them We Change Them and Are Changed," whose title repeats a line in several poems in *Desire,* Bidart maintains that

> what is not language finds embodiment in language by struggling to inhabit the forms—multifarious shapes, images, bits of language, patterns of language and gesture—that not only the world of art but the entire perceived world offer it. Inhabiting the forms inevitably means *changing* the forms. (118–9, Bidart's emphasis)

10. Sacks elaborates a psychoanalytically inflected analysis of imagery of breakage, thwarting, and substitution in the accounts of Daphne and Apollo and of Pan and Syrinx in Ovid's *Metamorphoses* (*English* 4–8),
11. Bidart edited Lowell's 2003 *Collected Poems,* a process that involved making choices among the many extant versions of Lowell's poems and an immersion in Lowell's revision practices, as Bidart indicates in the volume's Introduction: "rethinking work, reimagining it, rewriting it was fundamental to [Lowell] from the beginning, and pervasive until the end" (vii). Bidart was working on the Lowell edition while writing *Desire;* it is not surprising that *Desire* so directly considers form, revision, and poetic making.
12. In a discussion that refers to the repetitions of the fort/da game, Freud argues that "the compulsion to repeat [unpleasant experiences . . .] overrides the pleasure principle" (*Beyond* 16) and is connected with the opposing death drive, although repetition also defers death by unmaking chronological sequence. This opposition is central to Peter Brooks's association of these models with the paradoxes of narrative. While narrative "desire[s . . .] the end" (96), it also tends to "create retard [. . .] a postponement in the discharge which leads back to the inanimate" (103). This kind of retard is textually enacted through "repetitions that take us back in the text" (99). Brooks specifically associates "rhyme, alliteration, assonance, refrain, all the mnemonic elements of literature" (93) with the impulse to disrupt temporal sequences.
13. Hammer reads the use of the two typefaces in the poem differently, arguing that the poem contains two "voices" that belong to a single speaker (88). The roman repetition at the end of the poem of lines represented earlier in italics marks for Hammer the speaker's address to the reader: "The auditor the poem finally speaks to is—the reader. What the poet insists on, as he moves from italics to roman, is that the reader can hear him trying to speak to the dead" (89). Although the poem ultimately gives scant evidence of so dramatic a turn in address, Hammer's reading is appealing partly because it draws on Bidart's preoccupation with performance and thus with audience.
14. Bidart's poem fails to acknowledge that the end of Borges' piece, in undermining the opposition between "Borges" and "I" it has been elaborating, suggests that its opposition between a true living being and one committed to making art is inaccurate: "I am not sure which of us it is that's writing this page" (324). Bidart's essay, though, acknowledges this difference (111).
15. Chiasson usefully reads this moment in terms of the thematics of performance and drama in Bidart's earlier work, suggesting that here Bidart expresses the desire "to see someone else—an other—play him"; the poem thus reveals "the difficult necessity of playing himself" (138)
16. This passage enacts a tendency Melissa Zeiger has connected to AIDS elegies more generally: such poems, she claims, emphasize "the welcome return of the dead in dream, fantasy, and ghostly manifestation" while acknowledging

that "the desired moments of communion can only be temporary, so neither climax nor celebration can occur except under erasure" (108).

NOTES TO THE CONCLUSION

1. Shetley's transhistorical claim comes in the Introduction to his study of contemporary American poetry. Jeffrey Gray more directly associates a similar schism with the experimental or language-poetry "pole" of late twentieth-century poetry: essential to this poetry, he suggests, is the effort to "reduce[e] or at least assimilate[e] the problem of *subjectivity* to the status of *language*" so that poetry is "purge[d . . .] of origin, narrative voice, and affect" (714, emphasis added).
2. The OED's first definition of "efface" is "To rub out, obliterate (writing, painted or sculptured figures, a mark or stain) from the surface of anything, so as to leave no distinct traces"; the second is "To expunge, erase (words or sentences) in a written composition or document." In contrast, the first definition of "deface" is "to mar the face, features, or appearance; to spoil or ruin the figure, form, or beauty of; to disfigure."
3. While no other critics have examined self-effacement in American poetry, several have considered the deconstructive notion of erasure, a term that is more textual and less bodily than *effacement*. Jody Norton, for example, claims that in contemporary American poetry (which she defines as extending only until the late 1960s), "subjectivity is always under erasure, in that 1) it is structured as representation [. . .]; and 2) it is relational, and transformational, both as regards other subjectivities and as regards the modalities of memory and language through which it is constituted" (45).
4. As I discussed in more detail above, Frye insists categorically that "the lyric poet, so to speak, turns his back on his listeners" (20) and Culler similarly emphasizes the distinction between apostrophe and "direct address" (*Pursuit* 153). W. R. Johnson and, less absolutely, William Waters, are nearly alone in allowing that the lyric "you" may in fact function as reader address, although neither uses the term "apostrophe."
5. Strikingly, in a discussion of ancient Greek lyric, W. R. Johnson uses the same phrase, although he distinguishes the "twinship between writer and reader" (76) in Greek lyric from the "alienation" effected by modern lyric (72).

Works Cited

Altieri, Charles. *Self and Sensibility in Contemporary American Poetry.* New York: Cambridge UP, 1984
Annas, Pamela. *A Disturbance in Mirrors.* New York: Greenwood, 1988.
Ashbery, John. *Your Name Here: Poems.* New York: Farrar, 2000.
Auden, W. H. "Lay your sleeping head, my love." *Selected Poems.* Ed. Edward Mendelson. New York: Vintage, 1979. 50–51.
Axelrod, Steven Gould. *Sylvia Plath: The Wound and the Cure of Words.* Baltimore: Johns Hopkins UP, 1990.
Bahti, Timothy. *Ends of the Lyric: Direction and Consequence in Western Poetry.* Baltimore: Johns Hopkins UP, 1996.
Bawer, Bruce. "A Summoning of Spirits: James Merrill and *Sandover.*" *New Criterion* 2.10 (1984): 35–42.
Bedient, Calvin. "Birth, Not Death, Is the Hard Loss." *Parnassus: Poetry in Review* 9 (1981): 168–86.
———. "Oh Plath!" *Parnassus: Poetry in Review* 12 (1985): 275–81.
Berman, Jeffrey. *Narcissism and the Novel.* New York: New York UP, 1990.
Bidart, Frank. *Desire.* New York: Farrar, 1997.
———. *In the Western Night: Collected Poems 1965–1990.* New York: Farrar, 1990.
———. "Introduction: 'You Didn't Write, You *Rewrote.*'" *Collected Poems.* By Robert Lowell. Ed. Frank Bidart. New York: Farrar, 2003.
———. *Music Like Dirt.* Louisville, KY: Sarabande, 2002.
———. "Pre-existing Forms: We Fill Them and When We Fill Them We Change Them and Are Changed." *Salmagundi* 128–29 (2000–01): 108–22.
Blasing, Mutlu Konuk. *Politics and Form in Postmodern Poetry: O'Hara, Bishop, Ashbery, and Merrill.* New York: Cambridge UP, 1995.
Bloom, Harold. "Introduction." Harold Bloom, ed. *James Merrill.* 1–8.
———, ed. *James Merrill.* New York: Chelsea House, 1985.
Blosser, Sivianne. *A Poetics on Edge: The Poetry and Prose of Sylvia Plath.* New York: Peter Lang, 2001.
Borges, Jorge Luis. *Collected Fictions.* Tr. Andrew Hurley. New York: Viking, 1998.

Boothby, Richard. *Death and Desire: Psychoanalytic Theory in Lacan's Return to Freud.* New York: Routledge, 1991.

Bouson, J. Brooks. *The Empathic Reader: A Study of the Narcissistic Character and the Drama of the Self.* Amherst: U of Massachusetts P, 1989.

Brain, Tracy. *The Other Sylvia Plath.* New York: Longman, 2001.

Brisman, Susan Hawk and Leslie. "Lies Against Solitude: Symbolic, Imaginary, Real." *The Literary Freud: Mechanisms of Defense and the Poetic Will.* Ed. Joseph H. Smith. New Haven: Yale UP, 1980. 29–65.

Britzolakis, Christina. *Sylvia Plath and the Theatre of Mourning.* New York: Oxford UP, 1999.

Brock-Broido, Lucie. *The Master Letters.* New York: Knopf, 1995.

Broe, Mary Lynn. *Protean Poetic: The Poetry of Sylvia Plath.* Columbia: U of Missouri P, 1980.

Bronfen, Elisabeth. *Over Her Dead Body: Death, Femininity, and the Aesthetic.* New York: Routledge, 1992.

———. *Sylvia Plath.* Plymouth, Eng.: Northcote, 1998.

Brooks, Peter. *Reading for the Plot: Design and Intention in Narrative.* New York: Knopf, 1984.

Bundtzen, Lynda K. *Plath's Incarnations: Woman and the Creative Process.* Ann Arbor: U of Michigan P, 1983.

Burr, Zofia, *Of Women, Poetry, and Power: Strategies of Address in Dickinson, Miles, Brooks, Lorde, and Angelou.* Chicago: U of Illinois P, 2002.

Butscher, Edward. *Sylvia Plath: The Woman and the Work.* New York: Dodd, 1977.

Cameron, Sharon. *Lyric Time: Dickinson and the Limits of Genre.* Baltimore: Johns Hopkins UP, 1979.

Catullus. "I Hate and Love" (English transln.) Unattributed handout. "Translation—and a Poet's Project." Seminar led by Frank Bidart. Boston University. April 1994.

Chase, Cynthia. "'Viewless Wings': Intertextual Interpretation of Keats's 'Ode to a Nightingale.'" Hosek and Parker 208–225.

Chiasson, Dan. "Presence: Frank Bidart." *Raritan* 20 (2001): 117–138.

Culler, Jonathan. "Deconstruction and the Lyric." *Deconstruction is/in America.* Ed. Anselm Haverkamp. New York: New York UP, 1995. 41–51.

———. *The Pursuit of Signs.* Ithaca: Cornell UP, 1981.

"Deface." *Oxford English Dictionary.* <http://dictionary.oed.com/>

de Man, Paul. *The Resistance to Theory.* Minneapolis: U of Minnesota P, 1986.

———. *The Rhetoric of Romanticism.* New York: Columbia UP, 1984.

Dickinson, Emily. *The Complete Poems.* Ed. Thomas Johnson. Boston: Little, Brown, 1960.

———. *Selected Letters.* Ed. Thomas H. Johnson. Cambridge: Harvard UP, 1986.

Diehl, Joanne Feit, ed. *On Louise Gluck: Change What You See.* Ann Arbor: U of Michigan P, 2005.

———. *Women Poets and the American Sublime.* Bloomington: Indiana UP, 1990.

Works Cited

Dodd, Elizabeth. *The Veiled Mirror and the Woman Poet: H.D, Louise Bogan, Elizabeth Bishop, and Louise Glück.* Columbia: U of Missouri P, 1992.

Easthope, Anthony. "Reading the Poetry of Sylvia Plath." *English: The Journal of the English Association* 43 (1994): 223–35.

"Efface." *Oxford English Dictionary.* <http://dictionary.oed.com/>

Findlay, L. M. "Culler and Byron on Apostrophe and Lyric Time." *Studies in Romanticism* 24 (1985): 335–53.

Forbes, Deborah. *Sincerity's Shadow: Self-Consciousness in British Romantic and Mid-Twentieth-Century American Poetry.* Cambridge: Harvard UP, 2004.

Foucault, Michel. *History of Sexuality: An Introduction.* Vol 1. New York: Vintage, 1978.

Freud, Sigmund. *Beyond the Pleasure Principle.* New York: Liveright, 1961.

———. "Mourning and Melancholia." *Standard Edition.* Vol. 14. 142–58.

———. "On Narcissism: An Introduction." *Standard Edition.* Vol. 14. 73–102.

———. *The Standard Edition of the Complete Psychoanalytical Works.* Tr. and Ed. James Strachey. London: Hogarth, 1975.

Friedrich, Paul. "Dialogue in Lyric Narrative." *Dialogue and Critical Discourse: Language, Culture, Critical Theory.* Ed. Michael Macovski. New York: Oxford UP, 1997. 79–98.

Frye, Northrop. *Anatomy of Criticism.* Princeton: Princeton UP, 1957.

Fuss, Diana. "Corpse Poem." *Critical Inquiry* 30 (2003): 1–30.

Gervais, David. "Some Versions of Pathos." *PN Review* 28.2 (2001): 20–23.

Gilbert, Sandra M. "A Fine, White Flying Myth: The Life/Work of Sylvia Plath." *Shakespeare's Sisters: Feminist Essays on Women Poets.* Ed. Sandra M. Gilbert and Susan Gubar. Bloomington: Indiana UP, 1979. 245–60.

———. "My Name Is Darkness: The Poetry of Self-Definition." *Contemporary Literature* 18 (1977): 443–57.

Glück, Louise. "American Narcissism." *PN Review* 23.6 (1997): 10–13.

———. *Ararat.* New York: Ecco, 1990.

———. *Descending Figure.* New York: Ecco, 1980.

———. *The House on Marshland.* New York: Ecco, 1975.

———. "Invitation and Exclusion." *Proofs and Theories: Essays on Poetry.* New York: Ecco, 1994. 113–123.

———. *Meadowlands.* New York: Ecco, 1996.

———. *The Triumph of Achilles.* New York: Ecco, 1985.

———. *The Wild Iris.* New York: Ecco, 1992.

Gray, Jeffrey. " 'Necessary Thought': Frank Bidart and the Postconfessional." *Contemporary Literature* 34 (1996): 714–39.

Gregerson, Linda. *Negative Capability: Contemporary American Poetry.* Ann Arbor: U of Michigan P, 2001.

Gubar, Susan. "Prosopopoeia and Holocaust Poetry in English: The Case of Sylvia Plath." *Yale Journal of Criticism* 14 (2001): 191–215.

Halpern, Nick. *Everyday and Prophetic: The Poetry of Lowell, Ammons, Merrill, and Rich.* Madison: U of Wisconsin P, 2003.

———. "Louise Glück's I." Panel on "Lyric Utterance and the Reader: Overheard, Performed, or Addressed?" MLA Convention. Philadelphia. December 2004.
Hammer, Langdon. "Frank Bidart and the Tone of Contemporary Poetry." *Southwest Review* 87 (2002): 75–89.
Harrison, DeSales. *The End of the Mind: The Edge of the Intelligible in Hardy, Stevens, Larkin, Plath, and Glück.* New York: Routledge, 2005.
Hedley, E. Jane. "'I'll tell you something': Reader-address in Louise Glück's *Ararat* Sequence." Panel on "Lyric Utterance and the Reader: Overheard, Performed, or Addressed?" MLA Convention. Philadelphia. December 2004.
Hertz, Neil. "Lurid Figures." *Reading de Man Reading.* Ed. Lindsay Waters and Wlad Godzich. Minneapolis: U of Minnesota P, 1989. 82–104.
Holbrook, David. *Sylvia Plath: Poetry and Existence.* Atlantic Heights, NJ: Humanities P, 1976.
Hollander, John. *Melodious Guile: Fictive Pattern in Poetic Language.* New Haven: Yale UP, 1988.
Hughes, Ted. *Birthday Letters.* New York: Farrar, 1998.
———, ed. *Collected Poems.* By Sylvia Plath. New York: Harper, 1981.
———. "Sylvia Plath's *Collected Poems* and *The Bell Jar.*" *Winter Pollen: Occasional Prose.* New York: Picador, 1995. 466–81.
Hungerford, Amy. *The Holocaust of Texts: Genocide, Literature, and Personification.* Chicago: U of Chicago P, 2003.
Hutcheon, Linda. *Narcissistic Narrative: The Metafictional Paradox.* Waterloo, Ont.: Wilfred Laurier UP, 1980.
Jackson, David. "Lending a Hand." Lehman and Berger 298–305.
Jakobson, Roman. "Two Aspects of Language and Two Types of Aphasic Disturbances." *On Language.* Ed. Linda R. Waugh and Monique Monville-Burston. Cambridge: Harvard UP, 1990. 115–33.
Johnson, Barbara. "Apostrophe, Animation, and Abortion." *A World of Difference.* Baltimore: Johns Hopkins UP, 1987. 184–99.
Johnson, W. R. *The Idea of Lyric: Lyric Modes in Ancient and Modern Poetry.* Berkeley: U of California P, 1982.
Juhasz, Suzanne. *Naked and Fiery Forms: Modern American Poetry by Women.* New York: Harper, 1976.
Kalstone, David. "Evenings at the Ouija Board." Rotella 44–49.
———. "Persisting Figures: The Poet's Story and How We Read It." Lehman and Berger 125–44.
Keats, John. *Selected Poems and Letters.* Ed. Douglas Bush. Boston: Houghton, 1959.
Keller, Lynn. "'Free/ of Blosson and Subterfuge': Louise Glück and the Language of Renunciation." *World, Self, Poem: Essays on Contemporary Poetry from the "Jubilation of Poets."* Ed. Leonard M. Trawick. Kent, OH: Kent State UP, 1990. 120–29.
Kneale, J. Douglas. "Romantic Aversions: Apostrophe Reconsidered." *ELH* 58 (1991): 141–65.

Koch, Kenneth. *New Addresses: Poems.* New York: Knopf, 2000.
Kochhar-Lindgren, Gray. *Narcissus Transformed: The Textual Subject in Psychoanalysis and Literature.* University Park, PA: Pennsylvania State UP, 1993.
Kramer, Lawrence. "Freud and the Skunks: Genre and Language in *Life Studies.*" *Robert Lowell: Essays on the Poetry.* Ed. Steven Gould Alexrod and Helen Deese. New York: Cambridge UP, 1986. 80–98.
Kristeva, Julia. *Black Sun: Depression and Melancholia.* New York: Columbia UP, 1989.
Kroll, Judith. *Chapters in a Mythology: The Poetry of Sylvia Plath.* New York: Harper, 1976.
Lacan, Jacques. *The Psychoses. The Seminar of Jacques Lacan. Book 3.* Tr. Russell Grigg. New York: Norton, 1993.
Laplanche, Jean and J. B. Pontalis. *The Language of Psychoanalysis.* Tr. Donald Nicholson-Smith. New York: Norton, 1973.
Lehman, David. *Signs of the Times: Deconstruction and the Fall of Paul de Man.* New York: Poseidon, 1991.
—— and Charles Berger, eds. *James Merrill: Essays in Criticism.* Ithaca: Cornell UP, 1983.
Li, Victor P. H. "Narcissism and the Limits of the Lyric Self." *Tropic Crucible: Self and Theory in Language and Literature.* Ed. Ranjit Chatterjee and Colin Nicholson. Singapore: Singapore UP, 1984. 3–23.
Loeffelholz, Mary. *Dickinson and the Boundaries of Feminist Theory.* Chicago: U of Illinois P, 1991.
Lowell, Robert. *Collected Poems.* Ed. Frank Bidart and David Gewanter. New York: Farrar, 2003.
——. *Life Studies.* New York: Farrar, 1959.
Lurie, Alison. *Familiar Spirits: A Memoir of James Merrill and David Jackson.* New York: Viking, 2001.
MacDonald, D. L. "Merrill and Freud: The Psychopathology of Eternal Life." *Mosaic* 19: 159–72.
Macovski, Michael. *Dialogue and Literature: Apostrophe, Auditors, and the Collapse of Romantic Discourse.* New York: Oxford UP, 1994.
Markey, Janice. *A Journey into the Red Eye: The Poetry of Sylvia Plath.* London: Women's Press, 1993.
Materer, Timothy. *James Merrill's Apocalpyse.* Ithaca: Cornell UP, 2000.
McCorkle, James. *The Still Performance: Writing, Self, and Interconnection in Five Postmodern American Poets.* Charlottesville: UP of Virginia, 1989.
McHale, Brian. *The Obligation toward the Difficult Whole: Postmodernist Long Poems.* Tuscaloosa: U of Alabama P, 2004.
McMahon, Lynne. "The Sexual Swamp: Female Erotics and the Masculine Art." *Southern Review* 28 (1992): 333–52.
Merrill, James. *The Changing Light at Sandover.* New York: Atheneum, 1982.
——. *Collected Prose.* Ed. J. D. McClatchy and Stephen Yenser. New York: Knopf, 2004.

———. *Divine Comedies.* New York: Atheneum, 1979.

Middlebrook, Diane. *Her Husband: Hughes and Plath—A Marriage.* New York: Viking, 2003.

———. "What Was Confessional Poetry?" *The Columbia History of American Poetry: From the Puritans to Our Time.* Ed. Jay Parini and Brett Millier. New York: Columbia UP, 1993. 632–49.

Molesworth, Charles. *The Fierce Embrace: A Study of Contemporary American Poetry.* Columbia: U of Missouri P, 1979.

Nelson, Deborah. *Pursuing Privacy in Cold War America.* New York: Columbia UP, 2002.

Norton, Jody. *Narcissus Sous Rature: Male Subjectivity in Contemporary American Poetry.* Lewisburg, PA: Bucknell UP, 2000.

"Pathos." *Oxford English Dictionary.* <http://dictionary.oed.com/>

Peel, Robin. *Writing Back: Sylvia Plath and Cold War Politics.* Madison, NJ: Fairleigh Dickinson UP, 2002.

Perloff, Marjorie. "Angst and Animism in the Poetry of Sylvia Plath." *Critical Essays on Sylvia Plath.* Ed. Linda W. Wagner. Boston: G. K. Hall, 1984. 109–23.

———. *The Poetics of Indeterminacy: Rimbaud to Cage.* Princeton: Princeton UP, 1981.

———. "Postmodernism/'Fin de Siecle': Defining 'Difference' in Late Twentieth-Century Poetics." *Romanticism and Postmodernism.* Ed. Edward Larrissy. New York: Cambridge UP, 1999. 179–209.

———. "Sylvia Plath's 'Sivvy' Poems: A Portrait of the Poet as Daughter." *Sylvia Plath: New Views on the Poetry.* Ed. Gary Lane. Baltimore: Johns Hopkins UP, 1979.

Pinsky, Robert. *The Situation of Poetry: Contemporary Poetry and Its Traditions.* Princeton: Princeton UP, 1976.

Plath, Sylvia. *Ariel.* New York: Harper, 1966.

———. *Ariel: The Restored Edition.* New York: HarperCollins, 2004.

———. *The Collected Poems.* Ed. Ted Hughes. New York: Harper, 1981.

——— *Letters Home: Correspondence 1950–1963.* Ed. Aurelia Schober Plath. New York: HarperCollins, 1975.

———. "Ocean 1212-W." *The Art of Sylvia Plath: A Symposium.* Ed. Charles Newman. Bloomington: Indiana UP, 1970.

———. *The Unabridged Journals of Sylvia Plath 1952–1962.* Ed. Karen V. Kukil. New York: Anchor, 2000.

Polito, Robert, ed. *A Reader's Guide to James Merrill's* The Changing Light at Sandover. Ann Arbor: U of Michigan P, 1994.

Preminger, Alex, et al., eds. *The New Princeton Encyclopedia of Poetry and Poetics* Princeton: Princeton UP, 1995.

Rathmann, Andrew. "An Interview with Frank Bidart." *Chicago Review* 47.3 (2001): 21–42.

Ramazani, Jahan. "'Daddy, I Have Had to Kill You': Plath, Rage, and the Modern Elegy." *PMLA* 108 (1993): 1142–56.

———. *Poetry of Mourning: The Modern Elegy from Hardy to Heaney.* Chicago: U of Chicago P, 1994.
Redfern, Walter. *Puns.* New York: Blackwell, 1984.
Roberts, Neil. *Narrative and Voice in Postwar Poetry.* New York: Longman, 1999.
Rose, Jacqueline. *The Haunting of Sylvia Plath.* Cambridge: Harvard UP, 1991.
———. *On Not Being Able to Sleep: Psychoanalysis and the Modern World.* London: Chatto, 2003.
Rosenblatt, Jon. *Sylvia Plath: The Poetry of Initiation.* Chapel Hill: U of North Carolina P, 1979.
Rosenthal, M. L. *The New Poets.* New York: Oxford UP, 1967.
Rotella, Guy, ed. *Critical Essays on James Merrill.* New York: G. K. Hall, 1996.
Rubin, Stan Sanvel. "Introduction." *The Post-Confessionals: Conversations with American Poets of the Eighties.* Ed. Earl G. Ingersoll, et al. Rutherford, NJ: Fairleigh Dickinson UP, 1989.
Sacks, Peter M. "The Divine Translation: Elegiac Aspects of *The Changing Light at Sandover.*" Lehman and Berger 159–85.
———. *The English Elegy: Studies in the Genre from Spenser to Yeats.* Baltimore: Johns Hopkins UP, 1985.
Sadoff, Ira. "Louise Gluck and the Last Stage of Romanticism." *New England Review* 22.4 (2001): 81–92.
Saez, Richard. "'At the Salon Level': Merrill's Apocalyptic Epic." Lehman and Berger 211–245.
———. "James Merrill's Oedipal Fire." Bloom, *James Merrill* 35–56.
Scott, Nathan. *Visions of Presence in Modern American Poetry.* Baltimore: Johns Hopkins UP, 1993.
Selinger, Eric Murphy. "James Merrill's Masks of Eros, Masques of Love." Rotella 145–74.
Shetley, Vernon. *After the Death of Poetry: Poet and Audience in Contemporary America.* Durham, NC: Duke UP, 1993.
Spargo, R. Clifton. *The Ethics of Mourning: Grief and Responsibility in Elegiac Literature.* Baltimore: Johns Hopkins UP, 2004.
Spiegelman, Willard. "'Are You Talking to Me?': Speaker and Audience in Louise Glück's *The Wild Iris.*" Panel on "Lyric Utterance and the Reader: Overheard, Performed, or Addressed?" MLA Convention. Philadelphia. December 2004.
———. *The Didactic Muse: Scenes of Instruction in Contemporary American Poetry.* Princeton: Princeton UP, 1989.
———. "Repetition and Singularity." *Kenyon Review* 25 (2003): 149–68.
Staten, Henry. *Eros in Mourning: From Homer to Lacan.* Baltimore: Johns Hopkins UP, 1995.
Stevenson, Anne. *Bitter Fame: A Life of Sylvia Plath.* Boston: Houghton, 1989.
Sword, Helen. *Ghostwriting Modernism.* Ithaca: Cornell UP, 2002.
Travisano, Thomas. *Midcentury Quartet: Bishop, Lowell, Jarrell, Berryman, and the Making of a Postmodern Aesthetic.* Charlottesville: UP of Virginia, 1999.

Tucker, Herbert F. "Dramatic Monologue and the Overhearing of Lyric." Hosek and Parker 226–243.
Upton, Lee. *The Muse of Abandonment: Origin, Identity, Mastery, in Five American Poets.* Lewisburg, PA: Bucknell UP, 1998.
Uroff, Margaret Dickie. *Sylvia Plath and Ted Hughes.* Urbana: U of Illinois P, 1979.
van Dyne, Susan. *Revising Life: Sylvia Plath's* Ariel *Poems.* Chapel Hill: U of North Carolina P, 1993.
Vendler, Helen, "Divine Comedies." Polito 134–43.
———. "An Intractable Metal." *Ariel Ascending: Writings About Sylvia Plath.* Ed. Paul Alexander. New York: Harper, 1985.
———. *Poems, Poets, Poetry: An Introduction and Anthology.* Second Ed. New York: Bedford, 2002.
———. "A Quarter of Poetry." *New York Times Book Review.* 6 Apr 74: 4+.
———. *Soul Says: On Recent Poetry.* Cambridge: Harvard UP, 1995.
Waters, William. "Answerable Aesthetics: Reading 'You' in Rilke." *Comparative Literature* 48 (1996): 128–147.
———. "Poetic Address and Intimate Reading: The Offered Hand." *Literary Imagination* 2 (2000): 188–220.
———. *Poetry's Touch: On Lyric Address.* Ithaca: Cornell UP, 2003.
Wheeler, Lesley. "Heralding the Clear Obscure: Gwendolyn Brooks and Apostrophe." *Callaloo* 24 (2001): 227–35.
Williamson, Alan. *Introspection and Contemporary American Poetry.* Cambridge: Harvard UP, 1984.
Yenser, Stephen. *A Boundless Field: American Poetry at Large.* Ann Arbor: U of Michigan P, 2002.
———. *The Consuming Myth: The Work of James Merrill.* Cambridge: Harvard UP, 1987.
Zeiger, Melissa F. *Beyond Consolation: Death, Sexuality, and the Changing Shapes of Elegy.* Ithaca: Cornell UP, 1997.

Index

A

Absence/presence and "The Book of Ephraim," 63–64
Address, poems of, 4; *see also individual poem headings*
Agency/projection and "Daisies," 88–89
Alienation deriving from postwar prosperity/complacency/conformity, 6
Ambivalence to apostrophe, psychological/emotional, 3, 33–35, 71–72, 89
"American Narcissism" (Glück), 76–78, 81
Animation/apostrophe/death, *Ariel* and the connection of, 39–42, 44
Apostrophe as a viable/suggestive figure for post-World War II poets, 1–4, 6–8, 95; *see also* Postmodern poetry; *individual poem headings*
Ararat (Glück), 74, 79, 89, 93
"Ariel" (Plath), 37–44
Ariel (Plath)
    ambivalence to apostrophe, 71–72, 89
    "Ariel," 37–44
    Changing Light at Sandover compared to, 51–52
    "Cut," 44–47
    "Daddy," 29–36
    death/deadness, 31, 34, 36, 38–42, 44–45, 48
    dexterity, linguistic, 48
    Glück's (Louise) analysis, 27–29
    invisibility, Plath's belief that her poems will lift her, 48
    "Lady Lazarus," 28–29
    letters to her mother, Plath's, 47–49
    mortality, Plath's belief that her poems can release her from, 48
    "Ode to a Nightingale" compared to, 37–39
    overview, 22–23, 27–28
    Ramazani's analysis, 31
    self-destruction as a kind of aesthetic strategy, 124
Artificiality, standing outside apostrophe and exposing its, 53–54
Artistic creation/influence and *Desire*, 110–116
Ashbery, John, 25; *see also* "This Room"
Auden, W. H., 107
Autobiography and Bidart's poems, 98–100, 118–119
Autobiography functioning like posthumous utterance, 42

B

"Ballroom, The" (Merrill), 64–67
Bedient, Calvin, 75
Berlioz, Hector, 115–116
Beyond the Pleasure Principle (Freud), 41, 57
Bidart, Frank, 5, 22, 127; *see also Desire*
Binswanger, Ludwig, 98
Bishop, Elizabeth, 68–69
Bloom, Harold, 76
Bodily fragmentation and self-effacement, 124–125

"Book of Ephraim, The" (Merrill), 52, 54–66, 73, 124–126, 128
Borges, Jorge L., 110
"Borges and I" (Bidart), 110–111, 114, 117
Brainard, Joe, 96
Britzolakis, Christina, 44
Brock-Broido, Lucie, 17–22, 44
Browning, Robert, 10

C

Callas, Maria, 99–100, 115–116
Cameron, Sharon, 7, 89
"Catullus: Excrucior" (Bidart), 103–104, 110, 112
Changing Light at Sandover (Merrill)
    ambivalence to apostrophe, 71–72
    Ariel compared to, 51–52
    artifice, illuminating apostrophe by drawing attention to its, 54
    "Ballroom, The," 64–67
    "Book of Ephraim, The," 54–64
    "Coda," 54–55, 64
    embodiment of the addressee requires a violation of lyric itself, 132
    juxtaposing poems spoken by different speakers, 72
    Keats and "The Book of Ephraim," 65–66
    loss, position of, 53, 54, 65
    "Lost in Translation," 67–69
    lyric, affinity/nostalgia for, 53–54
    Ouija board, 52–53
    overview, 10, 23, 51
    standing outside apostrophe and exposing its artificiality, 53–54
Chase, Cynthia, 36, 66
Child enters into the language, Jacques Lacan's theory of how, 8–9, 71–72
"Coda" (Merrill), *Changing Light at Sandover*'s, 54–55, 64, 130
"Coin for Joe, A" (Bidart), 108–110, 114
Collected Poems (Bidart), 114
"Confessional" (Bidart), 106
Confessional poetry, 16, 35–36
Confusions in "Daddy," 30–31
Conservative "contemporary" from the experimental "postmodern," eagerness to distinguish the, 4–5
Culler, Jonathan, 2–3, 9, 29–30, 34, 52, 77, 132–133
"Cut" (Plath), 44–47

D

"Daddy" (Plath), 29–36, 45, 131
"Daisies" (Glück), 87–90
Deanimations and "This Room," 131
Death/deadness
    Ariel, 31, 34, 36, 38–42, 44–45, 48
    "Daddy," 31, 34
    Desire, 96–98, 101–103, 105–106, 109–112
    "First Hour of the Night, The," 114–115, 119
    oedipal relations, 15
    Wild Iris, The, 79, 89
"Dedication to Hunger" (Glück), 73–74, 77
Defacement, de Man's notion of, 123
de Man, Paul, 42, 44–45, 122, 123
Desire
    analogy between two modes of, apostrophe suggesting an, 10–11
    central to many poems of the authors in this book, 95–96
    Glück's poems mediating on the perils of, 73–75
    lyric desire fulfilled through the dislocation of the lyric subject itself, 124
    "The Ballroom," 67
Desire (Bidart)
    artistic creation/influence, 110–116
    "Borges and I," 110–111
    "Catullus: Excrucior," 103–104
    "Coin for Joe, A," 108–110
    contradictions of desire, 116–118
    death/deadness, 96–98, 101–103, 105–106, 109–112
    echo and refrain, 105–106
    elegiac desire, redeeming, 96
    embodiment connected with erasure, 98, 113–114
    excruciation, desire's, 104

formal questions of lyric/elegiac concerns, 100
forward motion, impossibility of, 100–101
"Homo Faber," 111–112
"In Memory of Joe Brainard," 112–114
isolation connected to desire, 104–105
italicized passages, 106–107
knowledge, the opposition of desire to, 102–103
loss, desire associated with irrevocable, 96
lyric/grief/memory, connections between, 96
narrative and stasis, contradictory impulses toward, 105
overview, 24–25
paradoxes about desire, 120
pathos, preoccupied with, 95
performance: to forgo performance, 114–116
physical absence and voice, 100
reimagining the nature/function of desire, 96
repudiation connected with desire, 98
"Second Hour of the Night, The," 114–120
"Yoke, The," 101–103, 106–108
Detachment and *The Wild Iris,* 92–94
"Deviation, The" (Glück), 73, 122–124
Dickinson, Emily, 4–5, 8, 19–20
Distance, all address in motivated by desire to unmake, 51
Doubleness in "Daddy," 34
Dramatic monologue, 98–100
"During Fever" (Lowell), 13–17, 98, 131

E
Echo and death/deadness, 105–106
Echo and Narcissus, 106
Effacement, *see* Self-effacement and lyric space
Ego development, Freudian notion of, 40
Elegy, *see* Death/deadness
"Ellen West" (Bidart), 98–101, 105, 115, 120
Embarrassment and reading apostrophe, 2, 3, 48–49, 52

Erasure/abundance, "In Memory of Joe Brainard" and interplay of, 113–114
Evasiveness and "The Book of Ephraim," 57–58, 73
Exclusion of the reader, 28, 94; *see also* Overhearing and apostrophic hearing, lyric; *individual poem headings*
Experimental "postmodern" from the conservative "contemporary," eagerness to distinguish the, 4–5

F
"First Hour of the Night, The" (Bidart), 114–115, 119
Form involves damage/loss, the process of granting, 20–21
Foucault, Michel, 35–36
Free association permitting recuperation of what was lost/absent, 7–8
Freudian relations/relationships, 15–17, 40, 41, 54–57, 73
Frost, Robert, 21
Frye, Northrop, 11–12, 75, 94, 103

G
"Garden, The" (Glück), 92–94, 103
Gendering and *Ariel,* 46–47
Glück, Louise, 5, 22, 27–29, 36, 48, 49, 134; *see also* Wild Iris, The
"Golden State" (Bidart), 97–98, 110, 111
Gray, Jeffrey, 5
Grieving, elegiac desire transformed through the process of, 96

H
Hearing, *see* Overhearing and apostrophic hearing, lyric
"Her Habit" (Brock-Broido), 17–22
Hollander, John, 105
"Homo Faber" (Bidart), 111–112
House on Marshland, The (Glück), 73

I
Identifications of "This Room," the multiple, 133–134

Identity of protagonists in "Daddy," 29–30, 33
Impossible imperatives, apostrophe characterized by, 77
Inanimate entities, the personification of, 86–87; *see also Wild Iris, The*
Incarnation and withdrawal, "The Book of Ephraim" and the interplay of, 57, 58
Inferno (Dante), 115
"In Memory of Joe Brainard" (Bidart), 112–114
Intersubjective, the, 10
Intertextual, the, 10
Intimacy
  "Untrustworthy Speaker, The," 74–75
  Wild Iris, The, 90–91
Irrelevance of the written word in a post-industrial/literate culture, 6
Isolation connected to desire, 104–105
I subsumed in we, "Ariel" and the, 37, 40, 43

J
Jackson, David, 52
Johnson, Barbara, 8, 15, 16, 41–42, 58
Johnson, Thomas, 18

K
Kalstone, David, 54
Keats, John, 34–36, 65–66, 108
Koch, Kenneth, 1–4, 6, 7, 9, 44
Kristeva, Julia, 53, 58, 67

L
Lacan, Jacques, 8–9, 43, 71–72, 78, 96
"Lady Lazarus" (Plath), 28–29, 36, 48, 73, 93
Language limitations and *Changing Light at Sandover*, 68–69
Life/death, *Ariel* and connection between figurative language and, 41
Loeffelholz, Mary, 8, 9
Loss as productive poetic terrain, 9–10; *see also individual poem headings*
"Lost in Translation" (Merrill), 67–69, 128–129
Lowell, Robert, 13–17, 104
"Lycidas" (Milton), 105
Lyric subject, position/stability of, 5–7, 10–13, 22, 35, 43; *see also* Self-effacement and lyric space; *individual poem headings*

M
Master Letters, The (Brock-Broido), 18, 19–20
"Matins" (Glück), 81–85, 90–91
Melancholia, 53, 89, 91
Merrill, James, 5, 22, 100, 127–128; *see also Changing Light at Sandover*
Metamorphosis and "The Second Hour of the Night, 114, 128–129
Metaphor
  "Book of Ephraim, The," 59
  "Coin for Joe, A," 108–109
  prosopopeia, 45
  Wild Iris, The, 80–85
Metonymic model of understanding and *The Wild Iris*, 80–85, 91
Mill, John S., 11, 16, 21, 28
"Mock Orange" (Glück), 73
Mortality and the possibility of circumventing it, 121; *see also* Death/deadness
Mourning and "The Second Hour," 116

N
Narcissistic tendency to convert others into mirrors of the self, 73; *see also Wild Iris, The*
New Addresses (Koch), 1, 2, 19

O
"Ode on a Grecian Urn" (Keats), 109
"Ode to a Nightingale" (Keats), 34–39, 66, 102
Oedipus complex, 15, 56, 73
"On Narcissism" (Freud), 78
Other, the, *see* Overhearing and apostrophic hearing, lyric; *individual poem headings*
Ouija board and *Changing Light at Sandover*, 52–53

Index

Overhearing and apostrophic hearing, lyric; *see also individual poem headings*
  "During Fever," 13–17
  Frye, Northrop, 11–12
  "Her Habit," 17–22
  "Lady Lazarus," 28–29
  pathos of overhearing, 12–13, 22
  self-effacement and lyric space, 122
  "This Room," 132–134
  Tucker, Herbert, 12
  Wild Iris, The, 94
Ovid, 101, 106, 115, 116

P

"Palme" ("Valéry"), 128
Performance and *Desire*, 114–116
Perloff, Marjorie, 5, 37, 39, 43–44
Personification of inanimate entities, 86–87; *see also Wild Iris, The*
Physical dissolution/dismemberment and *Ariel*, 45–46
Plath, Sylvia, 5, 22, 86, 127, 134; *see also Ariel*
Pleasure principle, 41
Postmodern poetry, reconciling opposed notions of; *see also individual poem headings*
  apostrophe read as neither wholly literary/extraliterary, 7
  child enters into language, Lacan's (Jacques) theory of how the, 8–9
  desire, apostrophe suggesting an analogy between two modes of, 10–11
  free association permitting recuperation of what was lost/absent, 7–8
  identifications, multiple, 134
  isolation and the yearning for companionship, 121
  literal psychological models of apostrophe, avoiding overly, 9
  loss as productive poetic terrain, 9–10
  lyric subject, position/stability of, 5–7, 10–13, 22
  mortality and the possibility of circumventing it, 121
  overhearing and apostrophic hearing, lyric, 11–22
  overview, 5
  paradoxes confronting the post-Romantic apostrophic poet, 7, 129–130
Pound, Ezra, 5
Projection, Culler's notion that apostrophe is a form of, 132–133
Prose letter, 18, 21
Prosopopeia, 44–45, 48, 122; *see also Wild Iris, The*
Protolanguage and "The Book of Ephraim," 58–59
Psychoanalysis, apostrophe in close proximity to, 1–5, 7, 13–14, 55, 72, 78; *see also individual poem headings*
Puns and "The Book of Ephraim," 60–63

R

Radical from the formally traditional, eagerness to distinguish the formally, 4–5
Ramazani, Jahan, 31, 34, 96
"Raven, The" (Poe), 105
Readership for poetry, decline in the, 6
Refrain and death/deadness, 105–106
Refusal/persistence, "In Memory of Joe Brainard and interplay of, 113–114
Repetition connected to a reiteration of the loss, 105
Representation, apostrophe/language freed from the compulsion of, 58–59
Rilke, Rainer M., 8, 9, 20, 44, 72, 76, 78
Romantics, 1, 3, 4, 21, 72, 90
Rosenblatt, Jon, 45
Ruskin, John, 87

S

Sacks, Peter, 15, 96, 105–106, 109–110, 115
"Second Hour of the Night, The" (Bidart), 114–120, 126–129
Self-destruction, apostrophe flirts with, 36, 124
Self-effacement and lyric space
  acknowledgment of self-effacement permits/marks proximity to an other, 130

articulation, self-effacement allows the poem's, 122
bodily fragmentation, 124–125
"Book of Ephraim, The," 124–126
"Deviation, The," 122–124
"Lost in Translation," 128–129
lyric desire fulfilled through the dislocation of the lyric subject itself, 124
overhearing, clarifying pathos that inheres in lyric, 122
overview, 25
problems represented through poetry, self-effacement as answer to, 126
production, connection between self-effacement and poetic, 127–128
"Second Hour of the Night, The," 126–127
self and other, breakdown of distinctions between, 125–126
self-erasure and erotic meaning, connection between, 127
selfhood as a concept to be manipulated/dispensed with, 121
self-sacrifice and textual integrity, connection between, 122–124
subjectivity and language, conflict between, 121–122
submission requiring the permission of the other, 126–127
"This Room," 129–134
"Tulips," 125
Selfhood in *Ariel*, 33, 40
Self-Portrait of the Artist as a Young Dog (Thomas), 131
Self-sacrifice and textual integrity, connection between, 122–124
Separateness and merging, *Ariel* and, 42–43, 51
Seven Ages (Glück), 73
Sexuality
 "Dedication to Hunger," 73–74. *see also Wild Iris, The*
 "Second Hour, The," 115, 120
 self-erasure and erotic meaning, connection between, 127
Shetley, Vernon, 121–122

Silence in "Daddy," 33
Space, the intact but unreal, 130–134
Spectatorship/exclusion and "The Book of Ephraim," 63–64
Stevens, Wallace, 5
Subjectivity and language, conflict between, 121–122
Submission requiring the permission of the other, 126–127
Suicide and *Ariel*, 36, 41, 42, 46
Syntactic patterns in "Daddy," 32

T

Tempest, The (Giorgione), 60–61
Temporality of writing, 2
"This Room" (Ashbery), 122, 129–134
"To Psychoanalysis" (Koch), 1–4, 13–14
Traditional from the formally radical, eagerness to distinguish the formally, 4–5
Trancendence/death, "Daddy"/Keats and, 34–35
Transformations
 "Ballroom, The," 67
 "Daddy," 32–33
 "Second Hour, The," 117–118
Translation and "Lost in Translation," 67–69
Tucker, Herbert, 10–12, 17, 20, 94
"Tulips" (Plath), 48, 124, 125

U

Uncertainty and "Daddy," 30–31, 33
"Untrustworthy Speaker, The" (Glück), 74–75, 93

V

Valéry, Paul, 128
Vendler, Helen, 79, 134
Violence and *Ariel*, 44, 45–46

W

Waters, William, 11
"When I Have Fears" (Keats), 66
Whitman, Walt, 4–5
Wild Iris, The (Glück)
 "American Narcissism" and, discrepancy between, 76–78

condemnation of apostrophe, 72, 79–80
"Daisies," 87–90
death/deadness, 79, 89
detachment, 92
flowers expressing contempt of the human, 85–87
"Garden, The," 92–94
identification, outlining the dangers of, 76
intimacy issues, 90–91
loss, preoccupation with, 78–79
lyric, examining the self-absorption of, 72, 91
"Matins," 81–85, 90–91
melancholic elements, 89, 91
metaphoric/metonymic models of understanding, conflict between, 80–85
mortality, unmaking, 79
narcissism
    condemned/redefined/embrace, 75–79, 91
    narcissistic tendency to convert others into mirrors of the self, 73
orthodoxies of all kinds, suspicion of, 91–92
other is not there, possibility that the, 72
overview, 23–24
presence, speaker's longing for, 76
voice and autonomy, conflicted notions about, 80
Withdrawal and incarnation, "The Book of Ephraim" and the interplay of, 57, 58
Woodhouse, Richard, 65

Y

Yeats, W. B., 21
"Yoke, The" (Bidart), 101–103, 106–109, 111, 113, 119, 130
You of apostrophe, 8, 9, 20, 44, 72, 76; *see also individual poem headings*

For Product Safety Concerns and Information please contact our EU
representative GPSR@taylorandfrancis.com
Taylor & Francis Verlag GmbH, Kaufingerstraße 24, 80331 München, Germany

www.ingramcontent.com/pod-product-compliance
Lightning Source LLC
Chambersburg PA
CBHW051746230426
43670CB00012B/2178